A

NIGHTMARE'S

PRAYER

A Marine Corps Harrier Pilot's War in Afghanistan

Michael Franzak

Pocket Books

New York   London   Toronto   Sydney

Pocket Books
A Division of Simon & Schuster, Inc.
1230 Avenue of the Americas
New York, NY 10020

Copyright © 2010 by Michael Franzak

All rights reserved, including the right to reproduce this book or portions thereof in any form whatsoever. For information address Threshold Editions Subsidiary Rights Department, 1230 Avenue of the Americas, New York, NY 10020

First Pocket Books paperback edition July 2011

POCKET and colophon are registered trademarks of Simon & Schuster, Inc.

Cover design by Michael Nagin

Manufactured in the United States of America

10 9 8 7 6 5 4 3 2 1

For information about special discounts for bulk purchases, please contact Simon & Schuster Special Sales at 1-866-506-1949 or business@simonandschuster.com.

The Simon & Schuster Speakers Bureau can bring authors to your live event. For more information or to book an event contact the Simon & Schuster Speakers Bureau at 866-248-3049 or visit our website at www.simonspeakers.com.

ISBN: 978-1-4516-0807-6
ISBN: 978-1-4391-9499-7 (ebook)

*For those who didn't come home,
and for those who did but
who could not make the adjustments*

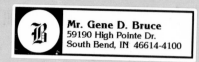

CONTENTS

INTRODUCTION
by Bing West

It is a testament to how much war has changed that the infantry on the ground don't even think about aviators. We grunts take it for granted that the big wings with the heavy explosives and the all-seeing eyes in the sky are hovering up there in the blue, beyond where we can see. We take it for granted that we can press a button to talk, or tap a computer screen and send a message, confident that it will be received. We know that the pilot can see more than we can; we know he packs a punch that brings silence to our battlefield. All we have to do is ask.

Now comes Mike Franzak to remind us that it's not automatic or easy. In fact, flying is damned hard work. Man wasn't meant to fly. It's an unnatural act. Any grunt will tell you that man was meant to keep both feet on the ground and dig quickly when the bullets crack by. Flying in a big, empty sky is injurious to your health. If something can go wrong, it will. You can't suspend gravity forever.

A Nightmare's Prayer is aptly named. In powerful, haunting vignettes, Mike explains why flying an AV-8

Harrier jet with tilt engines is like wrestling a Brahma bull. Sooner or later, the plane rears up and whispers, *Let's find out who's tougher.* On the ground, we've forgotten that a pilot risks his life every time he hurtles off the deck to guard us from above. Flight after flight, the plane must be tamed. No wonder AV-8 pilots have nightmares: it's reality waking them up at three in the morning.

Throughout Afghanistan, the grunts accept the fickle weather and the sudden crosswinds from the mountains as part of the scenery. When conditions get too tough or windy, we can hunker down.

There is no lee shore in the sky. Franzak's descriptions of landing in sharp winds are harrowing. Your knuckles are white, gripping the book as you wonder, *What idiot flies in those conditions, when the plane is trying to pitch over and squash you?* Then you realize that some platoon commander somewhere was in a fight, and someone had to help him out. You read how Franzak and his fellow pilots circle like sharks to make sure they know exactly where the fire support team is, how the planes roar down the valley to make sure the approach angle doesn't endanger the grunts, then pull up, turn around, and zip back in, hoping the laser-guided five-hundred-pound bombs don't malfunction.

The remarkable clarity of the communications is comforting to a grunt. When Franzak senses that the ground observer is under pressure or new to the job, he slows the action down, asking for instructions in plain English. Close air support seems so simple: all you have to do is ask, and you shall receive.

The Pentagon spends more than $150 billion a year on worldwide aviation, including the costs of the four services for items such as carriers, airfields, tankers, satellite linkages, training, and the like. At the peak, the wars in Iraq and Afghanistan cost about $70 billion a year. Aviation is the world's most expensive business, and it is dominated by Americans.

In the military sphere, this tilts all battlefields on land and sea in our favor. Our troops never have to worry about enemy aircraft; our enemies always have to worry about our aircraft. Almost no firefight in Afghanistan reaches the twenty-minute mark without air attacking the targets. That is a great comfort and decisive advantage for our troops.

The American response to 9/11 was to let loose the bombers. Confident and ignorant, tens of thousands of Taliban fighters, in support of thousands of Arab al Qaeda jihadists, manned their trench lines to repel ground attacks by a haphazard assortment of warlords who embraced America's cause (and money) in order to defeat their zealous foes. Thankfully, it wasn't a fair fight. Special Forces and CIA teams armed with satellite radios and laser designators stood off a few miles from the trenches and directed the air traffic. B-1 and B-52 bombers, F-18s, F-15s, and AV-8s like Franzak's queued up, peeled off, and dropped thousands of bombs.

Unlike during World War II and Vietnam, accuracy was not a problem. Electronic imaging and laser guidance had changed the term *aerial bombardment* into *precision air attack*. The Taliban and al Qaeda were routed by the end of 2001.

However, while technically the United States had advanced, it lacked strategic common sense. Consider an analogy: On December 7, 1941, the Japanese had struck at Pearl Harbor, killing some 2,400 Americans. The president declared that the American military response would not falter until the Japanese ruling order was destroyed. Seven months later, Admiral Spruance led three carriers across the international date line west of Hawaii to the island of Midway. There he fought the epic battle that decimated the Imperial Naval Fleet and sealed Japan's fate.

Now consider an alternate scenario: Spruance stopped his carriers at the international date line because he was concerned about treaties governing hostilities at sea. No one in the States protested, and the Japanese fleet sailed back to Tokyo in triumph.

Yes, that sounds preposterous. Yet on 9/11 more Americans died in New York City than at Pearl Harbor. However, when the Taliban were trapped by our bombing in late 2001, we suspended further air attacks to allow Pakistan to land airliners to evacuate the key Taliban and the Pakistani officers who were their advisers. A few months later, Osama bin Laden and his al Qaeda fighters were cornered in the Tora Bora mountains. Due to military error, they managed to escape in disarray to the Pakistani side of the border. No segment of American society urged crossing the border in hot pursuit to destroy al Qaeda—not the president, not the secretary of defense, not the Joint Chiefs of Staff, not the Congress, not the pundits, and not any grassroots public movement.

It's highly unlikely the Pakistani government or people would have reacted with rage had we destroyed al Qaeda. In its sixty-year history, Pakistan had never controlled the mountains to where Osama fled. The region was called the Tribal Area, distinct from Pakistan proper. We did not stop after a considered debate of pros and cons inside our government. We stopped because our shared intuitions about the nature of war had changed. Our culture was kinder, gentler, and richer.

The result was that the Taliban and al Qaeda regrouped safely inside Pakistan, sorted out their units, accepted refuge among the tribes, and prepared for the next battle. It is baffling why our leaders—military and civilian—thought the war was over in 2001. By 2003, when Franzak's squadron deployed to Bagram Air Base on the fringe of the northern mountain ranges, Afghanistan was in the midst of a false peace. The Taliban were infiltrating back from Pakistan, careful not to raise a profile that would again unleash American air attacks.

What Franzak encountered—long sorties with no authorized targets, punctuated by moments of fierce fighting—set the tone for the war that dragged on year after year. On the one hand, we did not want to employ bombs against compounds that housed civilians. On the other hand, the Taliban fought from those very compounds. They had learned not to mass in trenches. Aerial bombing remained our trump card, however, when our troops came under heavy fire. With that exception, the Taliban enjoyed the sanctuary provided by mixing with the people. True, there were five or ten missile strikes each month by unmanned Predator drones inside Pakistan. These caused a few dozen casualties, not trivial but also not a game-changer. It was a bit odd that the Pakistanis accepted being bombed by drones rather than by pilots. Perhaps next we will dispatch robot raid teams across the border.

For Franzak and the other fighter pilots stationed in Afghanistan, the mission became reactive. They could not bomb unless the mission accorded with a long list of rules—a sensible restriction, perhaps, but one that meant long weeks and months of staying alert, but with swords sheathed. The weather, combined with the idiosyncrasies of the AV-8 aircraft, instilled a tension into every daily sortie.

Yet there was no relief. Many squadrons did four-month tours and returned to the States. A lesser number did six months. Franzak's squadron endured eleven months, one of the longest deployments of the war. What the book brings home is the claustrophobia of the setting. The squadron had to keep up morale in the dust, the wind, the rain, and the mud. The aircraft were temperamental and unforgiving, demanding exhausting hours of maintenance from the rugged ground crews. They could expect no relief and take no days off. With only six planes and demands for aircraft patrols every day, there was no slack and no downtime to relax.

Franzak brings home the mounting stress. It's like he wrote a diary. You can see the tension building, day by day, without escape. As the executive officer, he faces a full agenda of problem-solving and of easing tensions between a driving commanding officer and a squadron of Marines who feel like they're living in a submarine that doesn't have a port. As a reader, you can understand the growing insomnia, the brain wrestling with too many problems. He's both a pilot concerned with keeping his edge in the air, and a manager/leader juggling tensions that can't be solved.

You don't expect it. You envision the squadrons that maintain and fly high-tech aircraft as having tolerable, perhaps flashy lives. Instead, you learn that they have it harder than the grunts. We in the infantry may live in the dirt, but we have moments of exhilaration, terror, bloodlust, relief, laughter, and goof-off time.

An aviation squadron can never let its guard down. There's no such thing as an aircraft not superbly maintained. There's no way to break the monotony and gruel of the daily routine. It's leadership and duty in tight quarters. Franzak has given us grunts quite a book. I always envisioned the pilots climbing out of the cockpits, sauntering to the O Club for a cold beer and hot steak, and stretching out on a mattress for a long winter's sleep.

Franzak has broken that mold. I can't work up a good, naïve, undeserved resentment about the cushy life of the aviator anymore. The images of the AV-8 tossing about in crosswinds like a rampaging bull, and of nights with too much pressure and no relief to a grinding routine, are too vivid. His squadron perseveres, despite suffering the disappointment of having been extended. What Franzak conveys most vividly is the squadron's dogged devotion to duty—when there's nothing else to fall back on, that is the time when character and the traditions of a unit provide a concrete floor that cannot be chipped away. Had Franzak's squadron been ordered to stay in their huts next to the flight line and continue a flight per aircraft per day, they would have scrounged that base and all of Afghanistan to find the spare parts, and they'd still be up over the heads of the grunts, waiting for their call, day after day after day.

PREFACE

They say there are no atheists in foxholes and to a certain degree I can affirm that, though my religious convictions are tepid at best. I don't remember when I began to question God but I know it was a long time ago. My parents are least to blame. They took us to church regularly. But as I grew older and introspective I came to question things, especially God. My church visits dimmed and nightly prayers became monologues in darkness. I wondered if my brother in the twin bunk below or my sister in the adjoining room was praying. *Was anyone listening?* I wasn't sure, so I stopped.

As years passed I prayed sporadically without much thought, more on a whim when I felt obliged to thank someone or something for the beauty of it all, but I refrained from asking anything—ever. And then one day I prayed very hard and I asked for something. I wasn't in a foxhole. I was above it. I was safe and comfortable in my sheltered cocoon 20,000 feet over the Hindu Kush. But I prayed. I prayed when I heard the muted cries of men who at last understood their fate.

In combat, there is a haunting sound a man may give when he is certain of his end. To those who hear it, everything changes. It does not matter if you have never met this man other than the radio contact you established with him ten, twenty, or sixty minutes prior. In that short period, a bond is built. You come to know him and he, you. Because you are critical to him. You are essential to his being. He needs you. He needs you because you have something he does not. Perhaps it is situational awareness, perhaps it is a mode of transportation—a lifeline out of his demise—or perhaps, as was my case, you bring death. You bring the means to kill, to buy time if time can be bought.

My squadron, VMA-513,* the "Flying Nightmares," deployed to Afghanistan in late 2002 with the following mission statement: "On or about 7 October 2002, VMA-513 squadron (-) (REIN) with six AV-8B aircraft will deploy to Bagram, Afghanistan, for a period of approximately 180 days to conduct expeditionary based air support for the Coalition Forces Air Component Commander (CFACC)." Put simply, we were sent to Afghanistan to support the grunt. To provide air cover—a protective blanket—over soldiers as they patrolled the inhospitable Hindu Kush.

---

* For an explanation of *VMA* and many other terms used in this book, please consult the glossary.

Located on the other side of the world, Afghanistan is eleven and a half hours behind the United States in time zones. Add to that another two thousand years. No one knows exactly why Afghanistan chose a half-hour time zone, but as one journalist recently warned, "[N]ever get into a war with a people who live in a half-hour time zone. The reference is usually to Afghanistan, a country no one has ever been able to subdue, for long at least. And it's even more true for the Pashtun, the country's largest ethnic group, who don't seem to live in any time zone at all."*

The differences between the United States and Afghanistan are stark. Afghanistan's rugged terrain is dominated by a mountain range that stretches six hundred miles from northeastern to southwestern Afghanistan. Bulging 150 miles wide, the Hindu Kush, considered the western extension of the Himalayas, is crowned with peaks towering above 22,000 feet. Due to Afghanistan's semiarid steppe, in which cold winters and dry summers dominate, only 12 percent of the country is arable. But wherever crops are grown, one is sure to find opium. Comprising 22 percent of Afghanistan's gross domestic product (GDP) in 2008, opium production is at least down from its 2007 high, when the United Nations noted that it comprised 53 percent of Afghanistan's GDP. In 2008, the International Monetary Fund ranked Afghanistan's GDP per

* Robert Baer, "Avoiding a Quagmire in Afghanistan," *Time*, April 1, 2009.

capita at 172, out of 181 nations. A United Nations report in 2006 on world population prospects listed Afghanistan's infant mortality rate as the second highest in the world, losing ignominious first place to Sierra Leone.

Afghanistan's infrastructure is scant (when we deployed in 2002, there were only two paved highways in the entire country). Reliable electrical power—a myth. Economic prosperity and potential—dubious. By contrast, the United States is not only on the other side of the world, it's on the opposite end of the spectrum. Landlocked, isolated, and insulated from the rest of the world, Afghanistan resides like some giant time capsule that God buried several millennia ago.

In late 2002, when the Flying Nightmares deployed to Afghanistan, we did so from a nation with growing amnesia. The 9/11 attacks had occurred a little more than a year earlier. The Taliban and al Qaeda had been routed from Afghanistan, or so everyone thought. And for anyone in the know, we were being sent to do what most termed "mop-up" operations. The focus was elsewhere: the Senate had recently passed a joint resolution authorizing the use of military force against Iraq.

When I returned home from Afghanistan a year later, in 2003, people asked me about the war, about our strategy, how things were going, what I had seen. I tried to describe these things but was not very successful. Trying to understand Afghanistan is akin to trying to understand Vietnam, and trying to simplify it is likely to end in frustration. With an ever-changing object and strategy to obtain it, the mission in Afghanistan may have been best described as "a war in search of a strategy."*

Seven years have passed since my return but I don't think much has changed, except of course U.S. troop levels and fatalities. I hope this changes, but I'm not optimistic. In 2002, U.S. troops in Afghanistan totaled 5,200. That doubled by the end of 2003, to 10,400. By the end of 2008, U.S. troops in Afghanistan numbered a little more than 30,000. A year later, at the end of 2009, the number again doubled, to 62,000. And in 2010, we shall see that number increase another 30,000. Criticized by some as a dithering and lukewarm response, the current administration's investment of U.S. forces in Afghanistan is not small, nor should it be. But there will be more fatalities.

As historian Stephen Tanner has noted, "Afghans have honed their martial skills by fighting among themselves, in terrain that facilitates divisions of power and resists the concept of centralized control."† Afghanistan has seen one invader after another—Alexander the Great, Genghis Khan, Tamerlane, Babur, the Brit-

---

* Carl Conetta, *Strange Victory: A Critical Appraisal of Operation Enduring Freedom and the Afghanistan War* (Cambridge, Mass.: Project on Defense Alternatives, 2002), p. 10.
† Stephen Tanner, *Afghanistan: A Military History from Alexander the Great to the Fall of the Taliban* (Cambridge, Mass.: Da Capo, 2002), p. 1.

ish, the Soviets, and now the Americans. In each case Afghanistan has been able to defeat its invaders with patience—patience that lasts through generations. Perhaps Afghanistan's violent history is, as Tanner also noted, "due in equal measure to the nature of its territory, which has in turn influenced the nature of its people.... [The] bulk of the land is unrelentingly harsh, and where it does not consist of jagged, successive range of heights it is largely desert.... It is a land that can be easily invaded but is much more difficult to hold—and to hold together."*

There are new generals in charge and I believe they are smarter and have more support, but Americans don't like long wars. I wonder if our patience can persist. I know the enemy is patient and more Americans will die. Yearly U.S. fatalities in Afghanistan reached 317 in 2009, out of more than 900 killed since 9/11. By all accounts the casualties and fatalities of Americans in Afghanistan are infinitesimal compared to other wars, but how does one measure the value of just one American serviceman—or woman? And what does one say to the widow, the parents, the children? Or does one not say anything, except maybe "I'm sorry"?

* Stephen Tanner, *Afghanistan: A Military History from Alexander the Great to the Fall of the Taliban* (Cambridge, Mass.: Da Capo, 2002), p. 3.

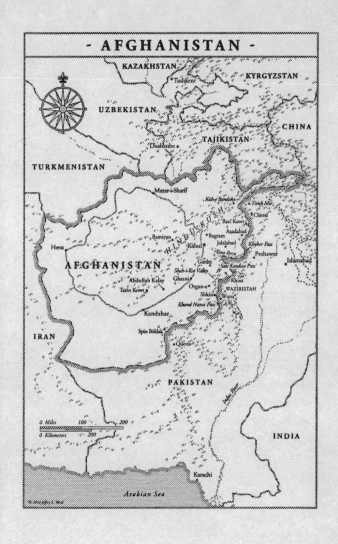

I

DEPARTURES

There are certain events in life one never forgets. The morning of October 7, 2002, was one of those times. I was deploying for combat. I was stepping inside the ring.

During my seventeen years of military service as a navy enlisted man and later as a Marine officer, I had deployed overseas five other times. I had served on the USS *Ranger* in the Persian Gulf in the early 1980s as a young sailor, loading bombs and missiles on jets. After earning my commission and wings, I flew Harrier jets across the Pacific Ocean, island hopping from California to Hawaii, to Wake, to Guam, to Japan and back the other way—twice. I had also spent months at sea, flying Harriers from small deck carriers supporting operations in Somalia, Kuwait, Australia, and other locales.

Those deployments and the men I had served under helped shape me for what I was now going to undertake. But some things can't be taught. This deployment was different. Secrets buried deep floated upward, echoing the promise I once made. No one knew the promise except me, but that was enough. The product of a transgression in a dark past, the promise was an attempt to escape guilt.

It happened in flight school, shortly before my winging in 1990. A moment of indiscretion and everything changed. I hardly knew the woman but she bore my son some nine months later and named him so. Though her aim was that of greater intentions, I had no such notions. But I loved the boy. I tried very hard to be a good father, writing letters and making telephone calls and visits as the years passed, but the reality I learned was that I was a father in name only. I was hardly there. Visits once, perhaps twice a year could not forge the bond a boy needs from his father.

As time wore on I swore to never fail any future child of mine, to always be there—physically there. Now, as I prepared to leave, the promise and guilt returned. I was a father again, happily married with an eleven-month-old son, but I was leaving him. Though the reasons appeared valid, I questioned my motives. Was I going because my country needed me or was I going for selfish reasons?

I turned and looked at the jets glistening in the morning sun. As the Arizona dawn breathed light into a new day, my thoughts swirled in the guilt before finally deciding to settle on a moonless night some ten years earlier.

My relationship with the Harrier was different

from that of most pilots. It was love-hate. I loved the airplane for the thrill she gave, but I hated her for the friends she took. My bond with her had been forged in blood on August 16, 1992, in Kuwait, just south of Iraq. It was my first deployment as a pilot. I and nine other pilots formed the Harrier contingent of the 11th Marine Expeditionary Unit (MEU) aboard the USS *Tarawa*. As our ship entered the Persian Gulf, the detachment of AV-8B Harriers was granted a two-week training hiatus in Kuwait. It was a place for us to hone our "night attack" skills. Then, on one hot August night, three of us landed and waited for the fourth. But he never returned. We waited and joked that he must have had a total electrical failure and landed at some obscure airfield—that he would have the last laugh. As the minutes turned to hours the impending doom became palpable, but no one spoke of it. Then reality struck. News arrived that a fireball had been spotted in the desert just south of the Iraqi border. The words froze each of us in that second, time stopped, and silence consumed us. Then we separated like remnants of a meteor bursting in the sky, each fragment on its own disparate vector, no one saying a word, each within his own gravity and guilt. I opened the door and stepped back into the unforgiving night, unsure of my destination. Hot, humid blackness devoured me, the tarmac sticky and warm against my soles. I shuffled forward toward the jets. I found her at the end of the row—the girl I had just flown. I didn't cry. I just talked to her. Rip was gone. His flesh and bones, torn to pieces no bigger than his hand, lay strewn across miles of desert he neither knew nor loved. I wondered how it happened. The investigation in the following days only raised more questions. But the thoughts that haunted me that night were of the wife who would give birth again in three weeks and a three-year-old son who would never again see his father.

That was ten years earlier. Now it was 2002 and I was deploying again. I was also wondering if we'd all return. I turned my gaze away from the flight line and toward the shouts and yells that surrounded me, mostly kids playing.

It was strange to see so many civilians in the hangar, especially women and children. Once or twice a year they filled the hangar, usually at the squadron Christmas party, air show, or change of command. But the women and children were strangers here. That was clear to the Marines who slaved in its confines, the mechanics who kept the troublesome Harriers aloft, who spent more hours inside the hangar than they spent at home. The floors had been mopped clean of JP-5 jet fuel and hydraulic fluid, leaving the hangar pretending to be something it wasn't. Tables filled with cookies, coffees, and Cokes replaced the jets, forklifts, and cranes. On the walls banners hung: "Good Luck Nightmares," "We love you Gunny Rod," "Semper Fi Nightmares." There was even the ubiquitous "Let's Roll."

Kathleen Dixon, the wife of my boss, Lieutenant Colonel Jim "Grouper" Dixon, pulled a Kleenex from her purse, knelt down, and wiped it against the face of her youngest son. The boy seemed annoyed by the gesture as he tried to pull away from his mother's strong grasp. "Hey, Kathleen, how are you?" I asked. Kathleen had been the focal point for the squadron wives over the last three months. She dealt with the countless complaints and meaningless gossip that can cripple a unit before or during a deployment. As the emotional storm swirled around her, she appeared calm and not the least bit frazzled by tugging currents. While the commanders reaped the accolades, their spouses never received enough recognition for their mystical and often unseen labor.

"Shit, Zak, you know how I am. But thanks for asking." Kathleen's candor was always refreshing given the number of pretentious spouses who attempted to wear their husband's rank on their collar.

"Kathleen, it's going to be OK. Grouper didn't leave anything to chance. He rode us like dogs over the last few months."

"You don't have to tell me, Zak. I live with the man."

Kathleen's banter had a way of reducing the stress. She understood that. She had to. The crashes and funerals endured over the years created a callous layer—a shield—but it did not deter her purpose. Kathleen's role was as critical as that of her husband, the two of them holding the squadron together, although at different ends. Grouper with the Marines in Bagram, Afghanistan, and Kathleen with the families in Yuma, Arizona.

The pilots suited up and climbed into their jets. I wanted to be in that first wave, but Grouper had directed me to remain behind and secure the hangar after everyone left. I would be the last Nightmare to leave. I was in charge of locking the doors and turning out the lights.

I pulled the small digital camera from my flight suit and began taking pictures. I felt uneasy, like an intruder, as I captured the sobbing eyes and tearful hugs of families saying good-bye. But I had promised myself two things regarding this deployment: take pictures and keep a journal.

As a young boy, I had listened to the stories of my grandfather. He had fought on Iwo Jima as a navy Seabee during World War II. His stories enthralled me with adventure as he described driving a bulldozer while enemy Japanese shot at him. But memories fade with time. Facts become distorted and the lines between reality and fiction blur. I wanted a way to preserve the present without relying on aging memory. Starting the journal would be easy. Maintaining it, harder.

The Harriers cranked up on cue. Within a few minutes, the radio in the squadron ready room crackled. The lead tanker aircraft was "up." The mission was a "go." Captain Toby Moore and I were the designated backups. I'd jump into the ground spare if anyone went down in the chocks while Toby would fly the airborne spare to the first refueling point. If the primary jets' aerial refueling systems checked out airborne, Toby would return to Yuma, shut down, and jump into the C-130 with me and twenty other Marines designated as trail maintenance crew.

The Harriers taxied out single file as families waved frantically. I watched my wife, Katie, tighten her arms around our son, Caleb. Her eyes narrowed as the jets roared down the runway. A tear came to her eye. I looked away and toward the Harriers. The jets circled around to the south and passed over the airfield in a tight wedge formation. The friends and families of the Nightmares waved as the Harriers rocketed overhead. But I knew the pilots didn't see anyone below. They stared intently to their left or right, maintaining a position so that wingtips didn't touch, while the thunderous roar of the Pegasus motors drowned out both the cheers and cries below. The noise faded as the jets climbed eastward, shrinking to dots in the dark blue, then vanishing.

Family members held each other in tearful hugs. The only ones not crying were children, who either played or stared vacantly upward as if searching unseen ground while those taller looked down upon them and thought silently—*Daddy is going away for a long time. He's going to war.*

"Well, babe, there they go. Do you want to hang out until I have to leave in the C-130?"

"No, Mike. I think I'll head home. Caleb's tired. It's been a long morning. You have things you need to do and we've already said good-bye." She was aiding me. I knew it, but my body froze and my eyes welled. Any previous excitement about untold futures faded. A helpless feeling overcame me. For the first time, I didn't want to go. I stared at Katie. I didn't know what to say or do. An uncomfortable silence hung there. Seeing my paralysis, she stepped forward. I gripped my arms around her and the boy, who was still wearing his yellow earplugs. Their touch brought me back to the moment and the crux of it all. *Why should others risk their lives and not me?*

I released them, Katie saying nothing but nodding slowly, a cautious smile on her lips. I kissed her and then Caleb. She wheeled around and I watched as her five-foot-one-inch, ninety-five-pound frame drifted away. Caleb, looking over her shoulder, stared back at me. He didn't smile or cry. He just looked at me as a one-year-old does—his head bouncing to the rhythm of his mother's steps, their bodies sliding off toward a distant door in the hangar corner. I choked back all sounds as if under the direction of some long-forgotten drill sergeant. Unconsciously my hand rose as if ignoring the script and waved good-bye to Caleb, who could see me, and Katie, who could not. Then the hangar door opened and closed and they were gone.

2

HAPPY HUNTING

I stood alone for some time, staring at the door, waiting for it to open as if something had been forgotten—an item, a word, a gesture. But the door didn't open. The hangar was mostly empty now. A few Marines, part of the trail maintenance crew, meandered around with wives or girlfriends awkwardly clinging on. Seeing nothing else on which to dwell, I ventured upstairs toward the Nightmare ready room like some despondent stray, seeking familiar ground.

I picked a chair in the back row and sat impatiently watching the TV in the corner but heard and saw nothing. I was alone except for the borrowed pilot who sat behind the wooden desk next to the radio. I thought about sending him back to his squadron but decided against it. Though we did not speak, I wanted the company. A static crackle forced my head to turn. "Base, Nightmare 11." It was Grouper somewhere over eastern Arizona leading the jets to the first aerial refueling point.

"Nightmare 11, this is base, go ahead," the borrowed pilot responded.

"All chicks have gotten a drink and are a 'go.' The spare is heading back," Grouper stated. The six jets would now make Cherry Point, North Carolina, sometime in the afternoon. The Marines, Toby, and I would follow closely behind in a C-130 transport aircraft.

"Roger, Nightmare 11. Solid copy, and"—the pilot paused for effect while smiling at me—"happy hunting."

The visitor's words struck me as odd. I was accustomed to farewells of "Good luck," "Have a safe flight," or "Be safe." I never heard anyone wish anyone "Happy hunting," but these were different times.

I headed back to my office and sent out a final e-mail to my parents. After closing my laptop and cleaning off my desk, I saw Caleb's half-filled sippy cup sitting on the windowsill. Katie must have forgotten it during the morning's fanfare. I placed the cup inside the small fridge in the corner of my office. As I flipped off the light and locked the door behind me, I wondered why I hadn't poured out the milk. It was going to be a long time before I returned. I decided there were forces I didn't understand—illogical forces that sometimes guided me.

Downstairs in the hangar, a few wives and children remained, spending the last family minutes together before the Marines boarded the C-130. I watched as Toby landed the backup Harrier and taxied into the line. In a matter of minutes, he shed his flight gear and ran across the tarmac to join us. The Marines quickly boarded the dull gray transport. Then it was my turn. I turned and looked at the Nightmare hangar one more time. It had become a second home over the last year, but I felt no remorse leaving it. Katie and Caleb were gone. Now it was my turn.

I squeezed into the main cabin, past the Marines and their gear, and looked for the first open seat. Pallets of toolboxes, spare Harrier parts, and cargo containers stacked on top of each other, held in place by chains and webbed nets, occupied most of the aircraft. The C-130 had been converted into a flying garage. Marines sat crammed next to each other in weblike hammocks that lined the inside fuselage. I fastened my seat belt, closed my eyes, and tried not to think of home. A few minutes later, we were airborne, flying east. When the flight engineer gave the "OK" sign, I unfastened my seat belt and climbed over the cruise boxes to the rear of the C-130. Next to a spare set of tires in between the rows of toolboxes, I stretched out on the hard steel deck. I rolled my flight jacket into a makeshift pillow and lowered my head. As I drifted to sleep, I reflected on the forces that had brought me to this point in time.

In what seemed like a few minutes but in reality was much longer, I woke to the prodding and rocking of someone against me. "Major Franzak, you OK? You're talking funny and kicking the toolboxes." I opened my eyes. A bald-headed, smiling Sergeant Harris stood above me.

"Where are we?" I asked.

"Sir, we're about thirty minutes out from Cherry Point."

"Thanks. Guess I was dreaming."

"Sir, you were dreaming some weird shit, then," the burly Marine stated, stepping over me and back to his confines.

"Yeah. It was weird," I answered, my voice lost in the noise of the humming props. Soon we would land in Cherry Point, our first stop. After one day of rest, we'd make the long flight across the Atlantic and into Spain. Then two nights in Rota, Spain, before flying on to Bahrain in the Persian Gulf. After one more night in Bahrain, we'd launch for our final destination: Bagram, Afghanistan. If all went well, we'd reach Bagram in five days. The Marines were hoping for a smooth trip. Yet those of us who had experienced deployments to far-off destinations knew such luck rarely occurred. There would be hiccups. It was only a question of when.

I sat up, searching for my green flight bag. Finding it at my feet, I reached inside and pulled out a small olive-drab logbook. Its first pages were filled with hieroglyphic scribble denoting duties and pilot landings aboard a boat a year earlier. The olive-drab book had an auspicious beginning in which fate intervened and prevented its premature departure. The book had been opened as an official record. It was then misplaced, another opened, and when found again, its utility was circumspect, as the record had been officially transferred to another. And since it had been marked on, written in, it was disposable. As the Marine cleaned the shelves and moved to discard the item the day before our departure, I intervened. I saw utility where others did not. I did not mind the fact that it was used. I simply skipped the first three pages and began, "Franzak, 7 Oct 2002. Day One. Our squadron deployed this morning for combat operations in Afghanistan. . . ."

As I continued my first journal entry I thought back on all that had happened in the previous year.

Katie and I had returned to the desert in July 2001 following my yearlong master's program at the Naval War College in Newport, Rhode Island. Upon my return to Yuma, the Marine Corps assigned me to VMA-513, the Flying Nightmares, where the commander who preceded Grouper tasked me with fixing his maintenance department. As the aircraft maintenance officer, I reported directly to VMA-513's then commander, Lieutenant Colonel David "Cow" Gurney. Cow wanted a quick turnaround. It wasn't happening. After two months, I was on the chopping block.

September arrived, and though the coolness of fall had yet to embrace Yuma, the oven days of summer were gone. I remember well that Tuesday morning. It was 5 A.M. and Katie lay awake next to me, swollen and sick, the baby due in a month. We rose as she prepared to drive me to work. I drank my coffee and watched the TV when it happened. News anchors rambled strangely about smoke pouring from a building. Katie walked over and sat down next to me. Then we watched the horror unfold.

I will never forget that Tuesday morning. Yuma, a new home. Katie eight months pregnant sitting next to me. The live picture. The second airliner colliding with the south tower in real time. People jumping. The towers collapsing. Innocent people gone in a flash. Perhaps every generation must suffer a shock that forever scars them—a threat to their way of life and the world they know.

On September 12, 2001, things changed. They changed everywhere. Dusty atlases were pulled from high shelves. Decorative furniture globes that sat untouched and unmoved in years were suddenly spun, as people sought to understand where these distant lands lay and what was there. Obscure names most Americans had never heard—*Bin Laden, al Qaeda,* and *Taliban*—were soon added to every American's lexicon. We all remained skittish, just waiting for the next attack. Then we responded.

On October 7, 2001, operatives from the CIA and Special Forces combined with the Afghan opposition group the Northern Alliance and attacked Taliban positions in Afghanistan, designating targets for the constant flow of American fighters and bombers that circled overhead. And while the attacks unfolded, I struggled forward as a failing maintenance officer, my two hundred Marines unsure of their leader, all of us wondering if we'd ever be called upon.

In late October, Katie gave birth to Caleb, who quickly consumed our lives. The days rolled into weeks and the weeks into months as work demanded more and more of my time. As fall turned into winter my maintenance department started its turnaround, a slow, almost imperceptible reversal of course. Soon after, the unit's next designated commander, Lieutenant Colonel Jim "Grouper" Dixon, arrived and settled in as the executive officer.

Grouper was an old-school Harrier pilot who grew up under pilots who flew the AV-8A, the original "Widow-Maker." Harrier pilots who had flown the "A" measured AV-8B pilots as something less, or so their actions conveyed. Grouper stood six feet, with a slightly muscular build. His head was capped snow-white with only the slightest shade of gray. He boasted a large gray mustache, a rarity for a Marine. The son of a career army man, Grouper saw life in simple blacks and whites. He rarely gave praise. A stickler for details, Grouper was one of the most passionate and ethical officers I knew. Marines generally feared him, especially pilots. Grouper and Cow were miles apart in thought and personality, and they worked together about as well as oil and water mix.

By late spring 2002, the squadron's maintenance department had managed a complete reversal. We now led the Harrier fleet in aircraft readiness rates. By summer, the media lost interest in Afghanistan and began covering the possible invasion of Iraq. According to many political pundits, major combat operations in Afghanistan were over. America's infatuation with its own success seemed premature, given Afghanistan's long and violent history regarding invaders. But most Americans are not well versed in world history, and those who sounded any warnings were drummed out by those lauding our success.

In June 2002, Cow turned the reins of the squadron over to Grouper. I expected reassignment, as it was customary for a new CO to emplace his own team. Much to my surprise, Grouper asked me to stay and serve as his executive officer. Things were going well in maintenance and I was happy. I enjoyed working with the junior Marines—the young lance corporals, corporals, and sergeants who carried the maintenance department on their backs. The job of executive officer focused on administrative matters, something I loathed. Nevertheless, the opportunity to remain in a gun squadron solidified my decision.

As I settled in as Grouper's XO (executive officer), rumors spread regarding deploying Harriers to Afghanistan. Most of the fighters supporting missions over Afghanistan were flying from bases in the Persian Gulf or from bases in one of the "Stans"—Kyrgyzstan and Uzbekistan being the primary locales. This equated to transit times of three and four hours before the jets were on station over the Afghanistan battlefields. The long transit times put additional strain on the tankers as well.

Military leaders wanted more efficient combat air support, but Bagram, Afghanistan, where most of the

American firepower was based, lacked the amenities that many fighters need. A lone A-10 squadron was based there despite requests for additional airpower. Navy F/A-18 and air force F-16 squadrons refused to base their aircraft in Bagram due to the lack of infrastructure and the poor runway condition. The Marine Corps stepped forward and played up the Harrier, boasting it could handle the assignment.

Rumor became fact. The Pentagon issued a "warning order" that trickled down the chain of command to Marine Air Group (MAG) 13 in Yuma. The MAG-13 commander reviewed his squadrons and chose ours, VMA-513, for the mission. Things happened fast. The change of command occurred in June 2002. In early July, Grouper and several staff officers from 3rd Marine Aircraft Wing traveled to Afghanistan to conduct a site survey. After Grouper's endorsement that the mission was doable, the decision to deploy the Nightmares was finalized, but with one caveat. Because of Bagram's limited space, the squadron was directed to deploy with only six aircraft and ten pilots. Difficult decisions were made as the squadron split. Half the squadron would deploy to Afghanistan and combat, while the remainder would deploy aboard the USS *Belleau Wood* for a normal Western Pacific (WESTPAC) assignment.

In August, attachments from other units joined the Nightmares. As a gun squadron, we had pilots, maintainers, and aircraft. But we didn't have cooks, engineers, military police, electricians, radio operators, or other job specialties needed to operate in an austere location like Afghanistan. Thus forty Marines from MALS-13 (an aviation maintenance and logistics squadron) and MWSS-373 and MWSS-374 (aviation support squadrons) joined our unit. While we held meetings in Yuma, personnel in Afghanistan cleared a minefield, the location of our future home. At the end of August, we sent thirty Marines forward to build our camp and living quarters.

Before we knew it, October arrived. Pilot training was over. Our final flights in the simulator and at an outlying field were high-hot-heavy operations. This involved high-speed short takeoffs (STOs) and 120-knot landings. The short takeoffs were anything but short, and the landings failed to capitalize on the Harrier's ability to land vertically, something the Harrier couldn't do in Bagram. The Harrier's Rolls-Royce Pegasus motors didn't produce the same amount of thrust at an elevation of 5,000 feet that they did at sea level. The irony of this made me wonder if the Harrier was really best suited for the Afghanistan mission or if politics were at play. Specifically, defense budget justification—proving the Harrier could handle combat so the Marine Corps could buy more of them or its follow-on vision, the Joint Strike Fighter. But debating merits didn't matter anymore. We were on our way now. The Harrier and the Nightmares were either ready or they weren't. Only combat would reveal the truth.

3

LOSING SIGHT

It was 1 A.M. We had been in Cherry Point, North Carolina, for thirty-six hours. Two days ago, Yuma, Arizona. This afternoon, Spain. After that, Bahrain, then Afghanistan. The sooner we got there the better.

The pilots relaxed in the ready room chairs as the air force lieutenant colonel handed us our smart packs, manila envelopes stuffed with maps and in-flight cards for the nine-hour flight. The maps depicted our circuitous route up the East Coast, across the northern Atlantic, down the European coast, and into Spain, while the numerous in-flight cards provided administrative items: call signs, frequencies, waypoints, refueling points, airfield data, divert field data, bingo profiles (emergency fuel). All of them would increase our situational awareness as we crossed the pond. The route was designed not only to get us to Rota, Spain, quickly but to stay in range of emergency divert fields throughout the flight in case anyone developed a problem.

As I contemplated my future, it was the past that kept surfacing—the image of Katie sliding away from me with Caleb's tiny face bobbing on her shoulder, his eyes staring at me, expressionless. It was time to compartmentalize. There were times I let my mind wander, debating whimsical issues or reminiscing as it saw fit. I allowed it that luxury so when I called it to task, it responded. I had learned the trick in flight school long ago. The matter was simple and not debatable. Thus with a conscious decision I banished all thoughts except those of the mission.

The air force officer introduced himself, called roll, and then moved quickly to the weather. The forecast for Spain: clear skies. The forecast for our departure out of Cherry Point: broken clouds and intermittent showers, sketchy but not bad. But the weather over the Atlantic drew sighs. The pilots fidgeted in their chairs. A cold front stretched from Greenland south to the Azores. There was no avoiding it. There would be clouds, turbulence, and likely vertigo. I hated tanking in the clag and I dreaded the vertigo. Thick clouds necessitated tight formation flying while turbulence caused the big KC-10 tankers to bounce. And when the tankers bounced they shook the heavy refueling baskets that trailed behind them—baskets with whom our jets must mate. In-flight refueling was a process as simple as sex unless confounded with temperamental weather, for then the dynamic changed. Mature pilots were often humbled, appearing more like teenage boys trying to copulate with a teasing courtesan.

Once the air force pilot finished, he nodded to Grouper. Grouper stood and walked to the podium in regal fashion. No one doubted who was in charge, least of all Grouper. He began with a few admin items, followed by some stern warnings—"Don't do this. Don't do that." Then he briefed the details of the sortie, beginning with the takeoff. There were six Harriers in the flight. A common technique was to divide the flight into two three-ships that would take off separately and join en route. But that wasn't what Grouper briefed. Instead, Grouper explained that lead through dash four would take off on the primary runway, while dash five (me) and my wingman, dash six, launched simultaneously from a perpendicular runway pointing in another direction. Our two-ship would then join the flight of four as they crossed in front of us in a tight turn around the airfield. The plan was to join quickly, low to the ground, beneath the weather.

Nobody flinched. Everyone but Grouper thought the same thing: it was night and we had never done this before—no one was familiar with this strange procedure of a six-plane simultaneous takeoff, using two separate runways, joining below the cloud deck, at night, on night vision goggles (NVGs). I saw no need to rush the join-up. The tankers were a hundred miles away. I thought about the scud layer hanging over the airfield, the limited field of view of the

NVGs, the difficulty in seeing clouds through NVGs, as cloud layers obscured moonlight, thus masking their identity. But Grouper's swagger, though brash, was convincing. He was the commander and was leading the sortie. Foolishly, I put aside my reservations and said nothing.

"Hey, does anyone else want a diaper?" AJ called out. I turned and looked at Major Andrew J. "AJ" Heino, the squadron's operations officer, who was holding a box of diapers above his head. The only other major in the squadron, AJ was a peer and a good friend. He was also a practical joker.

"Sir, what the fuck are you talking about?" queried Captain Roger "Jolly" Hardy. A "sir" in any sentence always excused exclamatory words that might otherwise challenge one's authority. It also appeared the new pilots weren't taking the bait.

"Hey, I'm not going to crap in my flight suit. This is going to be a nine-hour flight." AJ looked at me wide-eyed, and I then realized he was serious. I turned away shaking my head, my thoughts to myself. I was excited to be flying again. It had been almost a week as the jets had been groomed for the transit and then left coldly in the stable for fear of breaking them. Having missed the first leg, I was glad to be back in the fray, even if it was a long trip across the cold North Atlantic.

We suited up in our thermal underwear, followed by our anti-immersion suits, referred to as "poopy suits." The poopy suits were skintight, rubber dry suits to protect us in case we had to eject over the North Atlantic. Pilots had mixed thoughts about wearing them. If anyone ejected, it would be a long time before help arrived. Most believed the poopy suit only prolonged the inevitable.

We finished dressing, climbed into our jets, and started on cue. The operations duty officer (ODO) notified us that the tankers were taking off from Dover Air Force Base, in Delaware. We taxied to our separate runways—Grouper in charge of his four-ship and me in charge of my two-ship. Tower cleared us for takeoff. I listened as Grouper directed his division on the takeoff, but I couldn't see them, despite contorting my neck and head to extreme angles. The NVGs' field of view was simply too narrow. It was then that I began to question the brilliance of the plan. The clock was ticking. I had to time my take-off correctly. Grouper's four-ship was airborne somewhere in the night and moving quickly away from me and my wingman. After fifteen seconds, I launched on a hunch, hoping my timing was not too late, or worse, too early.

Following a mishap, an investigation officer and his team sort through the aircraft wreckage, review all maintenance records, interview witnesses and any surviving participants, and collect and review countless other data to determine what happened. In a process that lasts several months, they eventually reach a conclusion after much rigorous debate. They then publish a report listing the causes of the accident in hopes that other pilots will learn from the mistakes and similar mishaps will be avoided. In almost every case the report cites a chain of events that led to the crash. The report also notes that any one person could have interrupted the chain of events by doing this instead of that. But as all pilots will attest, the trick of "doing this instead of that," of recognizing seemingly meaningless events as they unfold and knowing they are leading toward an impending disaster, is never as easy as it often later appears.

My jet rolled down the tarmac and rotated. Three flashing strobes appeared to my left. *But where was dash four?* I banked my jet smoothly to the right in an attempt to cut the corner and expedite the rendezvous. First dash two, then dash three reported joining. I watched the blinding strobes flash close together as they skirted low above the earth. I thought about asking lead and the others to kill their flashing strobe lights but was afraid they might evaporate in the blackness. "Four, state your position," I called out.

"Four is in trail, five Harriers in sight."

I had no idea why dash four had lagged behind, but there was no sense in asking now. The outlines of the jets took shape before me as I slid up next to them in loose formation. I reported joining, followed shortly by dash four stating the same. All six jets now tightened the formation, each squeezing closer to another as we entered a thin, wispy puree of moisture. Grouper leveled his wings, and the six of us rose as one. And for some unknown reason, through the green tinge of the NVGs, like some secret portal into the night, I saw the dirt and grime and black soot of exhaust trailing down the fuselages as I studied the four shapes to my left. The entities moved like a single, breathing mass, one jet bobbing up, another down, as they shifted about on the tiny phosphorous image before me.

Separated by a few feet, the jets responded to the skill of their drivers, each pilot intent on holding his line, not too close, not too far, the fear of swapping paint residing in each of us. Then suddenly the shapes vanished and my eyes grew wide. But they saw nothing except an empty green disk of scintillating electrons. Then the one closest to me—the jet I had been flying formation on—reappeared, then disappeared, then reappeared, as if it were unsure of the trick. Without warning, the wispy clouds had turned to cake batter. My breathing quickened and I waited, knowing the future and fearing its sure, brutal arrival.

"Two has lost sight."

Aw shit, here we go. I squeezed the stick tighter and focused on the only aircraft I could see. While procedures are taught and drilled early in flight school for losing sight when two, three, or four aircraft are flying formation in instrument conditions (proportionally complicated by the number of aircraft), no such procedures exist for more than four aircraft, because flying in instrument conditions with more than four is not allowed. Though these facts may not appear relevant to those who find themselves outside the confines of rules, regulations, or any written procedures, there is a tried-and-true system attested to by all who are able to return and speak of its success. Usually they do so quietly, as a pilot's superstition is exceeded only by his ego. Those who would argue against this proven system are never heard from, because it is impossible to conjure up their spirits and ask them, "Did you pray?"

My eyes remained glued to the airplane on my left. Suddenly the shadowy figure turned sharply into me and I knew what had happened. His voice confirmed it. "Four has lost sight." He was taking a separation maneuver from the other aircraft he could no longer see. I snatched the stick to the right to avoid certain impact, hoping my wingman responded likewise. The three of us banked in unison to the right, my jet squeezed between two Harriers, all of us moving away from our wingmen we could no longer see. My body tensed and my shoulders scrunched upward. My left and right hand strangled independent victims—the throttle and stick. Then, without warning, the apparition to my left vanished, reversing away as quickly as he came.

I thumbed the mike switch forcefully. "Five's lost sight," I called out as I shifted my eyes to my glass head-up display system (HUD) and instruments that told me which way was up—instruments that I and the other pilots, except Grouper, had not been able to reference since we had taken off, because we were flying fingertip formation on NVGs, in the clouds, preoccupied with not hitting one another.

As I glanced at my instruments for the first time, a mere second after losing sight, my fear was replaced by unbridled panic. To my horror, I realized my jet was in a ten-degree nose-down slicing turn, plunging toward earth. It had happened in the separation maneuver, but I had remained ignorant because in the clouds there is no horizon—no top and bottom, no up and down. I leveled my wings and pulled quickly back to the horizon—too quick. My wingman's call confirmed the basis of my anxiety.

"Six has lost sight."

Six Harriers now occupied the same space, flying at over 300 miles per hour with visibility less than thirty feet. But because we couldn't see one another, we were unsure where to move and how to avoid what we couldn't see. My right hand squeezed the control stick tighter and my breathing stopped as I awaited the arrival of unwelcome metal.

But through some benevolent force that protects the stupid, it did not come to be. First one pilot, then another reported in, stating an altitude and a reference from the last or next waypoint. Finally, after all pilots had established an altitude separation from each other, Grouper spoke. In a calm, melodic voice vacant of all fear, he reported clearing the overcast above 8,000 feet. And I wondered, *Does he know? Does he know? Does he fucking know?*

Slowly, one by one in the night silence, the Harriers popped free of that viscous moisture, and from a distant view it must have appeared as tiny night caddis lifting free of a pond's surface, having survived the fate that hunted them below. Having shucked their sacks of some previous life and finding new wings, they gladly floated upward, mesmerized and greeted by the smattering of tiny distant fires and a small white crescent that loomed above.

I found no comfort in that night despite its raw, naked beauty, for I found myself wondering over and over again how I would deal with the issue—how I would explain to Grouper the near tragedy. I feared his response. Grouper would not like the criticism, but his plan had nearly killed us. If Grouper did not mention the near calamity in the debrief, the pilots would look to me—the second in command, the tactician and night system instructor—to illustrate the fallacy. The burden was mine and I feared it. I reached into my lower g-suit and pulled out my Skoal. Not worrying about bad habits or what I should or should not do, I savored the fine cured leaves as the drug dispensed its venom. My body slowly unwound.

We finally joined as a six-ship upon reaching our tankers in the skies over New Jersey. No one said much, then or later, as there was not much to say. But I believe most felt as I did, not sure how they managed the escape and wondering if it was only a slight pause before some greater calamity. After the last Harrier refueled in the smooth air just south of New York City, the tankers turned east with us in tow. The twinkling lights of the city slowly disappeared beneath our wings, replaced by the ink-black Atlantic. It was cold and dark ahead—a black hole sucking us forward.

Looking down, I wondered when I would see those tiny, pretty lights again, and then for the first time I realized I might never see them again. A chill filled my cockpit as I thought about whether I had left everything in order and would they find it and was everything signed, and then it seemed the simplest thing—a good-bye—might never be given. And that seemed unfair. Then I wondered if fairness had anything to do with it.

So I looked back over my shoulder one final time to find peace, but I did not find it. Instead my eyes found the corner of the island where I had stood eighteen months earlier, and I recalled how I had looked up in awe, mesmerized by the towers' grandeur and simplicity. But they were gone now, gone with the innocence, innocence buried in rubble, buried with their good-byes.

Then my wing devoured the last of the lights and with nothing more to see or gleam below, I looked east toward my future—cold, dark skies and somewhere in that blackness, a storm.

4

LEFT BEHIND

The storms over the Atlantic were not as bad as had been forecasted. After spending several hours flying in the goo, we emerged in daylight somewhere east of Greenland and north of the Azores. With the jet stream aiding our journey, we landed in Rota, Spain, eight hours after taking off in what can be described only as a debacle. But despite the ugliness of the recovery no one was hurt. We climbed free of our cockpits and listened as Grouper debriefed the flight.

Much was said of the recovery, and the crossing, and the tanking, but the issue—the unconventional take-off plan and the near collision that followed—was not mentioned. It was as if it had never happened. Breaking all protocol, Grouper simply skipped debriefing the plan, the takeoff, and how it all unfolded. I watched as the pilots hung their heads, unsure what to say since Grouper's control of the conch shell was firm and un-wavering. I had seen the eyebrows rise, the heads shake, the innuendos as if to say, "Can you believe that?" or

"I can't wait to hear this one." As my eyes scanned the group, I guessed their thoughts. *By God, please someone mention the takeoff lest we ever have to do that again. Please someone point out the fallacy in that disastrous plan so that we may learn from it.*

As the second in command, it was my responsibility to highlight the issue if no one else did. It was my responsibility to say, "Sir, the takeoff plan was a bad idea and we should have never tried it, especially since none of us had ever practiced it during the day, let alone on NVGs with six aircraft joining under a low-lying cloud deck. And what was the purpose, the rush? And above all, what can we learn from it?" I had more hours on NVGs than anyone else in the squadron and more than most Harrier pilots. I was a weapons and tactics instructor (WTI) and former Marine aviation weapons and tactics (MAWTS-1) instructor. Though Grouper had more hours in the Harrier than I did, he did not have more experience in regard to tactics, especially night systems. I should have said something when the plan was briefed but I didn't. Now, as Grouper led us through the debrief, I prepared to speak. I raised my hand and then lowered it, shaking my head. "Nothing, never mind" was all I could utter.

In the days that followed, I tried to forget my failure, telling myself I would find an appropriate time to address the matter. But that was a lie and I knew it. Two nights later, Grouper briefed the next leg, another nine-hour flight from Spain to Bahrain. Much to the relief of all, Grouper briefed a simple takeoff

and rendezvous. No one asked any questions. After
engine start, Grouper's designated wingman, Captain Dan "Dano" Carlson, reported a problem. His
auxiliary power unit (APU), required for all night
and instrument flights, had failed to start. Dano was
down in the chocks and with him, Grouper, as we
never left one aircraft behind. And though Grouper
had specifically stated in the brief, "There will be no
switching of wingmen should anyone go down," he
soon directed me to fall out and remain with Dano.
We watched as the four Harriers, under the direction
of Grouper, launched and proceeded on.

The mechanics quickly fixed Dano's jet but our
departure did not hasten and there was nothing we
could do about it. Day after day we waited for the
diplomats in Egypt and Saudi Arabia to approve our
flight through their airspace. And though we were
needed in Afghanistan, there appeared to be no sense
of urgency within diplomatic circles. As we waited,
enjoying the comforts of Spain, our brothers flew
combat patrols in Afghanistan.

After a ten-day delay, Dano and I finally launched
behind a lone tanker. Neither of us spoke as we flew
east over dark Mediterranean waters. A giant white orb
glowed above like some keyhole to another world. I
looked down at the flat black water, dots of hot matter
reflecting in the glass. I shrugged. The seas ahead would
not be so kind. The guilt, stress, and possible impending doom seemed irrelevant at the time, for in that sol-
emn night, surrounded by beauty, I took it all in.

As our ships moved eastward, the horizon turned a purple, velvety hue, which slowly changed to bands of blue and orange. A small crimson smudge broke the eastern horizon. As it rose I looked north toward the home of Odysseus. Under a bronze sky, island peaks jutted through a soft white blanket, and I thought of the god-challenger and his adventures, and I wondered of my own tale and what fate had in store and how it would unfold and if it was already written and if so, could it be changed, or not. And if given the last chapter, would I read it or simply ask the number of the final page so that I might gauge the thickness.

As we flew farther east I saw waters of the deepest blue give way to brown rolling sands that extended forever in all directions. We flew on but the landscape didn't change and I wondered, *How far do these ends stretch?* And after more time had passed, I saw a crooked green stripe split a barren brown land. Next to it stood tiny pyramids. Looking down I contemplated the men who built them and why they did so. *Perhaps their gods were not much different from ours*, I thought.

We flew across another sea and another desert and eventually landed next to a blue gulf where the waters rested without motion in an air thick with salt. Climbing free of my confines I saw the orange disk hanging low in the west, our journey having hastened its course. And as I lay in my cot that night reflecting on all, I realized I was one day closer to my destiny, whatever that was.

5

DRIVEWAY ONE

Three of us stood on the tarmac of Shaikh Isa air base in Bahrain. The early morning sun was well into heating the day. Beads of sweat glistened on AJ's large tanned forehead. His black Oakleys covered his blue eyes. AJ had been stuck in Bahrain with a broken jet after landing there with Grouper a week earlier. The Nightmare jets seemed strung out across the world. With his jet fixed and impatience growing, AJ prepared for his journey.

AJ smiled as he thumped the Copenhagen can with several quick flips of the wrist. He looked at me, then Dano, and back, as he pinched the snuff tight between his thumb and forefinger. AJ shook it free in the air, discarding any loose tobacco, and then placed the plug deep in his lip as if performing for us. Dano and I watched in amusement. AJ then sanitized himself—removing his patches and all other forms of identification except for his ID card and dog tags. AJ handed the patches and his wallet to the plane captain, who in turn handed AJ his 9 mm Beretta. AJ took it, slammed the magazine into the gun, looked at Dano and me, and asked with a huge smirk, "Well, do I chamber a round or not? If I have to eject and I've hurt myself in the ejection, I may not be able to chamber a round."

"AJ, don't chamber a round," I said, shaking my head.

But AJ didn't listen to me. With a subtle smile, he pulled the slide of his M9 back and let it ride home. He nodded as if to acknowledge my concern. He then slid the pistol into his holster and climbed into his jet. Dano and I watched him take off. He was going solo to Afghanistan. Grouper had called the night before, directing it. Dano and I would follow, after a day's rest.

The next morning, Dano and I sanitized ourselves as AJ had done the day before. I took my pistol and shoved one of my three magazines into the hole, but I didn't chamber a round. If I had to eject and was injured in such a way that I couldn't pull the slide back—well, then I had bigger problems.

We climbed into our jets, completed our pre-takeoff checks, confirmed the tanker was ready, and launched. Joining on the tanker over the Persian Gulf, we learned that the refueling hose was giving the drogue operator fits. I wondered what Grouper would say when he discovered we had turned back. But there was nothing we could do. We were at the mercy of the tanker. Dano and I watched as the tanker cycled its refueling hose, trying to fix the malfunction. Eventually they allowed us to tank, but directed us to be smooth. Dano and I remained cautious.

The KC-10 turned north after crossing into Pakistani airspace at checkpoint Tunis. We changed frequencies and reported our position on a secure net. Each of the frequencies we now used had an associated number and color—Khaki 17, Burgundy 25, Magenta 12, Mauve 6, Ochre 9, Peach 4, Salmon 13, Plum 15. I found it ironic that as I entered combat airspace, the colored frequencies sounded more like paints chosen by an interior decorator.

We flew north, reporting our status using the day's designated code words. Code words delineated basic things such as "I'm out of ordnance," "I need fuel," "I'm at the tanker," "I need to go home," "Can I go home?" A code word for returning to base might be *Chevy* one day and *Ford, Jets,* or *Yankees* the next. Car models, sports teams, cities—all meant different things on different days. To aid us, we flew with classified cheat sheets to decode the numerous call signs, frequencies, colors, and code words. We used these preventive measures in addition to having the ability to talk "covered" (secure) over the radios using crypto gear. Unfortunately, the litany of call signs, colors, frequencies, and code words confused us. We stumbled through them, getting them right on some days and wrong on other days, forgetting that the code words had switched at midnight, or yesterday, or some other time for which our current cheat sheet was no longer applicable. Perhaps in the confusion of fooling ourselves we actually fooled the enemy.

As we crossed into combat airspace, our own call sign changed. We were no longer "Nightmare"—we became "Joliet." The aircraft call signs assigned on a random basis were important to pilots. We paid attention to such trivial things. It was our ego. "Joliet" was an acceptable call sign for an attack pilot—a reference to a tough Illinois prison and the cult classic film *The Blues Brothers*. Ironically, that film was also the theme for the Afghanistan AOR (area of responsibility) since the Dutch, Danish, and Norwegian F-16s were labeled "Jake," "Elwood," and "Blues," respectively.

I initiated my radio call in the blind, not knowing if the British AWACS aircraft known as Saxon could hear me or not. "Saxon, this is Joliet 61, heading zero-one-zero, driveway one, five minutes, flight level two-five-zero, three hundred knots true." Nobody responded.

Twenty minutes later, Dano and I peeled away from the tanker as it turned east to refuel a section of Jakes. The scenery below was changing. The Gulf of Oman had long since disappeared; the land beneath us now was barren. Small ridgelines swirled in parallel circuitous courses, as if the earth had been combed into a corduroy fabric. Soon small hills, mountains, and a few trees replaced the craggy rock outcroppings. The small mountains grew to bigger mountains. The bigger mountains became even bigger mountains and the clouds thickened. Tall granite peaks disappeared, but I knew they were there. We climbed to 27,000 feet to stay VFR, clear of the clouds. The radios remained silent except for my unanswered calls.

I radioed Texaco, the tanker from which we had separated a hundred miles back. I asked them if they had contact with Bagram. They answered, "Negative." We flew north. My anxiety grew. Our options were few.

In the United States and most other civilized countries, a pilot can always talk to an air traffic controller. At different locations they talk to each other through phones or computer networks, allowing pilots to stay abreast of the weather along their flight route and at their destination. This gives pilots options—an out. The words of my first flight instructor echoed in my head: "Franzak, always leave yourself an out—an option to prevent you from becoming a statistic." I soon learned that options were hard to come by in Afghanistan.

"Bagram Approach, Joliet 61 in the blind, fifty miles south, looking for a radar descent." Nothing. I double-checked the frequency and tried backup frequencies, without any luck. Then the radio sparked with a welcome response. "Calling Bagram Approach, say again."

"Bagram Approach, Joliet 61, flight of two, squawking four, four, two, one. Forty miles south for radar descent."

"Roger, Joliet, radar contact. Come left to three-six-zero. Descend and maintain one five thousand."

I completed my descent checks as Dano tucked up to my right wing. I pushed my stick forward and we plunged into the goo. We broke out and leveled off at 15,000 feet mean sea level (MSL), 10,000 feet above ground level (AGL).

Ten miles to our east, mountains rose to 10,000 feet. Directly behind them larger mountains surpassed 14,000 feet. Five miles to our west the mountain peaks climbed sharply to 15,000 feet, the eastern slopes of the Hindu Kush. To our north, the Hindu Kush peaks began at 15,000 feet, then jutted upward to 18,000 feet and higher, eventually assuming heights above 24,000 feet.

Bagram Air Base, located approximately thirty miles north of Kabul, sat in a small valley surrounded by unforgiving granite peaks.

"Bagram Approach, Joliet 61 visual underneath, request switch to tower."

"Joliet 61, roger. Switch tower."

We had created two recoveries for combat operations in Afghanistan: the "Stuka" and "Whirlpool." Both were designed to limit our exposure to the enemy, keep us at altitude as long as possible, and land the jets in the safest, most expeditious manner. The Whirlpool was a tight spiral flown from directly above the airfield. If the weather was poor but there was a VFR hole above the airfield, we would use the Whirlpool. Pilots preferred the other recovery. The

Stuka was a steep dive done in combat spread that ended in a break over midfield. We also enjoyed the bellicose word as it spit from our lips. It evoked a nature akin to our own.

"Joliet 61, currently landing runway zero-three, winds zero-two-zero at ten knots, cleared to break, report downwind," the tower controller advised.

"Joliet 61, roger." I pushed the throttle into the corner. Dano crossed underneath and positioned himself on my left side in combat spread—abeam me two miles distant. We pushed the noses of our jets over simultaneously and I felt the fire in my groin as we plunged weightless. The jets accelerated quickly. We pulled the power to idle to help cool our motors and lower both our infrared radiation (IR) and aural signatures as we screamed downhill. We broke over midfield at 450 knots, applying heavy g's to bleed our speed. At 250 knots, I lowered my gear and began my landing checks.

Gear four down and locked, flaps in STOL... My concentration broke when I brought my eyes from inside the cockpit to outside. As I assessed my downwind position and intended point of landing, the landscape below consumed me. Thousands of mud homes and buildings crowded one another in a rural setting. The huts blended perfectly with empty brown fields, void of life. No cars, no lights, only tiny mud structures and mud walls that partitioned the brown landscape into irregular fallow tracts. Welcome to Afghanistan. I felt as if I had flown back in time.

I rolled the jet level, lining myself up with the runway, and checked the gear again before setting the Harrier gently on the tarmac. The jet bounced and shook, finding every pothole on the decaying runway. I slowed to a stop and turned onto the taxiway. To my left lay a rusted Soviet T-62 tank. Its left track long discarded, the impotent gun barrel pointed awkwardly at me as I taxied by. Fifty yards away, in a twisted pile of metal, several charred ZIL-157 Soviet army trucks and Soviet APCs remained. Soviet fighter planes, MiGs, and Sukhoi jets lay strewn about, resting where their last flight had taken them—disposed, forgotten eyesores. Bagram bore the scars from decades of war. It was a graveyard of mangled military skeletons whose steel flesh rotted slowly in the snows and rains that dove off the high steeps to the west.

The taxiway was worse than the runway. As my Harrier rolled past piles of rocks and large concrete chips, I thought about notifying tower, but then thought better of it. The foreign object damage (FOD) was everywhere. *They had to know.* The Federal Aviation Administration would have condemned the airfield back home, but in Afghanistan it was the crown jewel. Ground control directed me to the Harrier ramp. Decrepit hangars lined the western edge of the airfield, where black smoke billowed up from smoldering fires. The black smudge hung in the air, suspended, refusing to move on, as if vestiges following a massacre in some godforsaken land. I hoped the cold gray skies, the black smoke, and the battle-scarred ground were not a talisman of things to come. For the welcome did not bode well for the soul.

The Marines waited for Dano and me as we slid in next to the other parked Harriers. I brought my right hand across my throat in a slicing maneuver. My plane captain returned the signal and I killed the motor. I cracked the canopy and smelled the rank air of Bagram. It smelled a bit like burning tires, but worse. "Well, how was your flight, XO?" asked my plane captain.

"Good, no gripes. Bird's up," I answered, handing him my pilot bag. My laconic reply masked greater concerns. *Holy shit. What kind of fucking place is this?*

6

A NEW HOME IN AN OLD LAND

As I settled into my new digs, thoughts of Katie, Caleb, and home faded. I became preoccupied with the strangeness of my new environment as I tried to absorb it and adjust to its rhythm.

At the foot of the Hindu Kush lay Bagram, a strategic locale that had served Alexander the Great, the British, the Soviets, and now the Americans. The base, extending in a large oval with a circumference of seven miles, sat like a gigantic alien spaceship on the Shomali plains. Inside the base, the Americans, technology, and the twenty-first century ruled. Outside the wire, the real Afghanistan breathed.

A large perimeter fence, consisting of Hesco barriers (large dirt-filled bulwarks), surrounded the imposing fortress. Overseeing the Hesco perimeter stood fifteen guard towers positioned around the base. Constructed out of sea-land cargo containers stacked on top of each other, the guard towers provided firing points that covered the perimeter. The minimalist structures had few creature comforts—protection from the rain, sun, and some wind, but not the heat or cold.

One road provided the only ground transportation route into and off the base. Cars, trucks, and civilians passed through a lengthy combination of barriers, switchbacks, and checkpoints to deliver supplies to the eleven thousand personnel who lived on Bagram. American soldiers clad in heavy body armor, camouflaged helmets, and black goggles, strapped with modified M-4s that had the latest day and night optics, watched as their Afghan counterparts worked the lines. Proud men with thick black beards, carrying Kalashnikovs, dressed in simple clothes, searched the workers as they moved forward one at a time. The sound of barking dogs echoed in the background.

Inside the base perimeter, each unit built its own mini-fortress and living area. Bagram was an enclave of fortresses within fortresses. The Marine camp, located on the north end of the base, was a small rectangle oriented east-west (two hundred meters long and fifty meters wide) and enclosed on all sides by ten-foot-tall Hesco barriers, the modern-day replacement of the sandbag. Razor-sharp concertina wire lined the tops of the Hesco walls surrounding the camp. The Marine camp had two entrances: the west entrance that connected directly with the north-south main thoroughfare, Disney Drive, and the east entrance that connected to the flight line. Marines guarded both entrances twenty-four hours a day. Nobody entered the Marine camp without permission.

Within the small perimeter, the advance party of thirty Marines had erected our living quarters, showers, restrooms, and laundry facility in the former minefield. There were thirty-seven "B-huts" in the camp, thirty of which housed the two hundred Marines. The remaining seven served as offices or storage. The B-huts, or "hooches," as we called them, were minimalist wooden structures, eighteen by thirty-six feet, with half-inch plywood floors and walls. A large canvas tarp covered the primitive structure in a failed attempt at weatherproofing. There were few amenities in the huts.

Each Marine received a small aluminum cot. The cots weren't comfortable, but they kept us off the floor and away from the local critters (spiders, snakes, and scorpions) that sought the B-huts as an upgrade to their living conditions. The base newspaper, *Freedom Watch*, ran stories about the local critters with photos of the Asian cobra and camel spider and warnings not to handle or disturb them, but with resolute stupidity some soldiers ignored the warnings.

I bunked with five other officers and one of two civilians who accompanied us on our deployment. The civilians were tech reps for the maintenance department and became an engrained part of our team as much as any Marine did. A total of seven occupied our cramped quarters: Major AJ Heino, Captains Toby Moore, Dano Carlson, Jolly Hardy, Chief Warrant Officer Bruce Jones, our civilian tech rep Ron Morehead, and me. When Dano and I moved in, everyone else had already begun to transform their tiny living space into something a little less primitive. The best spots—the corners—had already been taken.

A constant clamoring of hammers, drills, and power saws resonated throughout the camp. Marines acquired wood from undisclosed locations and used it to build bookcases, shelves, and an occasional desk. Every Marine attempted to surpass his neighbor with more outlandish home improvements. Wood was not free, and acquiring it was no accident. Experts at obtaining the unobtainable, the Marines' acquisition of items led to an early confrontation. An army sergeant major accused one of the Marines of stealing wood from his camp. Unfortunately, the evidence had already been converted into a bookshelf. The Marine claimed he had bartered for the wood from an army sergeant, but that did little to satisfy the irate sergeant major. Eventually he left empty-handed, threatening to bring ill will to the Marines. News that the Marines had landed in Bagram spread quickly.

I kept my living space spartan, erecting a small shelf above my rack where I placed some books and a picture of Katie and Caleb. I also bought a rug, as did most everyone, in a feeble attempt to reduce the dust—dust that was everywhere. Dust penetrated everything, invading our clothes, sleeping bags, and anything made of fabric. We attempted to sweep the dust out of our hooch once a day, but it only created a large cloud before settling back down fifteen minutes later. The insides of my nose became caked brown. Dust clouds followed pedestrians as if they were incarnations of the cartoon character Pigpen. Everyone warned us about the dust, but it took seeing and breathing the fine brown talcum powder to comprehend its torment.

Two engineering projects dominated the work effort on Bagram during our deployment. One was the laying of rock and gravel on the roads, footpaths, and anywhere there wasn't a standing structure, in an effort to keep the dust down. The other was mine clearing.

Warning signs posted around the base gave detailed explanations of the Soviet mines that littered Bagram's topography. Tacked up next to the mine identification charts were statistics and details of how soldiers had lost hands, arms, and legs scavenging for souvenirs around Bagram—the same people who liked playing with the local critters. Mine-clearing operations were a never-ending process. The loud unannounced explosions were unnerving. I never knew when the explosions were going to happen. No one did. Occasionally, base authorities posted a notice at the chow hall stating, "EOD will be detonating mines on the north end of Bagram tomorrow at noon," but that was a rarity. The bone-rattling explosions kept me on edge for several weeks until I adjusted somewhat to their frequency.

Bagram was loud. It wasn't just the mines constantly going off. Our living quarters sat a hundred yards from the flight line and several hundred yards from the runway. Harriers, Hogs, and helos came and went supporting ground forces in remote locations, while large cargo jets brought in supplies to sustain the war machine. It was a constant intravenous drip from an IV bag into the sick patient—Afghanistan. Beans, bullets, and Band-Aids flew in, while bad guys in orange jumpsuits and the unfortunate casualty in an olive body bag flew out.

7

CROSSWINDS

After I rested a day, operations scheduled me for my first combat mission with Captain Hardy. Jolly had been flying missions with the CO for the previous week while I was stuck in Spain. Jolly and I met in the base of the control tower, where we kept our one makeshift briefing room next to our operations department. We pulled two folding chairs around a metal cruise box, on which Jolly spread a 1:500,000 map, known as a TPC or tactical pilot chart, of Afghanistan. We were tasked to provide "fixed-wing" escort to two CH-47 Chinook helicopters transporting VIPs (the Polish president and his entourage) from Bagram back to Kabul. The Harriers were the muscle in case anything went wrong. The mission was a late afternoon sortie with a night recovery.

As Jolly briefed the specifics of the flight, I listened carefully to a pilot who was a rising star within the Harrier ranks. His brief flowed with the simplicity and confidence of someone who had been doing this

for years, yet he had been here only a week. He was
the squadron weapons and tactics instructor (WTI),
our tactics guru, and had recently replaced me as
the aircraft maintenance officer (AMO). As a former
WTI and AMO, I had endorsed Jolly for both bil-
lets, but Jolly didn't need me as a daddy. A competent
pilot and tactician, he looked more like an air force
officer with his unusually long hair, but his tempera-
ment was otherwise. He spoke of the weak as herbi-
vores, as if God had assigned them to a lower station
in life, a condition they couldn't help. Jolly viewed
the escort of the CH-47s as such a mission, and instead of choosing words such as "lead" and "dash
two," he used "Hunter" and "Killer" to emphasize
our role. "XO, I'm the Hunter today. You're the
Killer," Jolly said, winking with a slight nod.

With all six Harriers now in Afghanistan, the
squadron configured them into two basic variants.
The lead aircraft, or "Hunter," carried two external
wing tanks, 300 rounds of 25 mm for the gun, a GBU-
16 (thousand-pound laser-guided bomb), and the Litening pod for targeting. The wingman's aircraft, the
"Killer," carried two external fuel tanks, 300 rounds
of 25 mm, and two GBU-12s (five-hundred-pound
laser-guided bombs). Later we replaced one of the
GBU-12s on the Killer aircraft with a rocket pod, giving our customers a greater selection of weapons.

The AV-8B had six stations for ordnance. On two
of them we hung external fuel tanks known as "drop
tanks." A constant and valid criticism of the Harrier

was its limited ability to carry ordnance, especially when it carried external fuel tanks. By removing the fuel tanks and loading more bombs, we gained fire-power, but at the expense of fuel—fuel that equated to "range" and "time on station," which were essential to supporting operations in Afghanistan. Thus we kept the fuel tanks and flew with less ordnance.

After the brief, Jolly and I checked out with the operations duty officer (ODO) and walked back to the Marine camp where our flight gear and aircraft were located. We donned our forty pounds of gear and sanitized ourselves, removing all forms of identification except for our military ID card and dog tags. I then stuffed six evasion charts into my lower g-suit pockets.

I had never seen an evasion chart until my arrival in Afghanistan. It was also something I hoped I never had to use. Printed on waterproof paper, the charts contained detailed terrain and survival information, with pictures and descriptions of edible and nonedible plants found in the local area, celestial navigation diagrams, survival tips, and even an evasion checklist for the forgetful pilot printed in the lower right-hand corner:

> Evasion Checklist: Assess immediate situation. THINK BEFORE YOU ACT! Treat life-threatening injuries. Assume someone observed your parachute descent and move away from the landing site. Seek a concealed site. . . . Do not leave evidence of travel. Use zigzagging move-

ment techniques. Use terrain to mask your movement. Avoid lines of communication (roads,
rivers, railroads, and powerlines). Notice. This
chart is intended for survival situations. Refer
to current editions of appropriate aeronautical
charts for flight planning or operations.

I found the warning especially amusing, indicative
of our litigious society and its desire to avoid culpa-
bility. The chart, four feet by five feet when opened,
folded into a small rectangle, the size of a paperback
book. Six of the charts covered our operational area in
Afghanistan, an area equivalent to the state of Texas.

After stuffing my g-suit pockets with the evasion
charts, I strapped my 9 mm Beretta to my left side. I
asked Jolly to snap the pistol securely in the pouch because my hand couldn't reach the fastener due to my
bulging survival vest. I was a walking Michelin Man.
In addition to my survival gear and six evasion charts,
I carried a host of other maps, all of different scales:
an operational navigational chart (1:1,000,000), two
tactical pilot charts (1:500,000), a box of 1:100,000
maps of eastern, southern, and central Afghanistan,
and a classified folder that contained satellite imag-
ery of our forward operating bases (FOBs). I carried
so many maps it bordered on ridiculous, but I didn't
want to be caught needing a map I didn't have.

The Harrier had its own map as well, an electronic display that relied on GPS signals for its precise location. It was impossible to get lost with

the moving map. But as a young pilot, I had been schooled by crotchety old men who flew with paper maps and stopwatches. I learned from them never to rely on the Harrier's technology, because it would fail me when I needed it most. Thus out of habit I crammed the redundant maps into my pilot bag and flight suit pockets.

Jolly and I walked across the crumbling concrete ramp to our jets, which sat exposed on the flight line. In the background stood three usable hangars that had survived inside war-torn Bagram, the nicest of which housed the headquarters of the 82nd Airborne. Inside the hangar, a deluge of wooden buildings served as the workspaces and command operation center for the army's conventional forces in Afghanistan. I wondered why tents and B-huts, not airplanes, filled the hangars. Not everything made sense inside the spaceship. In fact, many things didn't.

Jolly and I started our jets, finished our final checks, and taxied to the arming area. I waited until Jolly's jet was clear before I signaled to my plane captain that I was ready. We maintained excessive separation between aircraft so that jet exhaust from one didn't FOD another.

Once Jolly cleared the arming area, I pulled in. Three ordnance Marines with red cranial helmets and black goggles waited for me. The sergeant directed me to stop and raise my hands. Once the senior ordie saw both of my hands, he directed his two younger Marines to proceed under my aircraft and arm my gun and bombs. The senior ordie then gave me a thumbs-up and a salute that I promptly returned in good military fashion.

We taxied the short distance to the runway using two separate taxiways, stopping with 2,500 feet between us. Cleared for takeoff, we ran up our motors, finished our pre-takeoff checks, and signaled over the radio that we were ready. Jolly released his brakes and began a slow roll. He soon disappeared in a large dust cloud as the Rolls-Royce engine responded to full power. Once he was airborne, I released my brakes, letting the jet roll forward at idle speed. The aircraft bobbed up and down on the rough tarmac as it gained speed. At 50 knots, I pushed the throttle into the corner. The telltale acceleration of the Harrier was gone. I expected the jet to throw my head back against the seat, but there was no sudden acceleration, only a slow wobble and mild surge. I checked my RPM gauge, verifying I was at top end. The jet's additional ordnance, fuel, and the mile-high elevation, where less air feeds an oxygen-hungry motor, tamed the Harrier's sudden acceleration to a sluggish roll.

My Harrier lumbered down the runway, rocking back and forth as the speed increased—100, 120, 140 knots. At 140 knots, I moved my hand from the throttle to the nozzle lever and yanked it rearward, executing the Harrier short takeoff, commonly referred to as a STO. The jet lurched upward in flight after consuming most of the 10,000 feet of runway for its short takeoff.

"Joliet one-two airborne, three-mile trail, visual," I announced after getting airborne. After accelerating to 450 knots at 200 feet, I pulled the stick back. The jet climbed upward, but the airspeed bled off rapidly. I lowered the nose in a feeble attempt to keep my airspeed above 400 knots—maneuvering speed required to defeat missiles. Our nimble, sleek little fighters behaved like fat sows with the extra weight and drag.

After climbing to 24,000 feet, I joined on Jolly's left wing, crossed underneath, inspected his jet, and pulled into wingtip formation on his right side. Jolly held up his hand, palm outward, and gave the "push" signal. I took a cut away and positioned myself in combat spread, abeam but separated by two miles. The distance between aircraft in combat spread depended on the conditions and direction of the flight leader. I preferred maximum spacing between the jets—a more offensive posture.

We followed with our "FENCE" checks (combat checks of fuel, engine, navaids, communication, and equipment), ensuring our expendables worked. In addition to our offensive ordnance, we carried 160 flares and twenty chaff for defensive purposes. Each Harrier popped out two flares and one chaff on signal while the other pilot ensured a proper dispense. The flares provided a decoy to heat-seeking IR missiles, while the chaff, tiny aluminum strips designed to jam radar, blossomed into giant metallic clouds with the hope of predetonating any missile not fooled by the flares.

In training we completed these checks before crossing into enemy territory. If the expendables didn't work, one returned home rather than risk exposure to enemy surface-to-air missiles (SAMs), anti-aircraft artillery (AAA), and fighters. But there were no enemy and friendly lines in Afghanistan. Thus we completed the expendables checks shortly after getting airborne. If one's expendables didn't work, we kept that bird as high cover during the mission. It made no sense to send one jet back to Bagram if the expendables didn't work, because it had to land there anyway.

I followed Jolly on the radios as he moved us through the various control agencies, reporting our status using the day's assigned code words. We contacted the helo package and soon located the small black specks against the light brown Afghanistan hills. Their shadows gave them away. Flying south over the Shomali plains toward Kabul, we maintained a protective CAP over our package below. Jagged, snow-covered peaks glistened in the warm afternoon sunlight to our west. The valley below was green and fertile, a rarity in Afghanistan, since only 12 percent of the land is arable. The farmer fields fell into no particular pattern, only oddly shaped rectangles sprinkled with thousands of mud buildings. I pulled out my TPC map and found Bagram located near the center. The small towns and agricultural fields weren't depicted. Instead there was a short phrase: "Numerous Scattered Villages." Studying the map carefully, I saw the phrase repeated across the map. It was an accurate description.

After the helos landed in Kabul, Jolly directed us to our tanker located in the Poseidon track. The tanker tracks were large ovals in the sky, situated between 22,000 and 26,000 feet. We quickly joined on the large tanker and refueled our jets. The sun had now set and the dark purple luminance of evening nautical twilight began to fade into blackness. Jolly called for the flight to don the night vision goggles. I pulled my NVGs out of the foam case and mounted them on my helmet. It was still too bright for the NVGs to work when looking west, but soon all light faded, resulting in a black, moonless night and a crisp bright green image through the NVGs. We contacted our package for their return trip but they advised us they no longer needed us. We still had another hour of "on station" time to fill in our three-hour block, known as a "vul period." With time to kill, Jolly showed me the Big Cat training area.

Big Cat was the only aviation training range in Afghanistan. Unfortunately, fixed-wing aircraft were not allowed to drop bombs in it—we had to simulate target attacks with "dry" deliveries. We also had a floor of 10,000 feet AGL, which we were not allowed to break without authorization. The floor kept us at 15,000–20,000 feet due to Afghanistan's high elevation and prevented any realistic training. The risk-mitigation factors imposed by higher headquarters had serious unintended consequences. They prevented pilots from training the way we fought. They didn't reinforce proper switchology—the muscle memory of hands and fingers flipping switches, pulling triggers, pressing bomb-pickle buttons at the altitudes required to support the grunt. Worse, faking the movements bred bad habits.

The generals and policy makers had grown so risk-averse, they tied the hands of those charged with enforcing their policies. I understood the need to balance risk with mission accomplishment, but the pendulum had swung too far to one side. As I soon learned, maintaining our proficiency while deployed in Afghanistan was a constant struggle. When someone actually needed us, I hoped our skills wouldn't be lost in the abyss of political necessity.

After touring the Big Cat, Jolly led us home. We proceeded north back to Bagram, checking out with Warlord, the airborne early warning aircraft (AWACS), and prepared for individual recoveries. As we crossed the initial approach fix, Jolly kissed himself off and began his descent as a single. His lights disappeared into a black void. After completing one turn in holding, I prepared for my descent and first night landing at Bagram. "Approach, Joliet 12, out of two-four-thousand, Hi-Tacan, runway three," I stated.

"Roger, Joliet 12. Winds three-zero-zero at two-five, gusting to thirty. Altimeter, three-zero-one-zero. Report five-mile final," said the ATC controller.

I pulled my throttle to idle, popped my speed brake, and shoved the nose of my Harrier into the sucking hole beneath. It was black. I couldn't see the ground but I knew it was there—the unforgiving granite peaks that encircled Bagram. I had shot hundreds of night approaches in my career. Nevertheless, my anxiety was piqued a tad as my eyes began a dedicated instrument scan. A small cloud layer had settled into the valley, obscuring the airfield and base below. After descending 10,000 feet, I broke through the scud, promptly lowered my gear, and leveled off at 7,500 feet mean sea level (MSL), 2,500 feet above the ground. I saw the base clearly now.

The lights of the alien spaceship glowed prominently—the only lights in the entire valley. There were half a million people living around Bagram Air Base, yet there were few lights except those of the base itself. Electricity was a rarity outside Kabul, since only well-to-do Afghans had generators. But Bagram had lots of generators powering thousands of lights, letting everyone in the valley know we were there. Though I saw the base, I didn't see the runway, a dilemma I had never before encountered. Runways were always the brightest, most well lit item at any airport—that is, I learned, unless you're in combat. My GPS alerted me I was five miles from the runway. I advised approach of my location. "Approach, Joliet 12, five miles with the gear, request P-A-R."

"Roger, Joliet 12, switch to three-seven-nine-point-three for G-C-A pickup."

Great. Switching radio frequencies in the Harrier was usually simple, but we had had new radios installed before our deployment and the software for them was incomplete. The program office ran out of money during flight tests. Thus, instead of using our up-front control to change frequencies, we did it "heads down" on the backup radio in the right console. I looked down and punched in the new frequency. Looking up, I realized the spaceship had shifted left, something it could not do. I was drifting right. *Winds.*

The controller's voice came back to me now. The winds were 25 knots, coming from 300 degrees—a 90-degree crosswind for runway 03—and they were gusting. The crosswind limit for the Harrier at night and at our gross weight was 10 knots. The engineers had designed the Harrier to land vertically, not for roll-on crosswind landings. The Harrier performed poorly in crosswind landings, threatening to flip over. But the "any clime, any place" jump jet couldn't land vertically at Bagram.

I contemplated my predicament and options. I had to land the jet outside its designated crosswind limits by a factor greater than two. This was the realm of test pilots, something I was not. Bagram had one runway. The only suitable divert, Kandahar, was 310 miles and four thousand pounds of fuel to the south—four thousand pounds of fuel I didn't have. "Approach, Joliet 12 up three-seven-nine-point-three," I stated, still unable to see the runway. I waited but heard nothing—only the loud whine of the Rolls-Royce behind me as I added power to maintain my altitude and airspeed. I thought of Jolly, who must have made it down safely. *What did he know that I didn't?*

I repeated my call with more inflection. "Approach, Joliet 12 up three-seven-nine-point-three."

Again, no response. Now at four miles, I began my descent. I was high and right of course, trying to land on a runway I didn't see. I looked back down to my radio and dialed in the previous frequency. I repeated my call, my voice no longer controlled. "Approach, Joliet 12, no joy, three-seven-nine-point-three. Request P-A-R pick up this frequency."

"Roger, Joliet, stand by," said the approach controller.

Finally, a response, but it didn't help. My next call registered the fear within and clearly denoted it to all listening. "Approach, Joliet 12, I need a P-A-R pickup now!"

"Roger, Joliet, unable at this time. Switch tower."

You're fucking kidding me. There is a golden rule that pilots learn early. It is the first and most important rule of aviation: "Aviate, Navigate, Communicate," in that order. Many pilots killed themselves because they confused the prioritization of this blood-written commandment. I quickly dispensed with any further communications or radio changes and frantically searched for the elusive runway among a sea of lights. I had done the one thing my first on-wing had warned me never to do: I had flown myself into a box.

"Joliet 12, Paddles contact," the radio squawked with the familiar and welcome voice of AJ. Grouper had insisted that a pilot who wasn't flying monitor the Harrier takeoffs and landings—a missile watch officer—someone who could warn pilots of threats when they were most vulnerable, low and slow. The CO had been adamant in his decision, much to the dismay of the pilots, who scorned the additional duty, viewing it as unnecessary and a waste of needed rest. Grouper's wisdom and experience were now my lifeline. The missile watch officer was also an unofficial landing site supervisor (LSS) who provided pilots with needed advisories, such as corrections for landing. We referred to the missile watch officer as "Paddles," a reference to the landing signal officer we used when landing on navy ships. For me, the call from "Paddles" was the voice of an angel.

"Paddles, roger. I can't break out the runway. Am I right or left of centerline?"

"Joliet, come left," AJ responded. "I show you *well* right of centerline." I didn't miss the subtle emphasis in AJ's voice, his tactful way of telling me, *I was seriously fucked-up*.

The joy of flying was gone. Flying was one of my greatest privileges, and 99 percent of the time I loved it. But I was now in that 1 percent every pilot loathed. I subconsciously reflected on the aviation axiom "It is better to be on the ground wishing you were flying, than to be flying wishing you were on the ground." I dipped my left wing, establishing a turn to correct back to runway centerline. A centerline I didn't see. I put my trust in AJ to bring me down safely. My jet now pointed 30 degrees from runway heading. Instead of looking out the front of my cockpit for the runway, I was looking out the right side. AJ's voice returned.

"Joliet 12. I now show you on centerline."

I lowered my nozzles, slowing to 120 knots while smoothing my turn in a futile attempt to align my jet with the runway. At a hundred feet, I picked up the runway's faint IR lights. The spaceship's thousand other lights, which provided no purpose other than highlighting their existence, had obscured the tiny IR lights that lined the runway—IR lighting insisted upon by the air force to hide the presence of a runway (as if the enemy didn't know we were there). While the air force insisted on an IR-lit runway, they failed to communicate the necessity of dimming or turning off Bagram's thousand other lights controlled by the army. It was one of the many insipid battles resulting from competing services refusing to cooperate lest they appear weaker than the other.

With a 30-degree crab into the wind to keep myself from drifting off runway centerline, I stuffed the nose and dove for the deck. If I didn't maintain centerline, then I'd surely leave the runway. I would be in the infield—the dirt—the minefields. For a second I debated my chosen profession and wished I were somewhere else—anywhere but in Afghanistan, on short final staring out the right side of my cockpit.

But I wasn't, and that was the way of a single-seat fighter. One lived alone, either adapting or not.

The aircraft smacked the tarmac harder than I expected, rocking up on its right outrigger and threatening to flip over. I had done my best to kick out the crab with a boot full of rudder, but kicking out 30 degrees of crab was damn near impossible. It was an ugly landing. The jet bucked down the tarmac. I applied the brakes, but the Harrier refused to slow. I had landed long. I moved the nozzles into braking stop and prepared to fire the motor in reverse as a last-ditch effort to keep me free of the minefields. Finally, she eased. I stopped and stared at the overrun lights a hundred feet to my front.

My right hand fumbled at the bayonet fittings of my mask in a desperate effort to free myself of that ghastly gray snorkel. I tore it from my face and my throat heaved obscenities outward. They reverberated inside my cocoon, my ears hearing them well despite the thick padding of my helmet. My fists pounded the canopy glass as I felt the dreaded sobs rise from within. I ceased and my body capitulated into a gelatinous mass. The subconscious tension that had held every muscle rigid for the last two minutes simply drained out of me as the adrenaline dumped into my gut. I felt ill. It happened so fast. I had been on a routine night approach when suddenly I was faced with landing in crosswinds that exceeded the jet's limits and had almost exceeded mine. The radio crackled. "Joliet 12, clear at

Alpha. Report when clear," stated an agitated tower controller.

Fuck him. I paused a few seconds, then responded calmly, "Roger, Joliet 12 clearing at Alpha." As a single-seat pilot I knew nobody had witnessed my collapse. I wanted to keep it that way.

The following day, I reviewed recent statistics. I had flown four times in the last ten days, escaping seemingly inevitable crashes twice. With those odds I wasn't going to last a month. I dismissed the six-ship takeoff out of Cherry Point as an anomaly, but the landing in Bagram was different. *Was this going to be the norm?*

I decided to visit the weather office located in the Bagram control tower. I wanted to learn how the weather genies did their magic. In a decrepit building, a set of concrete stairs led up three stories, reversing back and forth before ending at a solitary door. A balding, academic-looking air force tech sergeant, in his early thirties with horn-rimmed glasses and a thick brown mustache, greeted me amicably. I explained my curiosity and asked if he would entertain my inquiries. Without hesitation, he agreed.

He quickly explained the tools at his disposal. Wind, temperature, and barometric gauges on top of the control tower provided readouts on a computer screen. "But what about measuring visibility, ceiling, or more important, predicting the weather and winds?" I asked, not revealing my circumstances the previous night.

He explained that he didn't have any tools other than his own eyeballs to guesstimate the actual cloud ceiling or the visibility at the airfield. If he could see the end of the runway, he knew visibility was at least one mile. If he could see only the ATC compound at midfield, he knew visibility was at least a half mile. To measure the ceiling, he guessed because there were no known vertical reference points except for the high mountain peaks, which became obscured when weather rolled in.

Determining the ceiling at night proved impossible without the assistance of a pilot actually flying. When an airplane took off or landed, the meteorologists requested pilot reports (PIREPs) of when pilots entered the clouds and when they broke out. If an airplane hadn't taken off or landed in a while, or if the weather conditions changed rapidly, which happened frequently in Afghanistan, the actual conditions rarely matched what was reported.

The air force meteorologist then explained that the weather forecasts for Afghanistan were done back home in the United States using computer models. "But," he added, pausing slightly, "unfortunately we don't have good models for Afghanistan because no weather balloons are released into the atmosphere here. Instead, we rely on the data that comes from weather balloons released in Iran. Of course by the time those weather patterns cross the Hindu Kush, a lot can change." *Balloons—of all things.* And I thought of a shoe lost for want of a nail and wondered of changing paradigms or if things really changed that much or at all.

All of us learned not to trust the weather forecasts. Instead we did our best to keep abreast of the current conditions through radio communications with approach control or base, but that wasn't always possible. The distances we flew to support our brethren often took us out of radio range. When the weather deteriorated, it was smarter to return home and land rather than chance it. Unless the grunts needed us, we tried not to push it. But at one time or another, all of us pushed it. As our time in Afghanistan grew, so too did our confidence and with it, perhaps, our demise. Afghanistan's fickle weather held the upper hand. Shamals—hot, dry northwesterly winds—appeared without notice, picking up quickly, and ceilings deteriorated rapidly.

Every landing at Bagram was rough and dangerous, but the ones at night, in bad weather, were age-makers. They turned hair gray and added lines to the face. Over the next year, several airplanes crashed trying to land on Bagram's shoddy, dimly lit runway. And as the months passed I would learn that my greatest threat in Afghanistan wasn't Taliban or al Qaeda, it was granite, weather, and sometimes ego. Despite all our technology, pilots still had their limits tested regularly in that land where God and Mother Nature ruled indiscriminately.

8

DROPPING BOMBS

The first month of combat operations came and went quickly. Each flight provided excitement and something new to learn. We became intimately familiar with aerial refueling operations both with and without NVGs. We learned the limitations of air traffic control and weather forecasters in Afghanistan and how best to work with them. We studied the Afghanistan geography from big to small—the mountain ranges, passes, and cities—memorizing the location of our forward operating bases (FOBs) throughout the vast country. FOBs, also referred to as safe houses or firebases, provided locales from which U.S. and coalition forces conducted ground operations against the enemy.

We worked with joint terminal area controllers (JTACs) assigned throughout the area of operations (AO). JTACs, mostly enlisted air force personnel assigned to army units, directed the air strikes from the ground and indoctrinated us to their turf—the roads, rivers, bridges, canyons, cliffs, valleys, and hills that dominated their surroundings. Most of our missions were along the Afghanistan-Pakistan border, working with our ground forces and waiting—waiting for the inevitable call to respond to a TIC, troops in contact, the result of an enemy ambush.

The war in Afghanistan over the previous year had transformed from high-intensity conflict to stability and security operations. The enemy no longer gathered in large troop formations with tanks and trucks. Instead they dissolved into small bands of insurgents that fought the war on their terms: quick raids, ambushes, sniper fire, and lots of indirect rocket and mortar fire. They swam among the population, making detection and identification difficult. The enemy that had defeated the British in three wars lasting over fifty years proved patient. I wasn't sure we would.

The one thing we expected to be doing in combat, we weren't—dropping bombs. Slowly over the coming months, our attack-pilot skills began to decay due to the lack of training on air-to-ground ranges. The decline was gradual and therefore insidious. It lulled pilots into thinking they were better than they were. When the grunts called on us for real—when lives were on the line—all of us were challenged not to screw up.

In the early days, the excitement of combat provided a stimulus that propelled us forward, allowing us to work twelve-, fourteen-, sixteen-hour days, sometimes longer. But after a few weeks, the buzz faded and fatigue set in. We then learned the importance of rest. In mid-November, I awoke to the obtrusive shaking of my rack. Opening my eyes, I saw Dano standing above me, smiling. He leaned over and whispered, "Sir, the OPSO [operations officer] and Wiz just dropped bombs." I returned the smile, closed my eyes, and pulled my sleeping bag back over my head.

The next day I talked to AJ, who recounted the story. He and Captain Geoff "Wiz" Warlock had been diverted to support troops under attack at FOB Lwara. The Harrier pilots held overhead, listening to the JTAC as he directed a section of A-10s in multiple attacks. The Hogs dropped several five-hundred-pound bombs, but the incoming mortar fire continued. After the A-10s dropped the last of their ordnance, they passed control to the Harriers. With incoming fire still harassing the FOB, the JTAC requested that the Harriers drop the biggest bomb they had on the suspected enemy position. Using his Litening pod, AJ designated the target and confirmed its location with the JTAC. After a "cleared hot," AJ released a thousand-pound laser-guided bomb (LGB). The ground erupted in a large ball of flame, dirt, and debris. The attack on the FOB stopped. The following day we read about the attack in the press.

U.S. war planes bombed and strafed enemy positions after rocket and ground attacks on two bases in southeastern Afghanistan and at least two attackers were suspected killed, the U.S. military said on Friday. There were no U.S. casualties. The attack on Thursday night was one of the largest and most concerted on U.S. positions in Afghanistan in months and came two days after the emergence of an audio tape believed to have been made by al Qaeda leader Osama bin Laden vowing to continue his struggle.*

Morale within the squadron skyrocketed. AJ and Wiz's attack provided a redeeming sense of comfort for the Marines. We had struck back. In my journal, I noted the incident: "According to the JTAC, the bomb hit right where the two attackers were standing. Shack! Fuck them. I had no idea war could bring out so much hate in me, but I feel no sympathy or pity for the enemy. I don't care if they are fathers like me."

Years later as I read my journals, those words embarrassed me. Nevertheless, they accurately depicted my thoughts and feelings in the fall of 2002. I concluded the journal entry with a prescient view of the future: "I believe the dropping of bombs will be the exception vice the norm."

Our victory at Lwara was short-lived. A few days

* "Heavy fighting after U.S. bases in Afghanistan attacked," Reuters, November 16, 2002, Afghan News Center Archives, http://www.afghanistannewscenter.com/news/archive/archive_2002.html.

later, we abandoned the Lwara safe house. Although strategically placed to oversee one of the many smuggling routes from Pakistan, it was too close to the border. The FOB was within easy range of indirect fire launched from positions in Pakistan, making response impossible, at least in 2002 and 2003.

But our leaving Lwara didn't prompt the enemy to do the same. Al Qaeda and Taliban continued to use the area around Lwara to stage attacks as well as smuggle men and arms into Afghanistan. We returned several months later and dropped more bombs there, but it was after the Nightmares had returned home that real tragedy struck. On April 22, 2004, Pat Tillman, an American patriot and NFL football player who left a life of fame, fortune, and convenience for one of hardship and anonymity to serve his country, died from friendly fire in a firefight near Lwara. Today FOB Lwara has a new name—FOB Tillman. It's not the only real estate in Afghanistan with an American name.

9

DAWN PATROL AND SHKIN

The success of AJ and Wiz's attack quickly earned the Harrier notoriety as a precision killer, especially in darkness, where we could see and others could not. Ground forces began requesting air support with a "night attack targeting capability" and the staff officers of the combined air operations center (CAOC) responded. Located in Al Udeid Air Base in Qatar, the CAOC under the call sign K-mart (later it changed to Shadow) directed the air war over Afghanistan. K-mart scheduled the Harriers for an increasing number of night missions to support the grunts in places like Shkin.

Shitty, shifty Shkin, a place I came to loathe. I didn't even like the name. It made my skin crawl. Located in Paktika province several miles from the Pakistan border, Shkin was a hot spot. A small rural town from which evil seeped. We responded to more action around Shkin than any other location in Afghanistan. The area was fueled with insurgent activity from Wana, Pakistan, a Taliban haven we weren't allowed to reach.

After my initial flight with Jolly, AJ's Ops paired me with Captain Aaron "Boss" Haug as my wingman. Ops attempted to schedule the same two pilots together for thirty to forty-five days before rotating crews. Experience was paired with inexperience so that pilots developed an effective team within their section while the monthly rotations kept everyone fresh.

Boss was a quiet, blond-haired, blue-eyed Buckeye and devout Ohio State football fan. He looked every bit the part of the all-American boy. Everyone liked Boss because of his carefree attitude. He was impossible to rile. Sometimes I wanted to check his pulse just to see if he was alive. His subdued personality lacked the ooh-rah factor prominent in many Marines, but he did have a unique talent. Boss knew the most obscure sports facts. I chided him for missing his calling as an ESPN analyst. Once his roommates discovered his hidden talent, they quizzed him relentlessly, trying to stump the sports trivia expert. "Who won the 1992 Indy 500? Who won the 1999 Cy Young? Who won the Heisman but became a professional basketball player?" He answered these with ease. Not to be outdone, his bunkmates eventually stumped him with such absurd questions as "Who was the 1995 Putt-Putt champion?"

Ops scheduled Boss and me for the late, late go— dawn patrol. Dawn patrol required briefs around midnight, a launch at two or three in the morning, and a recovery shortly after sunrise. The dawn patrol schedule became grueling over time. I did my best to sleep in the day before the flight, but the constant buzzing of saws and clanging of hammers prevented any rest. Everyone was building something in the Marine camp and it seemed his workbench was directly outside our hooch. I conceded defeat, rose, and took care of paperwork, watching the hours tick away until our brief time.

Boss and I launched several hours before sunrise for our fragged mission, XCAS—airborne on-call close air support, a glorified version of flying around waiting to be needed. After getting airborne and completing our FENCE checks, Boss and I toured Nangahar and Kunar provinces from Jalalabad east to the Khyber Pass, then north to Asadabad. We circled each safe house to see if anything was going on. It was silent and peaceful. After an hour, a call from Warlord, the AWACS aircraft, broke the silence.

"Joliet 61, Warlord. Switch to Khaki 17 and contact Playboy 17 or Misty 31."

"Roger, Warlord, Joliet 61 solid copy. Flight push Khaki 17 on the left."

Playboy 17 was working a section of A-10s, Misty 31 flight, near Shkin in the Gatling Bravo/Charlie a hundred miles south of our designated area. When the opportunity presented itself, I interrupted their dialogue and asked Misty and Playboy if they needed our support. Without hesitation, Playboy 17 requested we back up the Hogs since they were almost bingo. We contacted Warlord and relayed Playboy's request. Warlord contacted K-mart back in Qatar before directing us to proceed south to Shkin and work with Playboy. There was a lot of oversight and micromanagement of air assets. One didn't fart without permission.

Misty quickly gave us an update of the situation. There were three suspicious vehicles driving through wadis (dry riverbeds) south and east of the Shkin safe house. Playboy 17 and a small team of Special Forces had left the safe house in two vehicles and were now watching the suspicious vehicles from a concealed location. Unfortunately, their concealed location prevented them from keeping their "eyes on" all three suspect vehicles. Playboy piped in and provided more details. His whispered voice had an intense quality that hinted toward action.

Boss and I quickly located the vehicles based on a description from Playboy 17. The A-10s reported bingo and headed for home. Now Boss and I circled overhead, waiting. As I watched the vehicles move slowly through the rough terrain and closer to our troops, I anticipated the engagement. But there was something I didn't understand. Why was the enemy approaching our FOB, readying for the attack with their lights on? But I was new to the game, so I kept my questions to myself and reported what I saw.

The signs of a coming dawn soon appeared. When the sky lightened, we stowed the goggles. I switched the targeting pod's optics from night to day and noticed that the targeted vehicles looked like jingle trucks—large, flatbed vehicles painted in bright colors and decorated with hundreds of tiny bells that "jingled" when the truck was in motion. They were the Afghanistan version of mass transit and as common as Dodge trucks were in America. I wondered why the enemy would attack in jingle trucks. I was learning quickly that the enemy possessed strange tactics. As I studied the vehicles, Playboy provided an update.

"Joliet 61, Playboy 17. We are going to proceed back into the wire."

Huh? What about the enemy vehicles? I had expected a call for an attack at any moment. This was combat. I was hunting and ready. *But instead we're going home?* I kept my thoughts to myself. "Roger that, Playboy. What would you like Joliet to do?"

"Joliet 61, continue to monitor the vehicles."

Monitor for what? I again checked my response. "Roger, Playboy. Joliet will continue to monitor the vehicles. We have twenty minutes remaining in our vul period. Do you want us to remain on station longer?"

"Joliet 61, that's a negative. You're cleared 'Colorado.' "

The adrenaline from the hunt that had consumed me over the last three hours subsided. After another twenty minutes, we proceeded home, leaving the jingle trucks to continue on their way. The trucks likely carried Pashtuns living the way they had lived for centuries with little regard for the border that divided their culture.

The border established in 1893 at the bequest of the English government provided a buffer for British India. But the border, demarcated by the Durand Line, split the Pashtun homeland in two, leaving 11 million Pashtuns in Pakistan and 10 million in Afghanistan. As one historian noted, Sir Mortimer Durand created the border by "cutting a nonchalant swathe through Pashtun territory, sometimes drawing the line through the middle of the villages, grazing grounds or in such a way that farmers lived on one side of the border while their fields were on the other."* A hundred and ten years later, the border presented a new set of problems and increasing frustration for the war in Afghanistan.

* Stephen Tanner, *Afghanistan: A Military History from Alexander the Great to the Fall of the Taliban* (Cambridge, Mass.: Da Capo, 2002), p. 218.

10

HARBINGERS

On the morning of November 29, 2002, I shed my flight suit, pulled on running shorts, and laced up my Asics. AJ drove me to the north side of the base to the starting line for Bagram's first marathon. Despite the four-hour flight and no rest over the last twenty-four hours, I felt ready. My training plan had been awful. I had completed my longest training run the week before at just over twelve miles, the farthest I had ever run. There were a number of reasons not to run the race, but to me they were all the same—excuses. Not sure what to expect, I would just do what I always did, gut my way through it. How naïve I was.

The race drew reporters from *Stars and Stripes* and other news agencies. *Runner's World* ran a feature article about the race several months later, in the March 2003 edition. The race was billed as the first ever "Bagram Minefield Marathon." The course followed the inner perimeter road that lined the base. One lap was six miles. Runners would make four and a half laps and finish at the hospital, appropriately chosen. Minefields bordered both sides of the road over half the route. As we waited for the gun, I heard several soldiers joke, "This is one race where no one is going to cut the course."

As an army Black Hawk helicopter hovered overhead, EOD set off a mine and with a loud "boom," the first annual Bagram Minefield Marathon began. Over 150 participants sprinted ahead, causing me to wonder if I was beginning too slowly. Following the advice of a friend, my plan was simple: start slow, stay slow, and at the twenty-mile mark, pick it up. Afghan soldiers armed with AK-47s lined the route while roving gun trucks moved back and forth along the road as a deterrent to snipers. Mine dog detection teams cleared fields as runners passed by a few feet away.

After my second lap, riding an endorphin high, I altered my plan and picked up my pace. Unfortunately, the endorphins lasted only another six miles. At mile twenty, when I was supposed to kick in, I bonked. My body shut down, leaving me frustrated and embarrassed. My strategy of willing my body to continue to run met the physical limitations of "Sorry, can't do that." I began walking. I couldn't believe that my body refused to do what I told it. I had always been able to "will" my body to do something—to follow the orders I gave it. But now it failed me.

As I hobbled along, an ATV approached. I waved the driver down and asked for some water. The soldier handed me two bottles of Gatorade. I held up three fingers and he produced another. I gagged the liquid down. My body, unsure of itself, spit half of it back up. I began to jog—slowly. I then walked and ran, willing my body forward, until crossing the finish line at 3:39:48. I had successfully completed my first marathon, albeit like an idiot.

I didn't know it then, but the race served as a metaphor for things to come. I would again ask my body to do things it could not. Just as in the marathon, I tried to pace myself in the early days of the deployment, seeking a rhythm—a comfortable pace that I could maintain. But I didn't understand the distance. I didn't understand that the monotony of the months accumulated like the miles in the marathon. Later they took their toll. I'd bonk again. I just didn't know it yet.

My body ached for days. I found it difficult to climb into and out of the cockpit, but I did so with the help of plane captains who took pity on me. When I wasn't flying or standing duty, I hobbled across Bagram to the numerous meetings that required our presence—force protection meetings, base construction meetings, airfield planning meetings, safety meetings, and others. I soon discovered that most meetings were a waste of time—products of people who didn't have enough to do. The meetings droned on for hours. It seemed everyone had to say something, lest they appear incompetent, not worthy of their title, position, or responsibility. I remained quiet.

As the executive officer of the squadron, I was second in command, which in reality meant little.

But it did mean I had to work closely with Grouper and do my best to execute his plans. I sought ways to add value and not just more work for others. It was something with which I was struggling. Before leaving Yuma, Cow had pulled me aside.

"Zak, you know that Grouper is going to keep you as his XO."

"Yes, sir. I do."

"Zak, you know that executive officers are traditionally the ax-men, who enforce the rules and discipline amongst the officers and make the CO look like the good guy."

"Yes, sir. I suppose they do."

"Zak, Grouper is already an ax-man. You're going to have to find a way to toe the line without becoming another ax-man. The squadron doesn't need two of them."

"Sir, how do you suppose I do that?"

"Zak, I don't know."

That was it. That was the only advice I received for being XO. I was learning the Marine Corps way— on the job. The issue I soon confronted was that of working for a man whom I didn't like. I respected Grouper, but I didn't like him. I kept my feelings to myself, not sure in whom to confide. I found myself alone with an internal conflict that grew each day.

Grouper called me into his hooch, saying he needed to talk to me. I sat down and pulled out my notebook and pen. As I looked at him, I noticed a single white hair in his right eyebrow that jutted straight out—one long, crazy-looking hair. My eyes dropped to the empty paper as I prepared to take notes.

"Zak, the Marines aren't taking care of the camp. The crapper looks like shit. No pun intended. There are some fucking pigs around here. If someone soils that crapper again, I'm going to post a watch that has to inspect it after everyone takes a dump. And the camp, it looks like crap with all the trash blowing around. I want the Marine camp to be the cleanest compound in Bagram. In fact, I want the trash outside of our camp on Disney Road cleaned up. I want those lazy-ass soldiers to know, when they pass by our camp, that Marines respect themselves and keep themselves clean. Zak, we need another formation. I need to spell it out for the Marines—again!" Grouper paused, took in a breath, and then asked, "Zak, what do you think?" Before I answered, he continued. "Zak, we have it good here. Have you been to the hospital? I tell you, there are some unfortunate people in the hospital. You know, all of us should go to that hospital. We should. It would help remind people why we're here. You know, we could fly more as well. I talked to AJ and told him to look at scheduling more events. To let the CAOC know we could provide another section every other day. Maintenance is holding up with Bruce overseeing things. I don't think AJ gets it, Zak. This is combat. We're here to fly missions. Do you think AJ gets it? I don't. I don't think he gets it."

I interrupted. "Sir, I got LSS duty. The Harriers are probably getting ready to taxi."

"OK, Zak. Come see me when you get done. I got some other things to go over with you."

I headed outside to the green Nissan pickup, our Paddles truck. The keys were in the ignition. I drove out onto the taxiway and positioned myself at midfield where I could best watch the Harriers take off. My thoughts churned on Grouper's words. He was driving the squadron hard. He was getting the most out of everyone, but he was alienating them. Grouper said he didn't care what others thought of him, but I didn't believe him. I thought he was missing something. Love, respect, acceptance, appreciation—I wasn't sure which. Grouper talked a lot about his dad and his mom. His mom was ill now and his dad appeared to do little in caring for her. Grouper was mad at him. I had sat frequently in Grouper's hooch, listening to him vent.

I could see his dad, a man whom I never met. I could see the army man looking down at his young son and pushing him—telling him that he needed to try harder, run faster, do more, make better grades. I suspected that anything young Jim Dixon brought home wasn't good enough. My thoughts turned inward. *What kind of a father was I? Would I be there for Caleb as he grew up, providing sage advice and a father's comfort?* I thought of Michael, my twelve-year-old son who lived in Texas with his mom. I hadn't been there for him and now I had left Caleb. *Did I have my priorities right? Was I being a good man or was I just trying to prove something?* My concentration broke when the radio crackled.

"Paddles, Joliet."

"Go ahead, Joliet, this is Paddles," I responded.

"Dash two has a problem and is switching to the backup."

"Roger," I acknowledged. I called tower on my handheld radio and asked them if I could do a runway sweep. They quickly approved my request. I wheeled the LSS vehicle onto the runway and drove down to the south end, stopping along the way to pick up broken concrete and large rocks. The runway's condition provided a constant challenge to all who operated on it.

I parked the truck at the end of the runway and waited for the Harriers to taxi. With time to kill, I turned my eyes toward the infield. Several broken MiGs and Soviet tanks sat rusting in the open space. Near the discarded Soviet junk, a group of twenty Polish and Danish soldiers, clad in heavy bomb-protective clothing, moved slowly forward, clearing one of the many minefields that plagued Bagram.

Half the soldiers controlled German shepherd dogs on long retractable leashes. I watched the dogs move from side to side, their noses hunting the ground, seeking the minutest trace of RDX, TNT, or some other explosive residue. Then one of the dogs stopped and sat. The dog handler slowly approached, scanning the ground carefully as he moved forward. When he arrived at the dog's position, he removed a small yellow flag from his bag and placed it in the ground directly in front of the dog. Then the two moved on. The teamwork between man and animal appeared flawless and precise. I watched as the dogs stopped every twenty feet in a seemingly random way. I counted about thirty yellow flags in the small area they had marked thus far.

A row of soldiers with metal detectors followed the route of the dogs and their handlers. They were also clad in heavy bomb-protective clothing with big helmets and thick plastic face shields. The second group moved slowly, sweeping the ground with their metal detectors focused mostly on the areas with tiny yellow flags.

As I waited for the pilots to sort things out with maintenance, I watched the mine-clearing operation with increasing fascination. When I had parked my LSS vehicle, the mine-clearing team was fifty yards away, but now they moved closer. I watched as the nearest Alsatian approached. He seemed impervious to all except his task. His muscles rolled slowly underneath his thick, golden-black coat. His ears pointed high. His moist nose twitched rhythmically while his black snout moved back and forth centimeters above the ground, hesitating here, then there, then moving on. The dog stopped and sat down next to me. I stared at the dog's controller, who approached slowly and placed a yellow flag in front of the dog, a few feet from me. As he bent over, turning and looking at me through my open window, all slowed. His face was unmoved, expressionless behind the thick plastic shield. He said nothing.

I watched as the pair moved on, my thoughts returning to home, to Katie and Caleb. I missed them. Back home in northern New Mexico the aspens were turning gold, providing a rich contrast of colors. Not so in Bagram. The lack of color in Afghanistan became readily apparent as I scanned the horizon. As I waited for the Harriers to taxi into position, I pulled out my journal and made an entry:

There are four colors that dominate the Bagram canvas—gray, green, white, and brown. The sky and all the aircraft are a dull gray. The military vehicles, mostly different types of trucks, are a flat green. The mountaintops are white. Everything else, which is about 95% of the visual scene, is brown. It's either a light brown or a dark brown. The light brown is the light, talcum powder-like dirt that is everywhere. Even the few evergreen trees on the base have a light brown hue to them from all the dust that blows and collects on their needles. Dark brown is where water has spilled on the light brown dirt. The dark brown is mud and I expect to see more of it come winter.

The Harriers took off and quickly became tiny dots disappearing in the gray sky. Once they were gone, I unwillingly headed back to camp and to Grouper's tent.

11

NIGHT ATTACK

By late November, our Indian summer in Bagram was over. Gone were the days when the warm Afghanistan sun hovered above the high peaks, casting long shadows across Bagram before retreating for the night. Storm clouds moved in and the cold steady rains began. But flight operations continued unabated. Our boys were still out there, policing the Afghanistan-Pakistan border and patrolling deep into the Hindu Kush. Miserable as I was, I at least had a roof over my head and hot army chow twice a day. Compared to the grunt walking point in the cold, wet rain, I was living a life of luxury.

When Boss and I met to brief, Base Ops reported lightning within five miles of the airfield. We were in a Thunderstorm One (TS 1) condition. Boss and I briefed anyway. Thirty minutes later, the ODO interrupted us and advised that the air support operations center (ASOC) was considering canceling the flight schedule due to the weather. We finished our brief, not leaving anything to chance.

Jolly and Toby walked in from the rain having just returned from a mission. They reported the weather marginal but workable with ceilings at 4,000 feet and visibility three miles. The clouds were solid up to the mid-twenties, with a few sucker holes to the east. Jolly gave me a grid of a suspected al Qaeda hideout. "Sir, get some pod video if you can," Jolly said. "TF-5 wants it." I copied the coordinates before checking with our intel shop regarding the latest threats.

Intel briefed us that a Special Forces team had captured six Taliban near Gardez a few days earlier. We were picking up chatter that an attack on the Gardez safe house, to free the enemy prisoners, was "imminent." The CAOC wanted CAS assets airborne. Currently nothing was up. The Harriers had just landed and the A-10s were off until morning. Boss and I were the next ones in the chute. I turned to my wingman. "Boss, if the weather clears, we're going."

I told Boss to follow me as I headed up the three flights of stairs to the top of the control tower. The air force meteorologist, who saw me with increasing frequency, informed us that the airfield had just lifted TS 1. I requested the latest weather picture. Viewing the thirty-minute-old satellite photo, I saw the monster brewing to the west.

Boss and I out-briefed with the ODO, grabbed our pilot bags, extra maps, checklists, VRS tapes, and DSU bricks and headed out the door. Stepping into the cold darkness, I flicked on my thumb-sized keychain flashlight. The green light highlighted numerous puddles and mud pits from three days of steady rain. I moved cautiously across the mud parking lot and climbed into the back of the LSS truck. Boss and I slid all the way forward under a small tarp, where the seats were somewhat dry. Jolly drove slowly back to the Marine camp. The truck dipped and bumped along the potholed road, splashing mud and water along the way. Boss and I remained quiet. A few minutes later, Jolly flashed his lights and the guard opened the gates to the camp. Jolly maneuvered the truck through the maze of hardback tents and exited onto the flight line. The truck stopped. I jumped onto the tarmac and headed toward the soft glow radiating from a large tent.

In a Vietnam-era, general-purpose tent made of heavy canvas that didn't repel water but *absorbed* it, the Marines of the maintenance department toiled. Wooden pallets and boards, placed haphazardly on the ground, covered the inside of the tent in an attempt to keep the mud at bay. Desks, chairs, and bookshelves filled the limited space. Computers lined the desks, from which a dense thicket of extension cords and Internet cables protruded before snaking down to the ground and the shoddy wooden floor. Mud oozed up between the boards, nearly swallowing the power cords and pulling them underneath. Portable heaters blasted hot air within the tent, but it dissipated quickly. There were too many people crammed into too small a space, but it was cold and wet outside and the tent provided some protection from the elements.

I had become accustomed to operating in Bagram, taking for granted the efforts of our mechanics, who worked on the jets without the benefit of a hangar. I looked around at the Marines wrapped in heavy coats with black watch caps pulled tight over their closely shaved heads, their hands tucked into pockets or stuffed underneath armpits. Some jogged in place or stomped their feet in an effort to stay warm as the fog of their breath shot forward. It struck me then: this was it. This is why we came—to fight—to support the grunt in any clime and any place. No hotels, per diem, swimming pools, or booze. Only cold, wet, miserable Afghanistan. I felt good inside, proud.

We finished looking over the books and signed for the jets. As we stepped out of the tent into the damp blackness, Jolly called out, "Stand by. You're on hold."

I had seen this before too many times—stop, go, stop, go, stop, go. It lulled one into complacency. I told Boss to disregard. "Preflight your jet and be ready to go in case the word changes—again."

I found my jet at the end of the Harrier line, where a familiar voice greeted me from the darkness. "Good morning, Major Franzak." *Damn, it was morning, wasn't it?* My plane captain, Corporal Hamilton, took my pilot bag and began to set up the cockpit while I commenced my preflight with a red lens flashlight, more of the air force's covert lighting program.

As I walked around the jet, lightning flashed in the western sky. That was no doubt why the LSS had told us we were on hold. I finished my preflight and climbed into the jet. "Hey, Corporal Hamilton," I called down. "Call maintenance on your radio and ask them if we're still on hold."

Thirty seconds later, his red lens flashlight highlighted a bemused grin. "Sir, you're a 'go.' Base says the lightning is thirty miles away." He shook his head back and forth, emphasizing the same doubt I had.

Thirty miles? My ass. More like ten or less. I slammed the canopy shut, cranked up the motor, and prepared to launch. I donned my NVGs, which offered only a slight improvement. The fuzzy green image provided a general outline of shapes but little else. The NVGs worked poorly on stormy nights when the clouds blocked the light from the moon and stars. Nevertheless, without the NVGs I couldn't see my hand in front of my face.

We finished our cipher (secure radio) checks and taxied slowly around the poorly lit airfield. It was all too easy to taxi off the tarmac and into a minefield on a night like this. As we positioned on the runway, the tower controller cleared us for takeoff, then added, "Be advised. Lightning is now reported five northwest of the airfield."

No shit. The lightning's intensity increased as it moved across the valley. In a calm, reassuring voice, meant for me as much as my wingman, I keyed the back radio. "Well, this is what night attack is all about."

Jolly in the LSS vehicle responded with a long, drawn-out "Urrrrrrrrrh." My wingman said nothing.

After my run-up, I released the brakes and rolled northeast down runway 03. At 150 knots, I pulled the STO lever back and lunged into the darkness. Soon I was in the clouds flying the Bagram One, standard instrument departure. *Scan, scan, scan. Fly the instruments—be smooth—relax. Wiggle your toes, wiggle your toes.* As I passed 12,000 feet in a climbing left turn, my moving map revealed the 16,000-foot peaks a few miles to the north. I yanked my nose up, trying to climb higher, faster, and out of the soup. Finally, a few stars appeared through the milky clouds. At 23,000 feet, my jet popped into the clear, heading due south toward Kabul.

Now that I was clear of the clouds, I made out the subtle contours of the giant mass to the west. Its figure was obscured in the blackness, but I knew. I knew from experiences over the Far East—Korea, Japan, and Okinawa—as well as several hundred hours on NVGs in poor conditions. The leviathan awakened, shooting bolts outward from its core to the fringes of its mass. The veins glowed white-hot for a few seconds, outlining the goliath in a ghostly way, revealing the enormity, the billowing tops that reached upward beyond 40,000 feet. When the lightning stopped, the storm slipped back into the darkness, masked in the blackness of night. "Damn that's a big storm," I said quietly. The monster heard me and flexed its muscles again, frightening me before disappearing silently.

Once Boss joined, I gladly turned east and away from the beast. We checked in with Warlord, who told us to contact Playboy 14 on TAD 57. The "Playboy" call sign identified a JTAC attached to an army special operational forces (SOF) team. We proceeded east at 25,000 feet, dodging clouds as we attempted to contact the JTAC below.

Playboy 14 answered and provided his location as near the town of Gandomak. The irony of the location wasn't readily apparent, but I later read about the 4,500 British troops and ten thousand camp followers ambushed there in 1842. There was one survivor. Reaching the safety of Jalalabad on his dying horse, the severely wounded Dr. William Brydon recounted the story of the massacre. The episode became famous in the painting *Remnants of an Army*. Afghanistan and its people were no strangers to war.

As Playboy 14 briefed us, I found a small hole in the clouds and descended the section through the opening. The lights of Jalalabad—J-bad—appeared, then disappeared as the clouds enclosed us. At 4,000 feet, we broke out underneath. My moving map portrayed mountains several miles to our north, south, and west but I couldn't see them. Throughout my career, I had read mishap reports of pilots who flew into unyielding rock. The black boxes and tapes told the story. It was always the same. They remained unaware until the end. Until it was too late. Realizing their fate in the last seconds, the mistaken men yanked their stick hard, attempting to circumvent the inevitable, but physics prevents the impossible. And how the fear must have seized them in those final seconds. With slight comfort I thought, *At least it was quick.*

I was now tempting fate and I knew it. I was relying on the Harrier's technology to keep me safe, the INS, GPS, and moving map—the things I had been taught would fail me when I needed them most. I asked Playboy 14 to mark his position. Visibility was a few miles with no definable horizon—perfect conditions for a mishap. As we held in the narrow valley, it became increasingly difficult to cross-check my instruments while searching for the Special Forces team. Boss had it worse. He had to keep me in sight and maintain his position. Keeping the flight wrapped up with low, tight turns inside the small valley, I searched for the SOF team's IR light without success.

As we tried to sort things out, Playboy and I began "stepping on" each other's transmissions, effectively cutting the other person out. I became frustrated, and it showed in my radio calls. After a long pause, Playboy 14 responded, "Joliet 11, if I'm a little slow down here, it's because I have to put down the radio to work the IR pointer and vice versa. I'm working on no sleep and am a little tired."

I cringed, embarrassed at my loss of composure.

I had lost my perspective on who was supporting whom. In a disarming tone, I responded, "Roger, Playboy. Sorry. Joliet 11 standing by to work as directed." I scanned the ground carefully, then saw the tiny flashing strobe to the north. "Boss, hang on. Coming hard left," I stated. Flying over the position, I established a tight orbit above the team. Playboy 14 confirmed the visual and then proceeded with an update.

A few hours earlier, ten to twenty personnel armed with automatic weapons and rocket-propelled grenades (RPGs) ambushed the SOF team as they passed through a small village. During the shootout, the SOF team had killed one enemy and wounded two others. They broke contact and escaped to the south. With no casualties of their own, they were stuck with a disabled vehicle loaded with sensitive radios and other high-tech gear. They wanted to reenter the town at daybreak and requested our support. Low on gas, Boss and I needed to refuel. I informed Playboy of our status and peeled the section away to the south in a climbing turn. I promised to return quickly. Once level at 25,000 feet, I passed Playboy's 14's situation report (sitrep) to Warlord, who relayed it to K-mart and others.

To the east over Pakistan, a crescent moon sat low, cradling a tiny star on the violet horizon. Dawn was coming. The tranquility of the sight and the irony—the symbol of Islam—caught me off guard. I paused and absorbed God's beauty silently. Then I returned to my work, double-checking my weapons as I pulled into position behind the large KC-10.

Boss and I refueled quickly and then hurried back to Gandomak. The sky had lightened. The blackness of night was ceding to an eerie winter morning. We dropped down through a small hole and again found ourselves beneath a thick overcast where the gloomy light of predawn prevailed. The SOF team fired a flare. The glowing pyrotechnic burned brightly against the ashen gray countryside. We established an orbit and listened as Playboy briefed us on the team's plan.

"Joliet 11. After sunrise, we want you to establish a low-altitude CAP over the town as we sweep it. Break. We're going to talk to the town elder and tell him we mean business. Break. If they don't want to cooperate, we are going to tell them that you are going to bomb them. How copy, over?"

"Playboy, that's a solid copy," I acknowledged, recognizing the bluff. Thirty minutes later, Playboy announced the team was moving out. I directed Boss into combat spread as I set an east-west racetrack pattern over the town at an altitude of 4,000 feet. I pushed up the power and increased our speed to 400 knots due to our silhouettes against the gray clouds. I wanted more speed but the price was gas, and less gas equates to less time on station. It is a compromise required in combat, where the classic schoolbook answers meet the realities of supporting the grunt. Playboy 14 announced over the radio that our CAP was having its desired effect.

The SOF team moved through the village in a choreographed dance of cover and maneuver. Using my targeting pod, I called out danger points and possible ambush sights. Playboy 14 responded, telling us the team had uncovered large quantities of opium, automatic weapons, and an RPG hidden in a haystack. We watched the SOF team round up the village males and move them to the village center.

Boss and I remained wary of the prey below as the drama unfolded beneath us. And as my body tensed I realized I could not hear the sounds of the morning below and I wanted to hear them. Instead my eyes focused sharply, staring down, then up, then across, capturing all. I saw my wingman, his tiny jet chasing me and I him. We floated in a circle like a pair of lonely sakers, measuring the other in a game above the Gandomak plains, each searching for prey.

And so we flew, scouring the ground for another hour looking for squirters, runners, guilty voles, before the A-10s arrived. Playboy 14 thanked us for our work as we conducted a battle handover with Misty flight. We wished them luck and then departed to the west, dodging the remnants of a storm. We hadn't dropped a bomb, but our presence had made a difference. We had overcome the challenges of weather and terrain to support the grunts in a stressful four-hour mission. We had done what others expected us to do. And for the first time since arriving in Afghanistan, I felt I had done some good.

12

SCARS

The Marines' chatter from the ranks died abruptly when the sergeant major bellowed, "Squadron, ahhhh-ten-huh!" The inflection of his voice hammered the last syllable so that it resonated clearly. The sound of 180 boots slapping together in unison echoed through the newly erected hangar. Silence followed. When Grouper approached the sergeant major, I called the officers to attention in a more subdued tone. The sergeant major presented the squadron to the CO, and then announced, "Marines to receive awards, Cen-terrrrrrr, march." Five Marines marched forward, the last one calling a quiet cadence. The squadron adjutant read the award citations of each Marine as the CO pinned navy achievement medals on the first two and then handed the remaining three certificates for commendation. Once the formalities were complete, the CO called the squadron to attention and told them to fall out and form a "school circle" around him.

Once the Marines had settled around him, Grouper began. "Gents, we flew four hundred and thirty-one hours and one hundred and twenty-two sorties this month. We did that with only six jets and ten pilots. That's a testament to your hard work, to your dedication to the job, and to making the most out of what we have. Of course it's nice that we now have a hangar in which we can fix our jets, instead of pulling a wing in the rain, isn't it?" The Marines chuckled in approval. They were smiling. Grouper resumed. "But I want to talk about some other things." The smiles faded. "The porta-potties look like hell. Someone made a mess in one and failed to clean it up. It's simple. If I find another dirty crapper, I'm going to post a watch that inspects them after every use. I'm sick and tired of it. Do you guys want more duties?" It was a rhetorical question that the Marines knew better than to answer. "On another note, please take the time to answer some of the mail in the MWR tent. There are a lot of people back home writing us and thanking us. Write them back." The rant continued for a few more minutes before the CO dismissed everyone.

As the Marines filed out of the hangar, AJ grabbed me and pulled me aside. "Zak, Grouper wants to add more sorties."

"Yeah, I know, AJ. He talked to me the other day. He said he mentioned it to you."

"Zak, if we add more sorties, then we have to add more duties. We're pushing it as it is. Not only that, the jets won't hold up. Hell, this is only the second month. Do you think the CO is trying to impress someone?" AJ asked.

"Yeah, he probably is. I got a lecture on the meaning of a combat fitness report the other day. I'm guessing mine isn't going to look too good given the state of our crappers," I said.

AJ grinned and with a snicker said, "Fuck, this is going to be a long deployment."

"Yeah. It probably is," I said, walking away.

I felt sorry for myself as I began the long walk down Disney Drive. Several days earlier, I had received an e-mail from the MAG-13 operations officer, Lieutenant Colonel Paul "Rotor" Rupp, back in Yuma. Rotor was slated to take command of VMA-211, the "Avengers," in a few months. He asked me if I was willing to return home, be his XO, and take out his boat detachment for a summer deployment. I had worked for Rotor years before, when we were both Avengers—he a major, I a captain. I liked Rotor and was excited about the opportunity. Rotor said he wanted to check with me first before he approached Grouper. My elation at the offer was short-lived. The next day, Grouper told me that Rotor had e-mailed him regarding my reassignment. "I don't think it's a good fit," Grouper explained, before adding, "Besides, the MAG CO wants you to remain here." I realized then there wasn't going to be an easy out.

After a ten-minute walk, I reached my destination. The unique sound of my boots scraping against the plastic floor reminded me where I was. I thought it funny that I knew my location by the feel of my boots, but it was true. My Harrier had a metal skin. Our hooch, a wood floor. The flight line, concrete. Bagram's roads, fine, talcum-like dirt or hard gravel. But there was only one place with a plastic floor. And every time I stepped on it, the tiny rocks stuck in the treads of my boots scraped against the plastic like fingernails pulling on a chalkboard. The sound reverberated up my spine in chills. To avoid that nasty screeching sound, I picked up each foot deliberately as I pushed through the plastic tarp of a doorway. But the chalkboard scrape of my boots wasn't as bad as the noxious smell, a mixture of disinfectant, medicine, and human odors—sweat, waste, rot. I wondered if it was death.

I recalled my first visit a month earlier when the sticky sweet smell had surprised and almost overpowered me. I feigned composure as our squadron doctor, navy lieutenant Tim Marra, led me through the hospital entrance. I had asked him to take me there. He then left me with Captain Libby Dillon, an army nurse who entertained my questions and introduced me to the patients in the ICU. I spent an hour with Captain Dillon and the patients before leaving. Exiting the hospital into the warm Afghanistan sun, I inhaled deeply, sucking in the fresh air. I was outside and free from the horrors behind me. I made it fifty yards before I lost it. The tears poured forth as I struggled to breathe, bending over at the waist, holding my head in my hands. It took a few minutes before I collected myself. It was then I made the promise—to visit the hospital every day for as long as I was in Bagram.

That was five weeks ago and I was no longer true to my word. My visits had dwindled to every other day. Sometimes three or four days passed before I returned. My tears stopped after a few weeks. They returned when a new patient arrived, but then no tears came. I had begun the visits expecting to feel better about myself but that was an illusion.

As I pressed through the door, I thought about nine-year-old Ramin, who had lost his left arm when a rocket exploded. His left leg was in a cast to his waist. The doctors weren't sure how it would heal. His three friends weren't so lucky. Ramin was the only survivor of the children who found the unexploded rocket in their playground. There was three-year-old Hashmet, whose malnourished body resembled that of a one-year-old. The hospital had fought valiantly to restore the child's health with food supplements, but Captain Dillon knew it was temporary. Hashmet had been discharged the previous week. Shortly after his discharge, Captain Dillon spoke to me. "He's not going to make it. If he was in the U.S., he could make it. But not here."

"Why?" I pleaded.

"Even though we've explained to the father that Hashmet can't properly digest starches, the family can't afford to feed him anything else. They are poor. Naan is the common staple. I hope to God I'm outa here before he returns."

I was going to miss the auburn-haired nurse when she rotated home in another week. I turned right, walked down the hallway, and then turned right again and into the ICU. Dr. Hamed and Dr. Nasser were standing next to Ramin, translating for an army nurse who was changing the dressing on the boy's wounds. Once the nurse finished, Dr. Nasser walked over.

"How are you, Major Zak?" Dr. Nasser asked with a broad smile.

"I'm very good, Dr. Nasser. Very good. I can't complain, but I still do. How are you, and how is Ramin?"

Dr. Nasser's dark brown eyes and curly jet-black hair combined naturally with his light brown skin. His clean-shaven face and handsome features gave him the look of a GQ model. Dr. Nasser and Dr. Hamed lived in Kabul and worked several days a week at the army hospital translating for the American doctors and nurses. I had become friends with both Afghan doctors over the previous month.

"Major Zak, I am well, but Ramin is sad. He cried all morning, saying he misses his mother," Dr. Nasser explained. While I saw many fathers, brothers, uncles, and grandfathers visit their relatives, I never saw any women. They remained at home according to their strict Muslim beliefs. "We have two new patients as well. There is a young girl. She is probably three or four. They brought her in yesterday. She was bleeding in the ear. The doctors removed eleven maggots from her ear. Eleven! Can you believe that, Major Zak? Eleven maggots." I didn't say anything. I just shook my head. "There is a baby boy also. He is badly burned. A lamp caught his blanket on fire. He has third-degree burns over half of his body. I do not think he will make it, Major Zak."

No lumps filled my throat, no tears pushed from my eyes as I looked over Dr. Nasser's shoulder at the newly arrived patients. The little girl was asleep with a large teddy bear in her arms. The baby boy was in a plastic tent. I had become desensitized. I was beyond numb. The news simply rolled off me. I reached into my flight suit and pulled out several lollipops. They had become my trademark. "Dr. Nasser, can I pass them out?"

"Yes, of course, Major Zak."

On the walk back to camp, I voiced my anger. How vain and selfish I was. The fact that I didn't like my boss was a minor inconvenience and irrelevant given what others had—or didn't have. *Who the fuck was I to feel sorry for myself?* Grouper was right. I had it good. We had it good. No one worked harder than Grouper in looking out for the Marines. We had a hangar now, carpets in the tents, and he was pressing for an Internet cable in each tent so that the Marines could e-mail their families daily. Grouper was right. Seeing the hospital gave me perspective, but I didn't like the visits.

I came to view each visit as an inconvenience that disrupted my schedule. I no longer felt good after visiting the hospital. I wasn't changing anything. Instead I felt like hell after each visit, as if the children saw through my façade—my appeals for redemption. My visits didn't heal their wounds, aid their families, or remove their plight. Doubt consumed me. And as time wore on, my visits slowly diminished, withering away like a dying patient. I foolishly believed that by ignoring it, it would simply cease to be. But there was one thing I could not escape and the mere thought of the hospital caused its return, over and over again. It would be several years before that god-awful odor— that sickening sweet stench, of mixed origins—finally vacated the deep recesses of my mind.

13

VAMPIRES

On December 1, Grouper's desire for more flights became a reality. The CAOC ordered us into surge operations due to increased enemy activity at Shkin, Gardez, Orgun-e, and Asadabad. The enemy was testing each of the FOB's defenses in a series of attacks. Intelligence suspected a major attack was coming. We added two more sorties to the schedule. With our six jets, we flew six sorties every twenty-four hours, most of them at night. There was no room for error. Maintenance worked frantically to keep all six jets up. The tempo of operations became fly, stand duty, eat, sleep, repeat. Two pilots flew, two stood duty, two were in the chute, two prepped missions, and two slept. There wasn't any free time. After a six-hour mission and six hours of duty, we gladly hit the rack. The lights inside our hooch stayed off and the doors remained closed. When the door to our hooch cracked during the day, anyone awake squinted as the light peeked through. We became vampires in a darkened world, bleak and void of colors with the exception of the NVGs' green hue, which gave us our night-stalking eyes. A winter overcast moved in and the nights became darker—no moon, no stars, just blackness. We became our identity: Flying Nightmares.

Despite our nocturnal routine, the rest of the base remained on a working day schedule, including the de-mining crews. We resorted to sleeping with earplugs due to the constant explosions. Their frequency diminished for short periods, but as soon as one forgot about them—"Boom!" The unannounced detonations became nerve-racking.

In the early predawn hours during surge ops, a loud explosion jolted me awake. Explosions during darkness were unusual. I sat up feeling uneasy. My ears tuned to the sounds around me. A jet's engine whined in the distance. The sound of turning rotors signaled the departure of two, maybe three CH-47s. No gunfire and no more explosions. After a few minutes, I lay back down and quickly fell asleep.

Later that day, I asked Staff Sergeant Joy Wheatley, one of the Marines in charge of our security, about the explosion. She explained that base MPs had found a large crater on the eastern perimeter and footprints leading to it, nothing more. She said that local Afghans tried to sneak into the base at night to steal scrap metal for money. I thought about the children I knew in the hospital. Despite the surrounding beauty of the Hindu Kush, Afghanistan was a cruel and unforgiving place.

As surge operations continued, we streamlined our briefs from the normal 2.5 hours before takeoff to 1.5 hours. Many aspects of the missions were the same. Takeoffs, departures, tanking, recovery, landings were now standard operating procedures—SOPs. Our briefs focused on other essentials: whom we were supporting and how best to support them.

One unit we supported was Task Force 5 (TF-5), the "Snake Eaters"—the elite of the ground forces. Shrouded in secrecy with their own compound, the TF-5 guys were easy to spot on Bagram—beards, dark shades, Glocks on their hips, modified M-4s, and uniforms with no name tags or rank. They looked like mercenaries of death.

When the news of our targeting capability reached TF-5, they wanted to know more. A few of them arrived one afternoon for a brief on the Harrier and Litening targeting pod. They introduced themselves as Mark, Will, John, and Todd. After the introduction I said, "I'm sorry, I didn't catch your rank." The six-foot-three, 250-pound linebacker with thick blond hair and a full beard just smiled and said, "It's Will." An awkward silence followed.

A few nights later, Boss and I were airborne when we received an unexpected call from Warlord telling us to stand by for special tasking. They rolled us to a covered frequency and briefed us on our new mission. We were given a latitude and longitude (lat-long), a frequency, a call sign, and a time to be overhead the target. We were specifically directed not to arrive early so that the noise of our jets wouldn't tip our hand. It was a takedown—a time-sensitive target (TST) raid on a high-value target (HVT).

High-value targets and their status (live, dead, presumed dead, detained, and, most often, unknown) were briefed daily to the CJTF-180 commander and his staff. Shortly after we arrived, I sat in on a few briefs to get an idea of the bigger picture, to learn the mind-set of the senior staff. A petite woman with long blond hair and dressed in hiking boots, khaki pants, and a safari vest briefed the military audience. A friend who worked on the CJTF-180 staff leaned over to me and whispered, "She's OGA. You know— other government agency." The attractive woman looked out of place in the room full of middle-aged men dressed in camouflaged fatigues. She moved quickly through the list of targets—humans: Taliban and al Qaeda operatives whom we wanted to capture or kill. Though no one said it, most of us preferred the latter.

As Boss and I refueled behind the tanker, we plotted the target on our maps and assessed the terrain. The target was a small village in Nuristan province, Bâlâmurghâb, deep in the Hindu Kush. The landing zone was located on a small precipice at an altitude of 10,000 feet. The surrounding mountain peaks ranged between 15,000 and 18,000 feet. Most helicopters can't land in LZs at 10,000 feet, but TF-5's aviation element was different. They flew modified CH-47 Chinooks capable of performing these missions at night and in bad weather. TF-5 was the real "anywhere, anytime" response force.

As the seconds to the takedown approached, Boss and I added power and flew north. For once the skies were clear. The moonlight reflected off hundreds of snowcapped peaks that stretched to the horizon and beyond. The breadth of the Hindu Kush was daunting. As our jets skated the thin air over the wind-torn peaks, the helos landed. A whiteout ensued. I watched the drama as my targeting pod stove through the night. Tiny black figures, the IR images of the soldiers, swarmed from the back of the helicopters and into the snow. The images spread out and moved quickly to three mud houses adjacent to the LZ. I pulled my orbit tight, working my targeting pod and IR marker across the ground, looking, waiting, watching for squirters. The Disney-like show of green lasers danced across the houses, trees, and snow—each the deadly aiming dot of a TF-5 weapon.

We held for an hour as the Snake Eaters swept the buildings and nearby countryside, struggling as they moved through three-foot snow. Then we received the call "Dry hole." The intelligence was spotty and not always right. Sometimes chance benefited the enemy as well. TF-5 cleared us off and we began our flight home.

Our squadron SOP required us to return with a minimum of 1,200 pounds of gas and be on deck with 800 pounds, enough for one or two passes in case something wasn't right. In Afghanistan, most pilots padded their fuel because Bagram had one runway on which a number of things could go wrong. But tonight we had supported a major operation and were the only heavy firepower overhead. The weather was clear, so I opted to press our gas to the limit—not below "bingo" but right on it. As we maneuvered south toward Bagram, I asked Boss for his fuel state. He had a couple of hundred pounds more due to topping off last at the tanker.

I kissed Boss off, pulled the power to idle, pushed the nose over, and advised tower I was entering a high downwind from the north. As I turned final, I dropped the gear, stuffed the nose over, and pulled in some nozzles to slow down. I focused on my lineup.

Four in the green, STO stop clear, flaps in STOL . . . I stopped and looked back at my landing gear lights. A yellow light, indicating an unsafe main landing gear, glowed brightly. *Shit.* I grasped the landing gear handle and forced it down against the stop. Nothing. *Aw shit, not tonight.* I checked my gas. I had 1,000 pounds; enough to troubleshoot the problem for a few minutes.

"Tower, Joliet 11 waving off. Unsafe gear," I stated.

"Roger, Joliet. Say intentions."

"Joliet 11 entering the delta at two thousand." I keyed the back radio. "Paddles, Joliet 11 with unsafe main. Can you break out the checklist?"

"Roger, Joliet. Stand by."

Beads of sweat gathered on my brow. As the

ODO recited the emergency procedures, the main landing gear light turned green. I had done nothing. Perhaps there was a bug—a short circuit. I double-checked that the gear handle was firmly in the "down and locked" position one more time, and prayed. I turned final, rechecked my gear, and eased the Harrier onto the tarmac. The jet settled normally when I applied the brakes. I sighed in relief.

The next day Gunny Rodenkirk told me about the jet. "Sir, you were lucky. The mechs said that the doors were out of rig and that even if you had tried to blow the gear down, it wouldn't have worked. Damn, we dodged a bullet, didn't we sir?"

"Yeah, Gunny," I said, thinking about what might have been. "Yeah, we dodged a bullet." I walked away knowing it was better to be lucky than good.

14

MILK RUN

The expected major attack on one of our FOBs never came. After a week of surge operations, we needed a break. The pilots might have held up for another week, but the planes showed their wear. Maintenance was down to three jets. It was only a matter of time before we dropped a sortie. The CAOC recognized the drain they had placed on us and rotated us back to normal flight operations. The break in optempo gave me a chance to make a "milk run."

I met the Marines at our guard shack early in the morning. My body was accustomed to racking out at this hour, but coffee and the excitement of adventure moved me. Seven Marines and I jammed ourselves into a broken-down white government van while the gunny and staff sergeant manned a green pickup. Both vehicles were in sad shape— rusted frames, broken seats and springs, no seat belts, bald tires, and misfiring motors. The vehicles had been issued to us shortly after our arrival with the warning "Take care of them. There isn't anything else."

We fastened our flak jackets, secured our helmets, and loaded magazines into our weapons—nine Marines with M-16s and me with an M9 Beretta pistol. Our lack of armament and civilian vehicles gave the appearance of Marines going to the range—certainly not into a combat zone. We left the Marine camp and proceeded south on Disney Drive. Passing through the second checkpoint, the sergeant driving the vehicle looked back at everyone and said, "OK, boys. Lock and load." The sound of metal bolts slamming home, chambering rounds, echoed through the cab. I reached down and pulled my wimpy pistol from its holster, brought the slide to the rear, and chambered a round as well. I weighed the drama. *Aren't we going a little overboard?* I sensed the Marines wanted—needed—some action.

After clearing the base and the small villages to the south, we whizzed down a narrow road full of potholes. It was one of only two paved highways in Afghanistan. The road reminded me of Bagram's runway. I stared out my window, looking west at the Hindu Kush paralleling our track. I was glad to be out of camp, away from the meetings, the bullshit. The countryside reminded me of Mosquero, New Mexico, where I had spent childhood summers. The ground was brown and hard with a light covering of dry yellow grass. I recalled holding on to my grandfather's waist as we rode bareback on the cutting horse through the herd of cattle, counting them, looking for the sick cow.

Like northeastern New Mexico, there were scant trees, just wide-open, rolling plains of hard, dry earth. A few sheepherders moved their flocks along the road. Adobe mud homes with large mud walls appeared sporadically. Daydreaming of home and the smell of sagebrush, I returned to reality when my eyes glimpsed a rusted T-62 tank, its barrel pointing down at us from a small hill. Antiaircraft guns lined the highway where the hills pinched tight as the road twisted and turned through the narrow gap. There had been a fight here.

As we drove through the forgotten battlefield, something unique caught my eye. White and red painted rocks lined the road. Some were spaced two feet apart, others by ten feet or more. Perhaps they marked a future engineering project to widen the road. I turned and faced my driver, a shy, soft-spoken Marine who had driven this route several times.

"Hey, Sergeant Marquardt. What's with the red and white rocks?" I asked.

"That's a minefield, sir."

"You mean those rocks are marking mines?" I asked incredulously.

"Yes, sir."

"You're kidding me. All of those can't be mines," I protested.

"No, sir. Those are all mines. The red and white rocks mark the edge of a minefield."

"But they go on forever."

"Yes, sir."

I knew that Afghanistan was one of the most heavily mined countries in the world and that the area around Bagram was the most heavily mined area in Afghanistan. There were over 10 million mines in Afghanistan, which on average killed 100 and injured another 500 people each month. But seeing the never-ending line of red and white rocks, twenty feet off the broken asphalt, gave new meaning to my awareness.

Sergeant Marquardt swerved back and forth, dodging potholes as the van sped forward. If we blew a tire or Sergeant Marquardt lost control of the vehicle, we were going into the minefield. I quit looking out the side window and the minefields and stared directly ahead at the lead vehicle of our convoy.

When we reached the edge of Kabul, the mud buildings and sheepherders gave way to empty concrete buildings and burned-out factories. The architecture was devoid of creativity—simple, bland buildings built for function from a Soviet mind-set. They reminded me of the public schools back home built in the 1960s and '70s. But the buildings in Kabul bore the scars of war—big holes, small holes, missing walls, and collapsed roofs. The spray of machine-gun fire was stitched across the concrete fronts—7.62, 12.7, and the larger 14.5 mm holes. The signatures of light and heavy weapons pockmarked the walls in long, jagged lines. People were few.

We finally reached an Afghan paint store on the outskirts of Kabul. We posted a guard on the vehicles while the gunny, staff sergeant, and a few Marines went inside to purchase supplies. I remained with the guard and smiled at the children who gathered around us.

The Afghan kids quickly culled me from the herd. They saw that I was naïve—a sucker, vulnerable to their smiles and begs. They surrounded me and stuck out their hands. I raised my empty hands and shook my head, but my smile gave me away. It was no use. I turned and went to the back of the van, where I opened a box of MREs and began passing out sweets and other food to the cheering boys and girls. After a few minutes, I grabbed my camera and began taking pictures of the children.

A young girl in a purple dress with a silk scarf wrapped around her dark brown hair reminded me of Sharbat Gula, the "Afghan Girl," whose photograph had appeared on the June 1985 cover of *National Geographic*. As I knelt down to take the young girl's picture, she held tight to her baby sister's hand. Looking through the lens, I pondered their lives. *Who were they? Were they happy? Were they orphans struggling to survive?* But I didn't speak the language and their eyes revealed no more of their story than what I saw before me.

The gunny and his entourage emerged from the building with several cans of paint. We loaded into the vehicles and drove off to the center of town for more supplies. I waved to the children as we pulled away. They smiled and waved back.

As we drove farther into the city, it awakened. The narrow streets became crowded. Jingle trucks, taxicabs, and bicycles flowed without regard to any rules or organization while pedestrians scampered out of the way. At a few intersections men in uniforms stood on small stools, blowing their whistles and moving their arms frantically to direct the traffic that whirled around them. There were no traffic lights. An old man led his oxen down the street while taxicabs swerved to miss him. Other men pulled carts five or six times their size loaded with firewood. Cars, trucks, bicycles, pedestrians, and animals intermingled in a visual chaos accented by the din of whistles, horns, squealing tires, and the occasional shout.

An eclectic mix of people—Tajiks, Uzbeks, Kirghiz, Pakistanis, and Pashtuns—flowed back and forth on the sidewalks and streets in their various headgear. Turbans, qaraquls, and pakols, made famous by Ahmad Massoud during the Soviet-Afghan War, were everywhere. Massoud's picture hung on walls, buildings, and windows. The martyred hero—the "Lion of Panjshir"—remained an iconic figure, larger than life within Afghanistan.*

We stopped at an outdoor market, where an array of colors—reds, oranges, purples, greens—from

* Ahmad Massoud was an Afghan resistance leader who fought the Taliban. He was assassinated two days before 9/11 by al Qaeda operatives posing as journalists.

the fruit and vegetables contrasted sharply with the bleak buildings and muddy streets. The gray, overcast sky dropped low to the earth. A light rain began. As I walked through the open market and down the streets, the lack of women became apparent. There were men, children—boys as well as girls—but no women. Every now and then I merely caught a glimpse of a woman—rushing, moving quickly as though she was somewhere she was not supposed to be. I could tell it was a woman by the long chadri that covered her body, including her head. A small grille about the eyes allowed her to see, but not to be seen.

Watching the woman shuttle quickly across the street, I thought of Zarmina, the Afghan woman publicly executed in 1999 in front of thirty thousand spectators in Kabul's Olympic Stadium. I believed that our routing of the Taliban would improve the lives of the Afghans, especially the women. But as I looked around, I wondered if we were making a difference.

People moved around us but didn't look at us. Only the children approached us, pleading for handouts. There were no other soldiers or U.S. military. It was we ten Marines alone in the center of Kabul. I looked across the street at a group of young men who had formed a small circle. I could tell they were talking about us. They looked at us but didn't smile. No one smiled except the children. Kabul was a place on the edge—unsure of itself, nervous.

By late afternoon, the Marines climbed back into the vehicles and headed home. Before getting back into the van, I pulled Gunnery Sergeant Sanchez aside so that no one else could hear. "Gunny, I know there's a chance we could get hit with an ambush, so I understand the need to keep the speed up, but I think the chances of running off the road at high speed are far greater. If we don't kill ourselves when the vehicles flip, I'm sure the minefields will finish us off."

The stone-faced gunny looked at me and said, "Yes, sir." Then he walked away. I could tell by his face that he thought I "didn't get it." Perhaps I didn't. Three days after our milk run, insurgents ambushed two U.S. soldiers and their Afghan interpreter, leaving them critically injured. The attack took place in the Kabul open-air market where I had stood a few days earlier, admiring the colors in the vegetable stands.

15

LETTERS AND LOSSES

I watched the Marines pick through the envelopes one at a time, carefully inspecting each. They held them up and examined the handwriting closely. They were looking for soft cursive, or playfully drawn hearts, or smiley faces—anything cute that hinted of lace. They held the envelopes to their noses and sniffed. Was there a trace of perfume? If there was doubt, they tossed the unopened letter back into the box and pulled out another. I looked into the large box that contained hundreds of letters from strangers offering their support. A beautifully drawn American flag adorned one. I pulled it out and walked back to my desk in the S-1 (Administration) shop. Opening it, I read:

Dear Soldier:

My name is Kevin H. and I am an 11-year-old boy who goes to Brookside school in Allendale, NJ. . . . I heard you would not be able to be home during the winter holidays. If you can't

*go home for the holidays, what will you be
doing? Your family must be really missing
you. Thank you for protecting our country.
Remember you can make a difference in the
world. Have a happy holiday.*

*Your new friend,
Kevin H.*

I pulled out a piece of paper and began writing
Kevin back. I then printed a few pictures of the Harrier and me and pulled my squadron patch off my
flight suit. I enclosed the patch, pictures, and letter
in an envelope and turned to the young Marine who
worked next to me.

"PFC Atmore, will you see that this goes out in
the next mail run?"

"Yes, sir." He looked down at the letter. "Sir, I
didn't know you were from New Jersey."

"I'm not. What makes you think I was?"

"Sir, I'm sorry. I saw the address was in New Jersey.
Not to pry sir, but who do you know in New Jersey?"

"Nobody. I picked the letter out of the box in
the MWR shed. I'm taking the CO's advice and trying to respond to some of the people who are sending us their support. I chose this letter because the
sender had drawn a beautiful American flag on the
envelope." I picked up the envelope and showed it to
Private First Class Atmore. He examined it and then
gave it back to me.

"Sir, can I talk to you privately?" Atmore asked.

"Sure." I wasn't sure where this was going as I stepped outside and into the cold. Atmore followed me. Once he shut the door behind him, I asked, "What's up, Devil Dog?"

"Sir, I wanted to know if you could do me a favor." He hesitated before carrying on, perhaps gauging me. "I don't want to impose. Really I don't want to, but it would mean a lot."

"Well, what is it?" I was nervous now.

"Sir, could you write some friends of mine back home?"

I breathed a sigh of relief. "Sure. I'd be glad to."

"Sir, I'd like you to write Mr. and Mrs. Walcott. They have been friends of our family for a long time. They live in New Jersey."

"OK. Anything special you want me to say?"

"Yes, sir. They lost their son in the towers during 9/11. Can you tell them he isn't forgotten."

The unexpected blow drove deep. I had leaned into it, blindly—foolishly. I didn't feel worthy. "Sure. Absolutely. If you can write out their address and their son's name and anything else you think I should know."

"Yes, sir. Thank you. I know the Walcotts will be grateful." Atmore turned and walked back to the S-1 shop, leaving me standing in the cold Afghanistan air.

Wherever I went, I heard the same news. From AJ in Ops, Wiz in the Four, Gunny Rodenkirk or Gunner

Jones in Maintenance, it was the same. The Marines were privy to it as well. "Sir, the CO wants to see you." I sought him out, mostly behind his computer in his hooch, where he provided the latest updates to the generals. After being told to grab a chair, I broke out my notebook and pen and waited.

"Zak, we lost a Marine."

I looked at Grouper's face. Stoic, hard, sad. He continued.

"He fell overboard or at least that's what the Eleventh MEU presumes. Fuck. I got the e-mail this morning. It's the first fucking e-mail I've got from Screech in three fucking months. How about that, Zak? Three fucking months and now he has the gall to tell me he lost one of our Marines. What do you think of that? Isn't that fucked-up?"

It was a loaded question. Although I didn't like Screech, I didn't want to say anything. He was a peer. Our personalities had clashed frequently before Grouper joined the squadron, when I replaced Screech as AMO. I answered cautiously. "Sir, I'm not sure. He's no longer in your chain of command—"

Grouper interrupted. "I know that, Zak. I know he's no longer in my chain of command, but how about some courtesy. I'm no longer in General Amos's chain of command, but I provide him regular updates. I'm no longer in the MAG CO's chain of command, but I keep Ragu apprised of how his Marines are doing. When in doubt you keep everyone informed. You know what I mean?"

"Sir, perhaps he was giving the updates to the ACE commander, believing they were being forwarded on." I was boxing myself in, against my better judgment.

"Bullshit. He wasn't doing that." Grouper shook his head, visibly frustrated, partly by me.

I knew Grouper was right, but I didn't want to agree with him. I had lost my objectivity. I was failing him as an XO, but my ego prevented me from acknowledging it. I had believed him to be wrong too many other times. I sat there like a stubborn ass, waiting to take notes.

"We're going to have a memorial service. I'll work out the details with the sergeant major. We'll have it after our last night flight during shift change so all the Marines can attend."

"Roger, sir. Anything else?"

"No, that's it for now." Grouper looked up from his computer as I stood up. "Why don't you come by more often? It seems you're trying to avoid me."

"Yes, sir." I waited for more, pondering my Freudian slip.

"OK, Zak. Thanks." Grouper turned back to his computer and began typing another e-mail.

I found Lieutenant Joe Primeaux behind his hooch on the other side of the camp, next to the squadron's chapel. I watched as his hand traced the carefully scripted words on the large sign. Joe had been working on the project for over a week at the request of the CO. The sign was beautiful. It was almost finished.

Joe was painting the last of the black script that told the story of "Teufel-Hunden," the proposed name of the Marine Camp.

"Hi, Joe. How you doin'? The sign looks beautiful. You've outdone yourself," I said.

"Hey, sir. I didn't see you standing there. An artist I'm not. But I appreciate the remarks."

"Joe, can I talk to you?"

"Sure, sir. Go ahead."

I looked around to make sure we were alone. "Joe, I'm thinking about asking for a reassignment. I don't think I can take it anymore."

Joe stopped painting. He dipped his brush into the turpentine and then wiped it on the rag. "Let's go inside."

I followed Joe back into his hooch, where he closed the door and motioned for me to sit down. Joe was heavyset; not fat, just big. He was older but referred to me as "sir." He had joined the navy after a stint as a pastor in southern Mississippi. His soft Southern accent and disarming smile allowed me to continue.

"Joe, I'll be honest with you. I don't know where to turn. I don't know who to talk to. That's why I'm here. I'm gonna come clean." I paused, looking at Joe, then continued. "I know you're the chaplain, but I don't know who else to talk to. I can't stand the CO. I can't stand Grouper and don't know if I can take his negative bullshit anymore. He doesn't listen to anyone. AJ and Dano grabbed me yesterday and said they've had it. They can't stand the way the CO talks down to them—berates them and belittles them for their work. Nothing is ever good enough. He doesn't cut anyone a break. I'm supposed to be carrying through his orders but he's so damn busy doing it all himself that no one can do anything on their own. I just don't think I can work for him." I looked at Joe, who sat patiently waiting for me to go on. "Joe, I feel awkward talking to you."

"Sir, it's OK. This is between you and me." Joe got up and walked over to his bookshelf. He pulled out a book and sat back down. "I don't think your frustration is any reason to quit. You won't serve anyone well and you certainly won't serve yourself. You know, the CO has a lot on his plate and a lot of people leaning on him. He just wants to do well." Joe looked at me, seeing if I was taking it in. "I also think he has some issues with his father. Do you ever try just agreeing with him even when you think he is wrong?"

"Why would I want to do that?" I asked, confused.

"Well, if you agree with him at first, then you can avoid an immediate confrontation. You can then work with him on his proposal, slowly bringing him over to what you think might be better."

I mulled over the advice before saying anything. "Okay, Joe. I'll give it a go. What's the book?"

"Sir, you might like this. It's called *When No One Sees*. The author is Os Guinness. Have you heard of him?" Joe held out the book.

"No, Joe. I haven't," I said, taking the book. I read the title to myself. *When No One Sees: The Importance of Character in an Age of Image.* I stood up. I felt I had said enough, perhaps too much. "Joe, thanks. I suppose I can talk to you anytime."

"Of course, sir. Anytime."

Two nights later, the Marines gathered in the hangar in a large formation. Joe said a prayer, followed by Grouper, who offered words of encouragement about how Lance Corporal Robert Contreras had selflessly served his country. Corporal Lamphier came forward and spoke of his friend and the kind of person he was. He asked others to join in, to speak up about their fallen comrade, but the Marines were accustomed to standing quietly in the ranks. Few spoke or showed emotion. The awkward silence was broken when several Marines began singing "Eternal Father." When they finished, taps was played while the Marines stood at attention. The CO dismissed the Marines. We then formed a single line and took turns writing messages on a thousand-pound bomb at the back of the hangar. As Corporal Lamphier said, "It was what Contreras would have wanted."

As I stepped forward to write my message, I thought of the mother and father alone on the other side of world, receiving the news from a Marine in dress blues. I took the pen in my hand and thought of Katie and Caleb and a Marine in dress blues.

16

CLOSE CALLS AND MISHAPS

As Toby and I circled above the thick overcast at 25,000 feet, we realized our fate. There were no sucker holes tonight. Our only option to support the ground convoy below was to put our plan into effect. It seemed just, since I had proposed the plan and Toby had helped me build it. I drove east toward the Khyber Pass before completing my 180 and lining myself up for the descent. I keyed the back radio. "Joliet 22, are you ready?"

Toby answered with confidence. "Joliet 21, 22 in position. Ready."

I watched the miles tick away quickly until we were on top of the descent point, then I pulled my power to idle, popped the speed brake, pushed the nose over, and reset the power slightly above idle to give Toby something to play with. We descended into the soup.

I had never done this before. It felt strange—uneasy. *What if we had made a mistake?* No, Toby and I had been thorough. We had spent two days working the numbers and the charts. Then we had run the data by the CO, who approved it. I had to have faith. I felt the purr of the Rolls-Royce motor behind me as the altitude rolled down. We were passing through 20,000 feet now at 250 knots in a 10-degree dive. I waited for the radar altimeter (RADALT) to come alive.

The genesis of our plan had come a week earlier, over Shkin. It was my first flight with Toby, who had replaced Boss as my designated wingman. That night a solid overcast covered eastern Afghanistan. Playboy needed us below the weather, but there was no way to get down. After two hours of ineffective circles above the clouds, looking for the elusive sucker hole, we returned home. We had to find a way to get below the weather. It was then that the idea came to me: build our own approaches.

I pulled out the large TPC map and plotted each of our FOBs. Yes, it was possible. Each of the FOBs was located in a valley of some width and orientation. By aligning ourselves with the valleys, we could descend in a straight line until we broke out underneath. I ran the plan by Toby, who thought it would work. We plotted descent points, tracks, and endpoints that would place the pilots near the FOBs when they broke out—if they broke out. We measured the width of the valleys to account for pilot or system error—a little gravy. We ensured the tracks were long enough to account for the 3,000-fpm rate of descent. Then we created no-lower-than altitudes at the end of the tracks—2,000 feet above the ground. We could fly lower, but we needed at least 2,000 feet of clear weather to employ ordnance. If a pilot didn't break out by 2,000 feet, then he aborted, added full power, and began a 3–4 g climb back to sanctuary. It was risky, but options were few. Grouper double-checked our calculations and agreed with the concept. He added a few caveats. The GPS, moving map, and INS had to be working. It made sense.

I watched the altimeter spin down as I pressed the stick forward. I fought the urge to pull out of the dive. I had to stick to the plan. Never before had I descended into the goo without a clearance, without ATC providing me vectors, safety, steering me clear of obstacles, other aircraft—terrain. I looked at the moving map. My airplane was centered over the track. The endpoint was approaching. Sixty seconds out.

"Altitude, altitude," blared through my headset as the red warning light flashed ominously on my console. I was on the RADALT now. I reached up with my index finger and reset the red warning light by tapping my finger against it. Bitching Betty stopped. I reset the RADALT to 2,000 feet AGL. Thirty seconds to go. I prepared for the pullout. Then the clouds gave way and we broke out. I checked the RADALT. We were 2,500 feet above the ground in the J-bad valley. It was dark, blackness, nothing, no horizon. It was like my flight with Boss a few weeks earlier. Only the lights of Jalalabad, some fifteen miles to the east, provided any ground reference.

We quickly found Striker 15 and his convoy twenty miles east of Shahidan Pass. Toby and I held in a racetrack pattern 2,000 feet above the five-vehicle convoy as it crept westward along the road. Insurgents had mined and sabotaged the route the previous week. Striker reported he was glad to see us. Forty minutes later, as the convoy approached the pass, it became evident we could go no farther. The peaks disappeared into clouds to the west. It was a box canyon. There wasn't enough room to maneuver the jets safely between the cliffs that lined the route.

I briefed Striker on our plan. We needed gas. After we refueled, we would return overhead, serve as a radio relay, and pick up the convoy on the backside of the pass. Striker concurred. Toby and I climbed back up into the soup and headed southwest toward the tanker track.

"Warlord, Joliet flight is Dodgeball," I stated letting the AWACS know we were inbound to the tanker.

"Roger, Joliet. Be advised, Irate has repositioned from Poseidon to Athena."

"Roger, Warlord. Solid copy." I turned the flight south and toward the Athena track. I did the math. It was going to be close. The extra distance put us near bingo upon arrival in the Athena track. "Joliet 22, say state."

"Joliet 22, five-point-one."

"Rog. Thanks. We're going to be cutting it close tonight."

"Yeah, I know," Toby answered coolly. Toby was a first-tour captain who had impressed his previous bosses. They had seen his maturity and assigned him a department head billet, as the DOSS—director of standardization and safety. A farm boy from eastern Washington, Toby was a natural athlete. He sought competition. A former star baseball player, his wide shoulders and barrel chest looked better suited for the football field. A large nose and square jaw contrasted with his large, floppy ears. An anomaly—a child's face with a grown man's features. His giddy laugh often gave away his presence.

"Joliet 21, this is Warlord."

"Warlord, this is Joliet 21. Go ahead."

"New track, Joliet. Irate has repositioned to the Mercury track at base plus sixteen. Maintain base plus fifteen or less until joined."

"Roger. Joliet solid copy."

Shit. These guys are going to run us out of gas before we can refuel. I swung the section back to the north and pointed toward Mazar-i-Sharif. "Joliet 22, call home plate and get a weather update."

"Joliet 22, rog."

Toby called back a few minutes later. He said the ODO reported ceilings around 1,000 feet with visibility at least three miles. OK conditions but not great. As we drilled north at 24,000 feet, I couldn't believe we were still in the clouds. I looked at my air-to-air TACAN. Thirty miles separated us from Irate.

"Warlord, Joliet, request vectors to Irate 41, we're popeye," I stated, letting Warlord know that we were still in the clouds. We were going to have to join while IMC.

"Joliet 21, Irate 41 bears three-six-zero for thirty miles."

"Roger, thanks." I brought the section left 5 degrees to magnetic north. A few minutes later, I saw the flashing strobe directly ahead but the outline of the massive tanker remained hidden. More lights appeared. I approached slowly, bringing my wingman and myself forward as the giant ship came into view. I moved up to the KC-10's right wingtip. Tonight, because of the clouds, he was lit up like a Christmas tree.

"Irate 41, Joliet 21, starboard observation," I said.

"Joliet 21, cleared to the precontact position."

I pulled some throttle and dipped my left wing. I began sliding left and aft. It was then that I saw the snake. I had been so focused on flying formation, I hadn't noticed the hose. The sixty-foot-long, four-inch-thick hose with a twenty-five-pound steel basket heaved its head up and down like a cobra, its hood flared.

"Holy fucking shit," I said aloud. *There is no way. There is no way I am going to be able to get my probe into that basket.* The basket swung wildly about, vibrating side to side, hissing in the airstream, daring me to venture toward it. I looked down to my moving map. We were on top of the spine—the long back of the Hindu Kush where the peaks reached between 17,000 and 20,000 feet. Despite our altitude of 25,000, we were only 5,000 to 8,000 feet above the peaks where the winter winds howled and created turbulence that shot upward.

"Irate 41, Joliet 21 precontact," I said. "The basket is really bouncing out here. I don't think I'm going to be able to get in."

"Joliet 21, roger. Stand by. We should be entering some better weather in a few minutes." I held my position behind the tanker and watched the basket dance. It was taunting me—daring me to come into its range so it could strike.

A few weeks earlier, Toby had hit a dead hose when refueling with Dano. Neither Toby nor the KC-10 tanker crew knew the hose was bad. But when Toby hit the basket, a sine wave traveled up the hose to the tanker and then back down. The force of the wave sheared the hose from the basket, leaving it dangling precariously on Toby's refueling probe. Fuel spewed into Toby's canopy as he calmly declared an emergency and backed his Harrier away from the tanker. Toby and Dano recovered back at Bagram. After landing, the Marines easily pulled the basket free from the Harrier's refueling probe. Toby's smooth air work and calm demeanor saved a jet and prevented any further damage.

The menacing hose showed no fear. It threatened to strike anyone who came near it. Quietly and subtly its temper smoothed. We had crossed the spine. We were now north of the Hindu Kush. The KC-10 began a turn back to the south to maintain its position in the Mercury track. I figured I had a couple of minutes—maybe less. I drove forward at a closure rate of 3 knots, aiming at what I thought to be the middle of the basket's movements. I stared at the tanker's tail and not the basket that bobbed and weaved in sporadic, unpredictable swings.

As I neared the giant empennage, I glanced to my left at the last second. Smack. I felt the hit reverberate through the jet. I was in. I began taking my gas. It couldn't come fast enough. Within a few minutes, the turbulence returned. The KC-10 began bouncing. Its huge wings fluttered, bending in abnormal ways. The refueling hose shook violently as I struggled to maintain my formation. As I bumped upward, the KC-10 bounced down—its large tail filled the space above me. I ducked my head, anticipating the collision, and pulled the throttle to idle. The Harrier slid aft and the basket popped free. The black hose swung madly in the airstream, hissing and spitting residual fuel at me as I backed away.

"Damn, XO, that was ugly," Toby announced over the back radio.

"Yeah, Toby." I caught my breath before continuing. Unconsciously we had dropped the formalities of our ATO call signs. "This is going to be dicey tonight. If we can't clear this weather, we're going home."

"Roger. I'll give it at least one shot if the basket calms down," Toby said. Toby was aggressive and I liked it. I didn't want a fish as my wingman. I wanted someone who measured the risks and knew his limits, testing them every now and then. Toby was a good pilot. I trusted his judgment. We had guys on the ground who needed us. We didn't get paid to sit on the bench and cheerlead.

"Irate 41, Joliet 21 is going to reposition to the port reform position and let Joliet 22 top off."

I slid over to the KC-10's left wing and let Toby move into the refueling position. The tanker's long wings bowed in unexpected ways, metal bending, fluttering, like a diving board in the turbulence that tossed us. The basket swung up and down in large throws. Eventually it settled to moves of only ten feet. Toby's jet moved forward slowly, the basket threatening to punish the intruder. Then they connected. *Whew, maybe we'll get out of here with our fill of gas after all.* After Toby topped off, I switched positions with him and again took another stab at the basket. Somehow I managed to connect on my first attempt. Luck—I didn't complain. After topping off, I backed out and discussed with Toby the plan for filling the rest of the assigned ATO period. We agreed. It wasn't worth trying to tank again.

We called Warlord and advised them of the weather conditions both at altitude and on the deck in the valley. We recommended that we not tank again but conserve our fuel as best we could. Warlord relayed our information and recommendation to K-mart in Qatar, who approved it. Ninety minutes later, we checked out with Striker and recovered back at Bagram. Shooting individual precision approaches in a snowstorm, Toby and I both broke out around 500 feet. Landing on the slick runway, we discovered the braking difficult. I was glad to be back on deck. I could feel the age in my body, and knew that I had added lines to my weathered face.

The next day Toby and I heard the news. A Danish F-16 had crashed on Bagram's runway a few hours after we had landed. The section of F-16s had diverted to Bagram when the weather back at their home base in Kyrgyzstan dropped below minimums. The first F-16 landed uneventfully on Bagram's slick runway, but the pilot of the second F-16 was unable to stop his jet. Realizing he was going off the runway, the Danish pilot ejected. The airplane plowed directly ahead into a minefield, while the pilot floated down in his parachute. Amazingly, neither the pilot nor the airplane set off any mines. Bagram was a dangerous place. It was only a matter of time before a mishap occurred.

17

THE WIDOW-MAKER

By mid-December, the surrounding mountains were colored white, though it had yet to snow in the Bagram valley. Winter was coming. Under the cold gray skies, the Marines stood at attention. Charismatic Sergeant Walcott of MWSS stood in front, holding an 1850s British rifle instead of his Marine-issued M-16. He had purchased the weapon in Kabul on a milk run. Even the officers relished the irony. The color guard marched forward, the Marine Hymn played, and Private First Class Atmore removed the sheet that covered the sign. Joe's work stood before us all: CAMP TEUFEL-HUNDEN. Text below summed it up: "Devil Dogs. They symbolize the ethos of the Warrior culture of the U.S. Marines." Below the camp's name were the names of the Marines who had fallen on the Afghanistan battlefield. We didn't know them, but they were our brothers nonetheless. Grouper gave a short speech about naming the camp and then dismissed the Marines.

The Marine camp had improved greatly since our arrival, but it was the heaters we appreciated most. Base contracting finished installing the last of them shortly after the Marine camp dedication a week before the temperatures plunged to single digits. Then it became bitter cold. Due to the heaters' constant operation, they broke frequently. Several days passed before a contractor came to fix a broken heater. Meanwhile our hooch became an icebox.

Layered in thermal underwear, sweats, wool socks, polypropylene sock liners, wool gloves, and a knit watch cap pulled tight over my head, I climbed into my down sleeping bag. After a few minutes, I quit shivering. It was cold outside, but I had it good and knew it. The Marines were outside prepping the jets on the flight line: fueling them, loading them with bombs, performing the daily and turnaround inspections. And when it began to rain, the freezing drizzle soaked the Marines in hypothermic conditions.

But it wasn't just the Marines working on the airplanes who suffered. There was the soldier walking point—the grunt patrolling in the cold, in the rain, in the mud, with that huge pack on his back, climbing up steep ravines, working on little sleep, trying to help the locals, and hunting bad guys. When I felt sorry for myself, I thought about him, the "grunt": the anonymous icon of our foreign policy, carrying on his back a burden larger than his heavily outfitted pack.

"Hey, Zak. Grouper wants to see you."

I looked up through the tiny hole in my sleeping bag and saw AJ standing over me. *Damn, I just got settled.* I shed my warm cocoon and pulled on my flight boots, opting to keep my heavy sleepwear instead of changing into a flight suit. I grabbed my pistol, swung it over my shoulder, and headed out into the cold for the short walk to Grouper's tent.

"Sir, you wanted to see me," I said after knocking on the door.

"Yeah, come in, Zak. And shut the door. It's cold out there. Take a seat." Grouper was always cordial and friendly with me, even when he was mad, which he didn't appear to be. "Zak, the *L.A. Times* released a story today. It's going to be a four-part series about the Harrier. It's going to raise a lot of questions and, well, the wives might get the wrong idea. Some of the troops might as well."

I nodded and waited. Grouper turned back to his computer as if to read something. "Yes, sir. Is there anything you want me to do?" I asked.

"Not yet. Let's see how it plays out," Grouper said. "There is one more thing. There's an EEO issue that's come up. I swear they just don't make Marines like they used to. Anyway, one of the Marines in maintenance, the little Puerto Rican kid, can't remember his name, well, he got his feathers ruffled when I cursed about the jet not being ready. You know the damn thing was signed off, ready to go, and sure enough when I'm doing my preflight, I can tell the struts hadn't been properly checked. You know how I know? Well, there's grease on the back of the bolt. They haven't checked the strut if there's grease on that connecting bolt."

I nodded.

Grouper resumed. "Well, anyway, someone's trying to make a big fuss out of it now. Rat is the equal opportunity officer, so he's reviewing the complaint. I want you to make sure Rat is following the regs. I'm reviewing them here and am not so sure that Rat is going through the proper steps. Keep it low-key. Just look at the way he's doing things and make sure he's following the proper procedures."

"OK, sir. Can do. Anything else?"

"You know this shit didn't happen when I was a captain. Times have changed, Zak. You know what I miss?" Grouper looked at me and waited for an answer.

"Sir, your family?" I said shyly, unsure of myself. After I opened my mouth, I wished I hadn't.

"Yeah, Zak. I miss the family and my dog. I really miss Snickers. What a great dog. That dog is so loyal. It's always there for you. Always."

"Yes, sir. Snickers is a great dog. I miss Zeus as well." I thought about the black mastiff Katie had picked up from the pound a few months before my departure. "I haven't talked to Katie in a while, but of course I miss her and Caleb. It's tough around Christmas, isn't it?"

"Yeah, Zak. I know Snickers would just be curled up at my feet right now. Just a loyal dog that doesn't ask anything of you. It's just always there for you. Always."

"Yes, sir. Anything else?" I wasn't sure if the repeated references to the dog and loyalty were intended for me or were merely coincidence. I tried not to read anything into it.

"No, Zak. That's it. Fill me in when you can on the EEO issue."

"Yes, sir." I stood up, excused myself, and headed to the S-1 shop, where I asked Gunny Grivas to pull out the instructions for an EEO complaint. While I waited for the gunny to find the instructions, I searched the Internet for articles on the Harrier. It came up immediately. "Part 1: The Widow-Maker."

I read the article and found it informative. But I knew questions would be asked. The article seemed to fan the flames of the Harrier's less-than-impressive safety record as it stated, "Over the last three decades, it [the Harrier] has amassed the highest rate of major accidents of any air force, navy, army or Marine plane now in service. Forty-five Marines have died in 143 non-combat accidents since the Corps bought the so-called jump jet from the British in 1971. More than a third of the fleet has been lost to accidents."*

I called Katie and told her about the articles. She told me she didn't want to read them. I understood. I told her to be careful of reporters, since they

* Alan C. Miller and Kevin Sack, "Far from Battlefield, Marines Lose One-Third of Harrier Fleet. Part 1: The Widow-Maker," *Los Angeles Times*, December 15, 2002.

might call. She said she would. As I read the stories in the coming days, I found them interesting (the series went on to win the Pulitzer Prize). But it was the third article that got me. The obituaries. They were friends and mentors and they were gone. The articles brought forward forgotten faces and long-lost conversations—smiles, laughs, and practical jokes. But the faces were blurry now. At one time I could remember all of them. Then when I forgot some of the faces, I consoled myself that at least I remembered their names. There were too many of them now. Sometimes I forgot those, too.

A few days later, I received e-mails from staff officers in the Pentagon who were working Harrier issues. They were upset and felt the *Times* had double-crossed them on the story. One senior officer told me I needed to write a rebuttal. The e-mail scorched me, but I wrote an article anyway.

After reading the entire four-part *Times* series, I understood why the Marine Corps was mad. The series stated facts that embarrassed the Marine Corps. Most of the Harrier mafia attributed the bad press to the legacy of the first Harrier—the AV-8A. But the mishap rate for the current Harrier, the AV-8B, wasn't impressive, either.* Several days after the se-

---

*During my flying career, from 1990 to 2006, the AV-8B's mishap rate was 10.4 while that of the Corps' other fighter, the F/A-18 Hornet, was 2.88. Harrier pilots were three and a half times more likely to die or crash their airplane than were those flying the Hornet.

ries ran, the Harrier program office issued a "red stripe," grounding the entire AV-8B fleet due to a possible maintenance glitch. We inspected our Harriers according to the red stripe and determined our motors were OK. We resumed flight operations the following day. Nevertheless, the irony of the *Times* articles and the timing of the red stripe didn't escape me. Like much of the Harrier's history, it got the attention of the senior leadership only after enough jets crashed or the press ran a hard-hitting story.

18

DILEMMAS

There had been the announcement and request for silence at the morning meeting and later on the base's loudspeakers. The soldiers, contractors, everyone on Bagram stopped what they were doing and waited. They paused in respect, standing at attention. I stood alone on the tarmac behind the last Harrier, hidden. I didn't want company. My body snapped to attention, the leather of my boots making a dull thud when they hit. I pressed my arms tight against my sides, seeking what a drill instructor had instilled in me long ago— perfect alignment of my feet, body, arms, head— Marine Corps discipline, pride. Though no one saw me, I wondered if God did.

The cold wind dipping off the Hindu Kush stung my cheeks. Anger replaced sadness. I couldn't see the casket, but I knew it was there, being loaded aboard the C-17 in front of me. There was no sound except for the rippling of flags. My body remained rigid but my eyes glanced to my right, toward the flags. They pointed south, with the wind, rippling, beat straight like sheets on a clothesline in a coming storm. The C-17 taxied to the south end of the base, turned onto the runway, and took off to the north. Sergeant Steve Checo was going home. Once the C-17 was gone, I turned and walked back to the hangar. The sound of vehicles and people moving came alive again.

It had happened the previous night, during dawn patrol. Toby and I were airborne over Shkin with a half-dozen other aircraft—A-10s, Predator UAVs, AH-64s—all of us crowded into the same piece of sky, stacked on top of each other. All of us looking for the same thing: seven to nine insurgents evading, hiding in the wadis and bushes, moving east to sanctuary, to Pakistan. There had been the ambush, then the firefight. The medic bird had landed and the soldier had been evac'd. Now the killers hunted. We hunted. But after four hours of searching, we returned home empty-handed. The following day we learned the news. The soldier had died.

My ire grew slowly. With all the technology, all the money, all the power of the American military we put over that little piece of ground, we still couldn't find the enemy that had fucked us. We had failed. I took it personally and began to question our approach. Airpower and technology had its limits in a counterinsurgency fight. We needed more Special Forces or their equivalent on the ground, not just more airplanes.

I walked back to the hangar and found Rat in the

avionics ship. Warrant Officer Mark Ratledge was our avionics officer. He also was the equal opportunity officer. He knew I was coming. Seeing me, he got up and followed me to the green LSS vehicle. We got in and shut the doors. I handed over the files he had given me that morning.

"Well, Rat. I think it's pretty clear-cut," I said.

"Yes, sir. It seems that way." Rat nodded slightly as he spoke.

"What do you want to do?" I asked.

"Well, I'm being told by MAG-13 to close this thing up. They're telling me to note it in a file and close the investigation. I can't do that. The Marine Corps order doesn't give me that authorization. Because the allegations are against the CO, it has to be reviewed by a senior officer outside the command," Rat said.

The charges that Grouper was racist were ridiculous, but the Marines were angry. The pot had been brewing for a while. One Marine had come forward and now others were following. There were several complaints and written statements. They were accusing Grouper of things he wasn't, but they saw an opportunity for revenge and went for it. "Yeah, Rat. I know. Who is giving you the runaround back at MAG-13?" I asked.

"The female master sergeant who runs the EEO program back there. But I think she's getting her direction from someone higher," Rat stated.

"OK, Rat. I'll talk to Grouper. This might get

ugly. I'll tell him that he has to report this up the chain of command according to the Marine Corps order. Only his superior can close the investigation." I looked at Rat, who nodded back. I said, "You know the CO may be a lot of things, but the one thing he isn't is racist. He just said some things he shouldn't have."

"Yes, sir, he did."

"Thanks. I'll let you know what the CO says," I added. Rat and I got out of the truck and headed in separate directions, he back to his shop and I to my computer in the S-1.

It took an hour to compose the e-mail correctly, finding the right tone and citing the Marine Corps order appropriately. Content that I had covered the bases, I hit SEND. I would give the CO several hours to mull it over. Then I would talk to him.

I opened up a new Word document on my computer and began:

Dear Mr. and Mrs. Walcott,

I have the distinct pleasure of working with a friend of yours, Private First Class Jeriel Atmore. He is a fine Marine. The other day he told me the story of how you lost your son, Courtney Walcott, on 9/11 . . .

That was the easy part. Now what was I going to say?

*   *   *

I opened the box from my parents with a mix of excitement and trepidation. I removed the small Christmas tree and placed it on my shelf. There was a comforter, flannel sheets, a bag of lollipops, and candy canes. I put the lollipops in my flight suit, filling my left and right ankle pockets first and then my chest pockets. There were a dozen matchbox cars and several PEZ dispensers. I continued stuffing my flight suit pockets with the tiny Christmas gifts. I pulled out a large can of cookies and then saw the stockings. There was one for each pilot, their call signs stenciled in glitter. I was screwed. I took the tiny Christmas stockings out and placed them on the appropriate rack. Dano was sitting in his. "It's from my mom," I said, holding out the tiny red stocking with the name Dano stenciled in gold glitter. My look told him not to say anything.

AJ walked in, looked at his rack, and saw the tiny stocking lying on it. "What the fuck is this shit? Someone get a little light in the loafers around here?" AJ looked at Dano, who was holding his stocking, and me standing next to him, my face red. "Zak, the CO wants to see you," AJ added. I walked out, not saying anything.

Grouper told me to come in and take a seat. He sat back in his chair and crossed one leg over the other. He then rocked back and forth, looking at his wall. He pushed his silver hair back with his hands and with the palm of his right hand he pulled it down across his forehead, eyes, and mustache in one long, slow movement. I sensed danger.

"Zak, I asked you to check to see if Rat was following the regulations for an investigation on an EO incident. I didn't ask you to do Rat's job. It's not your place as XO to tell me what I need to report. That responsibility rests with the EO officer, Warrant Officer Ratledge." Grouper stopped and looked at me. His brow furrowed, his eyes narrowed.

Inside, I snapped. I had turned away too many times and there was no place left to store my rage. My lips pursed tight as my hands tightened into fists. I tried to hide them under my legs. The ire surfaced and burst forth. "Sir, you asked me to see if Rat was following the regs. That's what you asked me to do. And you know what, sir? That's what I did. But you didn't ask me what I did or the problems Rat might be facing. You didn't because you don't listen to anyone. You don't listen to anyone—"

Grouper cut me off.

"Zak, I asked you to ensure Rat was following the regs. I don't need two EO officers. You know I should have followed the MAG CO's advice and fired some people. This is combat. People around here seem to have forgotten that. I have reports of Marines acting inappropriately, some of them officers." Grouper stopped. He drew back his head with an air of confidence.

"Who, sir? Who is acting inappropriately?" I asked.

"Well, Zak, your name came up," Grouper snapped.

"What did I do, sir? How have I acted improperly?"

"I don't have the specifics of that. But apparently there have been rumors of removing me or hoping that I get relieved of command." Grouper continued for another five minutes, philosophizing about leadership and loyalty. When he finished I sat silent. The anger in my eyes spoke clearly.

"Sir, are you done?" I asked.

"Go ahead, Zak."

"OK, sir. I will, but it seems every time I start, you interrupt me."

"When do I interrupt you?"

I stared back, not saying a word. The tension mounted. I was no longer in control. "Like then, sir. Like five seconds ago," I began. "You might ask people's opinion but you don't let them finish. There are people here trying to help you. People who care about you. If you forgive me, sir, when I was a boy my dad told me a story about a little bird that flew too high and got ice on his wings."

I realized I was over the edge but saw no way out. My emotion carried me forward, unwillingly. I watched my career pass before me as my words spewed forth. "Because of the ice, the bird couldn't fly and fell to the ground. He lay dying in a pasture. A cow come along and shit on the bird. The bird was so happy because the shit melted all the ice and he could live. He was so happy he began chirping. He was singing about the joys of life and along comes a coyote and snatches the bird out of the shit and eats it." I could hear my father's words roll from my lips as my conscience told me to stop, but I couldn't. "My dad told me that just because someone shits on you, it doesn't mean they're your enemy, and just because someone pulls you out of shit, it doesn't mean they're your friend. And above all else, keep your mouth shut. Well, sir, that's something I haven't done today." I had gone off the deep end. My insubordination was grounds for firing. I had sealed the deal. Grouper just looked at me, perhaps dumbfounded at my outburst.

"OK, Zak. Thanks. I appreciate you stopping by." Grouper turned back to his computer. Unaware of anything other than my ire, I got up and left. I went the only place I knew I might find perspective, the hospital. As I stormed out of the camp, the toys and candy in my bottom flight suit pockets felt odd and heavy, like weights tied to my feet.

19

SNOW

I didn't see Grouper for a few days and he no longer asked for me. When we saw each other, we talked cordially and quickly, each moving on to take care of his own business. I expected to be going home now, but I carried on as if nothing had happened. I asked AJ if I should ask for a reassignment. He snickered as he always did, then said, "And what? Leave me here, alone? Fuck you. You're a pussy if you quit."

It was the morning of Christmas Eve. The pilots had decorated our hooch with Christmas lights while the Marines had tinseled the camp and hangar with various oddities sent from well-wishers far away. A Christmas tree erected in the middle of the hangar stood below a large inflatable snowman perched on top of the ordnance locker. Frosty looked over everyone. Grouper had arranged for a holiday celebration and the Marines prepared well. Then it snowed. Big, wet snowflakes dropped from the heavens. Perhaps it was the magic of the season.

The rough, macho personality of the Marines melted as the snow fell. Marines far from home in a combat zone seemed to find their childhood innocence. They stood outside with their hands outstretched, heads tilted back, mouths open, catching snowflakes on their tongues. A few built snowmen while others made snow angels. And the Marines, being who they are—fighters—had the inevitable snowball fights where errant snowballs purposefully hit several innocent passersby, especially officers.

Lieutenant Joe Primeaux opened the door and invited me in. "How are you, sir?" he asked.

I sat down on the cot and unzipped my coat. "Good, Joe. I'm good. Not really. Really I'm shitty, but how about the snow?"

"Missing the family, are you?" Joe asked.

"Yeah, but that's not really it." I didn't want to think about home. I was blocking it. Other thoughts consumed me. My thoughts churned on the boy who had lost both an arm and a leg. His family no longer wanted him. He was a liability. The father had told the nurse that the hospital could keep the boy. The father stopped visiting.

"Joe, do you believe in God?" I asked in all sincerity. I had read the book on character Joe had given me. We had talked about it and many other things over the last two weeks. And we had talked about God. Maybe if I had been in a foxhole under an artillery barrage the doubt wouldn't have been there, but the doubt was there and I couldn't escape it. I wanted

God. I wanted good. *But if God was all-powerful and all good . . .*

"Doing some heavy thinking, are you?" Joe looked at me. I felt empty. I couldn't say anything.

"Well, sir, I have my doubts, too," Joe said, sitting down and kicking off his shoes. "It's a damn thing, war. Dying children and all. Just doesn't make much sense. I get pretty mad at God sometimes. When I get mad, I try to think about Job. Now, there is a guy who got a raw deal."

Joe talked and I listened. He lifted the burden from me like a priest at confession, though I said nothing. He did the work. His wisdom and honesty comforted me. He worked the stones off my back and then aligned my internal compass back to true north. After a few hours, I walked home in the snows of Christmas Eve thinking about God. The snow crunched under my feet.

On Christmas morning, AJ and I went for a run. We shared our thoughts about how things were going. After reaching the north end of the base, we stopped and watched a CH-47 pluck the F-16 from the minefield at the end of the runway. The Chinook's blades bent upward sharply due to the weight of the F-16. The recovery operation had taken a week, most of it clearing the mines that surrounded the broken fighter, including one just inches from the right main tire. In the foreground, several broken MiGs lay discarded. I was glad the F-16 wasn't going to join them.

As AJ and I turned the northern corner, we saw

the C-130 resting midway on the runway, pointed crooked. It had crashed the night before, running off the runway on landing. Half the airplane was in the minefield, half on the runway. Bagram was claiming its victims quickly.

AJ and I went back to the hooch and took part in a white-elephant gift exchange organized by Toby. Needing to vent, I relayed my visit with the Afghan children at the hospital to Jolly and Dano. I felt guilty in the hospital. Guilty of being born in a prosperous country with a chance—an opportunity to live, not just exist. I described to Jolly and Dano the patients I had come to know. I explained how I handed out the gifts sent to me by my mom and Katie. One child, a ten-year-old boy who had had a tracheotomy, chose the PEZ dispenser from my hand. Jolly interrupted my story in mid-sentence.

"You what?" Jolly asked. "You mean you gave a ten-year-old boy with a tracheotomy a PEZ dispenser? Sir, you're kidding me. You mean you actually gave the poor kid, lying in his hospital bed with a bandage covering the hole in his neck, a PEZ dispenser? A PEZ dispenser, the kind where you push the head back and out of the neck pops a piece of pink candy. XO, you're sick!"

While Jolly raked me, Dano rolled over and howled. I laughed, too. I needed it. As I lay in bed and updated my journal, I contemplated the day's events and our mission in Afghanistan. Christmas 2002 was coming to a close. Twenty-three years earlier, Christmas in Afghanistan marked the beginning of something else—the invasion by the Soviets. The Soviets withdrew ten years later. Their foreign policy failure left a million Afghans dead and another 5 million as refugees. The Russian military also left 10 million land mines that continued to take the lives and limbs of innocent children. Perhaps in retrospect, the Soviets should have heeded the words of KGB chairman Yuri Andropov, who told his colleagues in March 1979, "Comrades, I have thought this issue over very thoroughly since yesterday and have concluded that we should consider very, very seriously whether it would make sense to send troops into Afghanistan. The economy is backward, the Islamic religion predominates, and nearly all of the rural population is illiterate. I do not think we can uphold the revolution in Afghanistan with the help of our bayonets."*

Soviet president Leonid Brezhnev and his colleagues later ignored the KGB chairman's prescient advice. I recalled Mark Twain's satirical assessment of man: "It is not worth while to try to keep history from repeating itself, for man's character will always make the preventing of the repetitions impossible." *Would the United States fall into the same trap in Afghanistan that so many others had?* I closed my journal not knowing the answer to that question. As I set

* Diego Cordovez and Selig S. Harrison, *Out of Afghanistan: The Inside Story of the Soviet Withdrawal* (New York: Oxford University Press, 1995), p. 36.

my journal down, my rack began wobbling. Everything was shaking. Across the room, another headlamp flickered on. It was Jolly.

"Earthquake?" I asked.

"Yeah. Earthquake," he responded. Lying back down, he flicked off his light. No one else stirred. The earthquake stopped as quickly as it came, over in fifteen seconds. Across the room, a small mirror above Dano's rack swayed back and forth, the light from my headlamp reflecting off it. I turned off my light and for the first time in a long time, I prayed.

The following day the *Washington Post* ran a story that asserted that the military had abused prisoners held at a detention facility in Bagram.* The U.S. military denied the accusations. Major Stephen Clutter, deputy spokesman at Bagram, stated that "there is absolutely no evidence to suggest that persons under control of the U.S. army have been mistreated."† The denials proved false. In 2005, the army disclosed that two prisoners had died in Bagram in early December 2002, after mistreatment and torture at the hands of their captors—American soldiers.

---

* Dana Priest and Barton Gellman, "U.S. Decries Abuse but Defends Interrogations," *Washington Post,* December 26, 2002.
† David Brunnstrom, "Army Denies Mistreatment of Prisoners in Afghanistan," Reuters, December 29, 2002.

20

PLAYING WITH FIRE

Grouper had grabbed me on my way back from the shower. He told me Major General James Amos was arriving soon. He expected to be relieved. He said I couldn't lead the unit. He was right, but it was something else that ate at me. I dismissed thoughts of work and pulled the gift out. I was alone in the dark—or almost alone. One could never really be alone in Bagram. There were too many people in too small a space. I worshipped any solitude. I had sought this moment since I had first opened the gift on Christmas. I didn't want to spoil it, so I waited until the time was right. I took up my journal and pen.

Sunday, 12-29-2002: 0620 Zulu—1050 local. I sit in my broken, faded fabric chair inside our darkened tent. The light burns bright outside. It seeps beneath the crack of the door. I close my eyes and smell the dust. I am alone except for two pilots sleeping. My headlamp lights the empty pages of my journal. My pen begins.

This morning we flew dawn patrol. We took off in the dark and landed shortly after sunrise. It was a beautiful, clear, cold Afghanistan night—black—an abyss except for a tiny sliver of moon and thousands of twinkling stars. God has the prettiest Christmas lights I know of. I'm glad he shares them with us the whole year and not just on Christmas.

The constellation Orion now rises in the east after sunset. Each night I welcome my friend. He and I are kin. I know it. Orion's brightest stars, Betelgeuse and Rigel, show brilliantly in the clear mountain air, unhindered by the light pollution back home. They are big, beautiful stars. Each would occupy half of our solar system. They are also distant. Betelgeuse, 500 light-years—Rigel, 900 light-years. Betelgeuse radiates a reddish-orange glow. It is dying. Its internal fuel almost depleted, Betelgeuse is in the twilight of its life. Yet, on the other side of the constellation, Rigel burns a brilliant whitish-blue. It is young, hot, exuberant, and jovial. I hear its yell. "Look at me. Watch me dance in the sky. See my twinkling blue light to those distant."

The stars, older than I can coherently conceive, are mortal as well. Time overlooks no one. Time. Time that intangible phenomenon, which allows measure and order in our universe. An unwelcome companion that reminds us, all beginnings have ends. We can't see it, hold it, hear it, feel it, smell it or taste it, but it exists. We can see its effects—feel its effects—and through them, we try to understand it.

I pick up the Christmas gift. It is a small book titled "The Joy of Fatherhood." Inside Katie has written my youngest son's name—Caleb—a gift to me from him on his first Christmas. I move through the pages looking for two specific photographs that captured my attention a few days before. I had briefly viewed the gift on Christmas. But due to the bravado that then surrounded me, I decided I could better appreciate the gift at a later time, alone. That time is now.

I find the first of two photographs I wish to ponder. Next to the first photograph is written "Sharing a Magic Moment." The photograph is of a newborn baby with his tiny hand wrapped around his daddy's finger. The baby is asleep, comforted by his father's touch. My breath draws short as tears build. Soon they run freely. I decide not to stop them. I think about the magical moment when my wife gave birth to the tiny baby.

His little body emerged from his mother so precious and fragile. The doctor held the baby while I sobbed in joy and cut the umbilical cord, forever severing his physical existence on another. "No turning back now, little guy," I said to him. His lungs bellowed out against the shock of this new and strange environment, and yet those same cries forced his lungs to accept the fluid of oxygen that fuels our lives. His one eye wide open, the other tightly sealed, perhaps reflecting his own trepidation on the path before him. The nurse carrying the tiny baby over to a table, his hand outstretched as if reaching for something. I offer my finger. He grabs it and wraps his tiny fingers around my single index finger. Tears of happiness flow freely from my eyes and my breath shudders in broken gasps both then and now as I cajole the past. He holds my finger. I don't want to pull away. I don't want anything to happen to this miracle that holds me. I only want to comfort and reassure him, all is okay. I cheat myself for a moment and believe that I can and will protect him from all.

I turn the pages of the book to the second picture I want to contemplate. It is toward the end of the book, second to last. Perhaps the author out of kindness didn't make it the last picture on purpose; the symbolism being too great. A middle-aged man walks with an elder man, his father. We stand behind them—unnoticed—watching their interaction. Their backs toward us, the middle-aged man's arm lies across his father's shoulder and back. The old man walks slowly with a small gait. The younger man is taller and has a spring in his step. Ahead of both men, a young boy leads the trio down a winding dirt road. The boy is walking playfully. His left arm extended, out and up, as if to maintain balance on some imaginary high wire. His right arm pushes a stick forward against the ground. Next to the photograph of the three males is the caption "Sharing the Love." The old man is telling his son something as the grandchild walks carefree in front of them. Perhaps the old man is reflecting on a similar time of his youth. The picture's yellow-orange color gives it a sense of age and contrasts sharply with the other photograph—the soft blue and green hues of the newborn clutching his father's finger.

Both pictures captivate me in their simplicity. They pull forth emotions that due to the current circumstances remain sheltered yet preserved. I decide it is healthy for me, in a quiet place and time, to reflect on those things I hold most important, but it is also dangerous. I play with fire.

It is my choice what I choose to remember and reflect upon. Memories remain immortal. I think I could live with that. Happiness and sadness without good or evil. The happiness and joy of a new star traded for the sadness and passing of another. I resolve I would only accept that universe if I knew the younger star was guaranteed the experiences of a full life. But time guarantees nothing. The conflicts of work compete for these precious seconds and sometimes they win. But today the visions of my family, stirred by the photographs, are vivid and crisp. I am alive. As the lactic acid pools in my calves from my morning run, I think to myself, Nothing is more important than love.

I set down my pen and journal, closed my eyes, and smiled.

21

"NO ANGRY REMARKS"

The pilots crowded around the small monitor, the video playback machine for the 8 mm tapes. The pilots' exclamations—the laughter, teasing, pumping of fists into arms—told the story. "Holy fucking shit. Look at that." As soon as one spoke, another interrupted. "Aw shit, dude. It's fucking vaporized. Dude, did you see the dog?" "Dog? That's not a fucking dog. It's a goat." "Bro, it's gone, that's what it is and so are those fucking assholes."

I waited until the hysteria subsided and then watched the video alone. The mud building and walls are there one second, gone the next. Shkin again. Only this time the target was Pakistani border guards. It had been coming. Too often we had chased the enemy to the border, where the guns of the Pakistanis pointed toward our soldiers, as if saying, "No farther." The intelligence suspected that in some instances the Pakistanis were collaborating—even aiding the enemy. Then it happened. A Pakistani border guard had fired on the Americans, hitting one U.S. soldier in the head. The Pakistani border guard fled to an abandoned madrassa, where he and others renewed their attack on the Americans. The Harriers were called in.

The JTAC requested that the Harriers strafe the madrassa. But the guns jammed, something they were prone to do if not exercised regularly on an air-to-ground range. The JTAC then asked the Harriers to fire a rocket, but the rocket went stupid. Exasperated and still receiving fire from the madrassa, the JTAC requested a five-hundred-pound LGB. The bomb eliminated the building, the Pakistanis inside, and at least one animal, probably a goat.

The next day the ruckus began. Pakistan accused the United States of dropping a bomb on its side of the border. There was talk of a formal investigation, which, to the relief of Dano and others, died quickly. The commanding general of the 82nd Airborne called and thanked Captain Dano Carlson for his work, but the rhetoric between the United States and Pakistan only grew more heated over the coming days. U.S. military spokesman Major Stephen Clutter stated, "We are not going to tiptoe and stop right when we get to the border, we do reserve the right to pursue them, and Pakistan is aware of that. There's no change there."*

The Pakistanis denied any agreement existed and

* Chris Kraul, "American Forces Claim Right to Enter Pakistan," *Los Angeles Times*, January 4, 2003.

tensions increased. Only Pakistani President General Pervez Musharraf and U.S. Secretary of State Colin Powell were able to cool things down. A Pakistani newspaper later cited an unidentified U.S. diplomat regarding the agreement: "This means that if a situation requires a hot pursuit, it will be done, but there will be no angry remarks from either side, as we saw after the Dec 29 incident."*

Funny, I thought. *Bombs, guns, death, but no angry remarks.*

As we passed into 2003, the luster wore off. It showed in the Marines and pilots. The missions— orbiting for hours, waiting, bored—were still there. The camp looked the same and the winter weather continued to harass us with low overcasts, rain, and snow. We began to look and act like the weather— gray, cold, depressed. Maybe Christmas away from home had sucked it out of us. We wanted to know we were making a difference, but the emotional high from an occasional bomb drop was fleeting. Jolly explained it well. "We came suited up in all of our football gear, but then ended up on the soccer field being outsprinted and outplayed by a more agile force. I don't even think we even understood the rules."

We heard news through our wives and friends

---

* Amine Tarzi, "A Weekly Review of News and Analyses of Events and Trends in Afghanistan," *Radio Free Europe/ Radio Liberty Afghanistan Report,* Volume 2, Number 2, January 9, 2003; "Hot Pursuit to Continue Quietly," *Dawn,* January 6, 2003.

that the remaining Harrier fleet was gearing up for war. But they weren't coming to Afghanistan. They were heading to Iraq. By mid-January, the tankers disappeared, followed shortly by the AWACS. The loss of these assets compounded our operations. We began flying two-and-a-half-hour missions without aerial refueling. To make up for the lost air cover, we added another section to the flight schedule. Missions became shorter but the frequency increased. The increased optempo aggravated the Harrier's temperamental mechanical status and wore on the pilots. Jets began breaking.

Captain Mike "Yap" Trapp's landing gear failed to extend, a problem I had experienced a month before. After six attempts, the landing gear finally extended, but with only a few minutes of fuel remaining. After touchdown, Yap's aircraft veered sharply to the right. Yap applied reverse thrust and kept the jet on the runway and out of the minefields. Boss, on the other hand, suffered a number-two hydraulic failure. His primary hydraulic system continued to function and Boss returned to Bagram without incident. Even Grouper received unwanted excitement as I stood ODO. I listened to the rising pitch of his voice as he described the blue smoke in his cockpit, the dimming of his lights, the unexplainable maladies, the first signs of impending doom. But Grouper made it home flying off his wingman. It seemed everyone was experiencing their fair share of abnormalities in the jets, most of them at night in nasty winter weather. But it was the monotony of operations that lulled us into complacency. It wasn't even February and yet we felt like we were stuck in a Bill Murray movie, doing the same thing day after day.

Kaboom! The shudder of the explosion shook the wooden frame of our tent, causing me to jump in my rack. *Goddamn it. I hate this shit*, I murmured to myself. This was the fourth attack in two weeks. The first time I had been fooled. Running to the guard shack in my shorts, boots, helmet, and flak jacket, I had burst into the command post, wondering if the wire had been breached. The Marines stared at me. "Sir, it's a drill," Sergeant Rapier said. "Good one, huh?" I turned and walked away in the darkness. I was tired and angry. It wasn't like we didn't have enough stress already. Sleep schedules were tough to maintain, but they were essential to our operations.

This time I knew it wasn't a drill. I listened to the gunfire: muffled caps and pops in the distance, the M240 machine gun's staccato firing off its retort. I didn't want to get up. *What if I just lie here?* That wasn't an option. Everyone had to muster in the camp's two bunkers and wait until "all clear" was given.

As I crowded into the bunker, I sat next to the youngest pilot in our squadron, Captain J. C. Banton. "What's up, JC? I guess we brief in a few hours, don't we?"

"Yes, sir. We're supporting the TF-5 raid." JC then added, "XO, it's a funny thing. When I go to my carpeted tent, lie on my cot, call my family, or e-mail them, I lose the perspective that this place is dangerous."

"Yeah, no shit." I was angry. I closed my eyes and selfishly thought of the sleep I was missing. It was the wear-you-down principle. The enemy launched a few rockets, fired some rounds, and then ran away, leaving us to pursue ghosts in the darkness. It kept us tired and off balance. Thirty minutes later, we walked back to our tents. I checked my watch. I had to brief in two hours.

JC's first name was Chris but he went by JC. Like Toby, JC didn't have a call sign, or at least one that stuck. He had replaced Toby as my dedicated wingman in mid-January. JC was as eager as a five-year-old on Christmas morning, only he was that way all the time. A devout Christian, JC was squeaky clean.

JC and I met in the tower and reviewed the mission data. We were supporting an operation in the Pech and Kunar valleys in northeast Afghanistan. The plan was to make a lot of commotion with jets and helicopters synchronized at a specific time over a specific location, making it appear as if a major assault were taking place. High overhead our electronic intelligence (ELINT) aircraft would orbit, waiting for the enemy to take the bait.

We proceeded to our assigned location over the Pech river valley, twenty miles west of Asadabad. The bright moon highlighted the dark green forests below. Forests blanketed in the freshly fallen snow.

In the middle of the valley a river raged, its rapids easily visible from our sanctuary above. The beauty of Kunar province disguised the nefarious subversion that stalked in the forests below.

At my designated time, I rolled inverted and pulled on the stick. I plummeted 15,000 feet before pulling out and leveling off 500 feet above the valley floor. JC remained overhead as high cover and followed my progress as I raced east in the valley, my wings knifing through the air, splitting the night. Under the glowing moon, I spotted my shadow ripping along the trees and rocks below. I was below the ridgelines to my north and south, moving through the valley at 500 knots, 500 feet above the ground. The green glow of my cockpit gave me an eerie feeling as the adrenaline pumped through me. I tilted my head up and peaked underneath the goggles. I did that every now and then when flying low on the NVGs because it scared the hell out of me. It made me feel alive.

It was a carryover from high school. I had learned the trick from my best friend in his 1970 Chevy Malibu. As we raced down Highway 39 between Roy and Mosquero, he turned off the lights. The Chevy 350 small-block and Holley four-barrel carb roared in the darkness. But we saw nothing. Even the dashboard was dark. There was only blackness and the sound of the supercharged Chevy speeding us forward into a void. Ten seconds later, when we could no longer stand it, he turned the lights back on.

Now some twenty years later I was doing the

same thing. Only this time there wasn't any booze. As I peeked under the NVGs for just a few seconds, I found what I knew was there. Nothing. A void, blackness. Yet the ground was there, big trees and bigger rocks rushing by. Speeding through the valley was an adrenaline high. At night, under the moon on NVGs, it was better. I devoured it with lust.

As I approached the junction of the Korengal valley, my left thumb triggered the flares. Red-hot fireworks popped into the airstream behind me, one after another, lighting up the sky as my Harrier remained hidden—a ghost itself. Only the roar of my motor and the flares I left in its wake gave away my presence. A small orange glow appeared in front and then passed quickly down my left side. Gunfire—but I wasn't sure. It was behind me before I knew it. As the Pech dumped into the Kunar, I pulled back on the stick and stood the Harrier on its tail, launching myself upward into the stars above.

JC picked me up visually and joined. We orbited overhead as the helos moved in and dusted off several landing zones. The A-10s, holding to our south, put out a long string of flares. Soon it was over. Bingo. Everybody headed home wondering if the guys in the ELINT birds had gotten anything.

After I landed, I saw AJ preflighting his jet for the next sortie. He came over after I shut down. "How did it go, Zak?" he asked.

"You know. Same old shit," I replied.

"Guess what?" AJ didn't wait for an answer. "We

got two of them fuckers tonight. Sergeant Wheatley filled me in. We killed one and captured one."

"No shit," I said, nodding in approval.

"No shit. Guess what else, Zak?" AJ's eyes opened wide.

"What?"

"The CO got an e-mail from the CG. They are looking at rotating us to Iraq and backfilling us with another squadron." AJ's eyes burned with fire in the Afghanistan moonlight.

22

GO AND NO-GO PILLS

It was as though a switch had been flipped in the Marines. Rumor spread quickly and the turnaround in morale was immediate. The officers began talking about deploying to two combat zones in one tour. The CO held a formation to quell the rumors. He went over the CG's e-mail and explained the possibility of redeploying to support combat operations elsewhere. We all knew where "elsewhere" was. Grouper closed by saying, "Be ready."

I thumbed through the threat manual, researching the Iraqi surface-to-air missile (SAM) systems we might face. The radio crackled, "Base, Joliet 21 flight is taxiing." I checked the secret chat room that connected us with the CAOC before picking up the handheld mike. "Roger, Joliet. Base copies. No updates. Mission remains as fragged." I set the mike down and returned to the threat manual. Although detailed, the material was two years old. I turned to one of our intel specialists. "Lance Corporal Duran, does CENTCOM have an updated surface-to-air threat analysis on their website for Iraq?"

"I'll check, sir."

"Hey, you guys need to clear out of here. Didn't you get the word?" I looked up and saw the soldier standing in the doorway. He was dressed in full battle gear—helmet, flak jacket, weapon at the ready. His animated face hinted of trouble.

"What word?" I asked.

"We found a UXO outside, right here at the base of the tower. We need to evacuate the building. EOD is on the way." The enlisted Marines stared at each other and then looked to me.

"OK," I began, not sure how to continue. "I got two airplanes taxiing for takeoff. I need to monitor the radios and computers in case something happens." The soldier looked at me dumbfounded but said nothing. I continued, "Well, are you going to blow it in place or remove it?"

"We are going to remove it."

"OK. Everyone else can clear out. I'll stay here and man the radios. Just make sure to let EOD know I'm still here. And let me know when it's clear."

"Yes, sir."

The Marines grabbed their gear and walked out with the heavily armored soldier, closing the door behind them. I put on a flak jacket and helmet and hunkered down in the corner next to the radio. I closed my eyes and listened. I heard voices outside, but then they grew faint. Silence filled the room. I sat and waited. Fifteen minutes passed and the door to the ready room flew open. AJ looked at me, sitting on the floor in the corner.

"Zak, what the fuck are you doing?"

"There was a UXO. Some soldier said that EOD was coming to remove it." I felt stupid trying to explain myself. I stood up, adding, "We have jets airborne."

"Hmm." AJ shook his head. The hazing was coming. "Well, I didn't see any EOD. Looks like ops normal to me. The Hog pilots are in their ready room. Where are the Marines?"

I decided that trying to explain further was pointless. I opted for another tack. "I sent them to chow."

AJ walked over, his face red. "You're not going to believe this, Zak, but we got to turn in our 'go' pills."

"What? What are you talking about?"

"Grouper got an e-mail from the CG directing us to turn in our 'go' pills. It's fucking Tarnak Farms. That's what it is."

"What about the no-go pills?" I asked.

"Just the go pills, Zak. Everyone has to turn them in. Word came from the commanding general. We don't have a choice. It's the fucking asshole F-16 pilots who killed the Canucks last year. One of them is now claiming that the air force issued him uppers, which made him overly aggressive and thus resulted in his, quote, lapse of judgment, unquote." AJ rolled his eyes sarcastically.

Before we deployed, our squadron doctor, navy lieutenant Tim "Doc" Marra, had issued each pilot two prescriptions of uppers and downers: Dexedrine and zolpidem. We used the uppers and downers when we needed them, while Doc kept track of how much each pilot used. In the previous four months, I had taken the uppers five times. The sleeping pills, a little more. We took the Dexedrine when we needed a boost. I had used them on the eight-hour flight when we crossed the Atlantic and on several dawn patrol flights when the sun just didn't rise fast enough.

We had all read the Tarnak Farms report before deploying. The report covered the friendly-fire incident when two Air National Guard pilots flying F-16s had engaged Canadian military personnel who were conducting live-fire training near Kandahar. The F-16 pilots killed four Canadian soldiers and wounded eight others. Every pilot in the squadron had the same opinion after reading the report: the two F-16 pilots were hell-bent on dropping their bombs on something in Afghanistan—anything. Both F-16 pilots were charged with articles 92 (failure to obey an order) and 119 (manslaughter) of the Universal Code of Military Justice. Now they were working their defense.

The incident stood as a stern warning to us all of what could happen in combat if we chose to act recklessly. The incident also robbed us of a tool we used to maintain our operational tempo. I knew for a fact the go pills didn't make me aggressive—they helped keep me awake, and, for that matter, alive.

"AJ, this is bullshit. It's because of Iraq and the gearing up for combat ops. The generals are covering their asses."

"Yeah, Zak. They sure as hell are."

23

THE MOST FAMOUS MILITARY OXYMORON

The winds beat the canvas siding against the plywood frame in a racket that made sleep impossible. I ventured outside to use the porta-pottie but couldn't see fifty feet in front of me due to the blowing dust. Yesterday it had been driving rain, the day before, snow. Periods of brief sunshine came and went. Afghanistan's fickle winter weather played havoc on us. Another day of standing "alert," hoping nothing happens. No one was flying in these winds.

I drove down to the control tower to review the latest intelligence updates. Once there, I read the intel summaries but hunted for news online as well. The two sides told different stories. My confidence was waning, especially concerning military intelligence.

I found a *Time* article that told me more about our current operation than anything I found on our classified website. It was last week that we had begun Operation Mongoose, the largest offensive operation since the overly hyped but ineffective Operation Anaconda in 2002. We were hunting for Taliban operating in southern Afghanistan, southeast of Kandahar near the town of Spin Boldak. Spin Boldak was a known smuggler's stop that held a large contingent of Taliban sympathizers, but instead of military intelligence informing us of the enemy, we found them by a stroke of luck.

On January 27, 2003, while U.S. and Afghan soldiers conducted random checks of personnel entering the country, a motorcycle zipped by with two turbaned men. American soldiers gave pursuit. One of the fleeing men attempted to throw a grenade at the pursuing Americans but fumbled it and blew off his own legs. His accomplice surrendered. During interrogation, the accomplice admitted to being part of a large Taliban force living in the caves of the Adhi Ghar mountains.

Assisted by Special Forces teams, army conventional forces began sweeping the mountains while droves of attack planes of all types appeared overhead. Harriers and Hogs, Falcons, Apache gunships, even the Bones—B-1 bombers flying out of Diego Garcia—came and dropped bombs. After the battle, eighteen enemy were confirmed dead, though a much larger force was suspected. Multiple caches of weapons were uncovered and destroyed. Vast stores of food and supplies were found, including a flock of sheep. As one Afghan soldier said, "They had mutton. They were eating a lot better than we were."*

* Tim McKirk, "What About the Other War?" *Time*, February 2, 2003.

I watched as our intelligence analysts changed the suspected number of enemy on a random, chaotic basis. They were guessing. But what disgusted me was the smugness and arrogance that surrounded the intelligence community when it was overcome with ignorance. Inside the big CJTF-180 compound, maps portrayed suspected enemy positions and numbers. Tiny red ovals on the maps denoted the last of the enemy near Tarin Kowt, Shkin, Asadabad, and Khost. These last vestiges were cited as "hardheaded holdouts" that would eventually see the light or be destroyed. At least, that's how it was conveyed.

Nobody saw, or cared to see, that a large majority of al Qaeda and Taliban had escaped to Pakistan. Only recently had we acknowledged that Osama bin Laden might still be alive. No one saw that large remnants of Taliban had withdrawn high into the Hindu Kush in southern, central, and northern Afghanistan. No one saw them, because they couldn't—because we didn't have the assets on the ground to report what was going on. It didn't matter how many Harriers, A-10s, AWACS, UAVs, and satellites we put overhead. High-flying technology didn't walk the dusty streets, climb the hills, look inside caves, visit villages, shake hands, pass out food rations, and have chai with the local honchos. All that high-tech equipment failed to tell us that the enemy was waiting patiently to strike again on their terms.

Frustrated with the contradictions, I headed to chow. It had been a bad week. Several days earlier,

I had learned about the space shuttle *Columbia* disaster. I had lost another friend—Wicky. Captain Laurel "Wicky" Clark had been VMA-211's flight surgeon in the mid-1990s when she was a lieutenant and I was a captain. We deployed overseas together and she became a close friend. *Rip, Pops, Gator, now Wicky*. We had all served together in VMA-211, the "Wake Island Avengers." They were gone now. As I placed my tray of powdered eggs and burnt toast on the table, I wondered who was next. *Would it be another Avenger or perhaps a Nightmare?*

In the background, I picked up the faint twang of George Strait singing "Amarillo by Morning." I had taught Katie to two-step to the song when we first dated. Without warning, I began crying. I struggled to get ahold of myself, but I couldn't. I was alone but ashamed for my loss of composure. I got up, took my tray to the kitchen, and left.

The crisp, cold air outside snapped me back to reality. My attack-pilot persona had cracked. Emotions were dangerous. I had played with fire after Christmas when I had spent time with the gift. But I had allowed that. This was different. I hadn't authorized this emotional venture.

We all missed home, but dwelling on it was unhealthy. All of us needed to bury feelings for home and our loved ones deep in a box and nail it shut. It was dangerous to allow those feelings out. It was dangerous because we didn't control our destiny. We were stuck in Afghanistan until we were told to go home. I didn't want my wingman thinking about home when the grunts called for air support. And he didn't want me daydreaming, either. By the time I reached camp, my thoughts were once again steeled, like the Afghanistan winter—cold, hard, and relentless.

24

NEWS

CJTF-180 headquarters provided the flag with the request that we fly it on one of our missions. I placed the flag under my ejection seat the following night. The stars were brilliant. Orion was high in the sky. As I scanned the heavens, I thought of my friend and wondered if she was looking down on me. I gave the flag and the certificate to the army colonel, but I included a letter as well. It began: "Dear NASA, I was honored to fly this flag in my Harrier over the Afghanistan battlefields. It was special because I knew Capt. Laurel Clark. She was a friend. . . ."

A few days later, CENTCOM released a message requesting six Harriers in Afghanistan from March 2003 until September 2003. No unit names were given. They didn't need to be. The delusion still existed with some that another Harrier squadron would replace us while we were moved to support the upcoming invasion of Iraq or sent home. It was false hope.

The day before Valentine's Day, we received official word tasking VMA-513 with supporting combat operations in Afghanistan another seven months. Morale plummeted. No one was going home. I called Katie on Valentine's Day and broke the news. I didn't want to tell her, but I knew the gossip back home was spreading like wildfire. As I told her the news, I heard the air sucked out of her small body.

A solid overcast moved in and the rains began. The rains turned to snow. Big, wet snowflakes fell, but the ground was too warm for any of it to stick. Bagram became a mud pit. Then someone found a UXO behind the provost marshal office shack in the Marine Camp. It had been there all along—next to the smoking pit. We evacuated the camp while EOD came and removed the old Soviet mine.

Over the previous month, Grouper and I had found a way to work, though I was surprised he never fired me. He changed, as did I. He asked my opinion on issues and sat quietly while I gave him my feedback. He exercised patience with me as I grew into my job and I quit trying to fight him. I discovered that his read on the issues was often correct. I came to see him as a good man in a difficult position. I wanted him to win. The general had stuck with Grouper and Grouper had stuck with me. For that, I came to trust him.

As we waited for EOD to clear the mine, Grouper walked over and pulled me aside.

"What is it, sir?" I asked.

"Congratulations, Zak. I received the news this morning. Tomorrow the message will be released. You've been selected for lieutenant colonel. AJ also made the cut." Grouper smiled and placed his hand on my shoulder. "You've done well."

As we walked back to camp after EOD cleared the mine, I thought of how my strange journey had begun. I had enlisted in the navy in 1981 as a way to stay out of jail. My first choice, the Marine Corps, had turned me down due to my naïve admittance of my past. To join the navy, I lied. Boot camp cleaned me up. I no longer had access to the things that were destroying me. After boot camp, I discovered the track, gymnasium, and library. I began working out and going to school at night. I applied for a commissioning program and was accepted. While attending Texas A&M on an NROTC scholarship, I changed my option from navy to Marine, my first true love. My grandfather pinned on my lieutenant's bars four years later. I never thought of making the military a career. It just happened. Twenty years had passed since I joined the navy. Where had that time gone?

I wonder what they're doing. Was she feeding him? No, it was too early for that. Was it Saturday and were they going to the beach with the Warlocks? No, today is Friday. No, it's Saturday, isn't it? It must be Friday back home. Cut it out. Get over it. I got to get over it. That's what I got to do. I have to. I just have to. I can't change anything. No sense bellyaching on

*this. Others are in it, too. Heck, Morrell's wife had a
baby in December and he wasn't even there. It was
his first. That's a lot tougher than what you're going
through. You can do it. You have to. Don't you dare
show any weakness. They'll see it. You know they'll
see it. You saw it in others and they'll see it in you.
Got to find the positive. Got to make it positive . . .*

"Hey, Zak, I'm heading to Ops, then chow. You up?
I hear you, so don't tell me you're not up." AJ's voice
rang clear. I wondered if I was murmuring.

"Yeah, I'm up."

"You wanna go chow?" AJ persisted.

"No, I gotta get ready for my flight with Stern.
We got the Fab Five meeting and the AOM as well."
Captain Joe "Stern" Bertagna had arrived a few
weeks earlier, one of two new pilots to help with the
optempo.

"Hey, your bag broke." AJ pointed above my
rack.

"Yeah, I know. Fuck you."

AJ walked out laughing. The wetness had woken
me, but I had stayed in bed anyway. I was too tired to
rise. I just lay there thinking. The storm had come in
the night, maybe at dawn. They were common now.
My temporary fix had failed. New measures were
called for. The rain had pooled until the taped garbage bag could no longer hold. When the bag broke,
the water spilled down the wall, onto my shelf, soaking my books. After pooling there, it dripped down

onto my cot. This had been my second attempt to fix the leak that plagued my new quarters. AJ laughed that his side didn't leak, while mine did. It was luck. Random chance as to who got what side. That's how life worked, or so I told myself. I grabbed some towels and dried up the mess.

AJ and I had moved into the split B-hut to make room for the new pilots a month ago. Grouper lived in the other half of the hooch. A thin wooden wall separated AJ and me from our boss. The new pilots, Captains Bertagna and Stricker, had arrived recently to help. We had requested them a few months earlier. I stepped outside and walked toward the porta-pottie. Behind the outhouse stood the Hindu Kush, highlighted by a deep blue sky.

"Good morning, Hindu Kush. How are you?" I was being positive. The mountains didn't answer. Gusts of wind whipped snows from the peaks, making slow white rollers that fell gently down the east face. The wind blew hard. Although the mountains remained covered in white, the Shomali plains had shed their winter fleece over the previous month. A beautiful green had overtaken the valleys of Afghanistan or at least those through which water flowed. It was the beginning of spring.

Flowers sprang up in Bagram's infield. Thousands of tiny poppies—red, white, pink, and purple flowers—enveloped the abandoned Soviet armament that lay rusting in the Bagram infield. A blanket knitted of ruby reds and bright pinks with a smattering of purple covered the hard brown earth, and the mines.

The previous week I had noted in my journal that March had come in like a lion and was leaving like a lamb, like the seasons I knew as a boy growing up in New Mexico. But I was wrong; there was no lamb—only more lion. As the snows melted, the winds returned and they roared. Despite the rejuvenation of life, the reality of war continued. The spring offensive was on.

The "show" had begun in mid-March. We watched the Secret Internet Protocol Router Network (SIPRNET) traffic and listened to the chat rooms as the attacks on Iraq began. Our friends were flying missions from ships in the Persian Gulf and airfields in Kuwait. They were also dropping bombs—lots of them. We all wished we were there—in the show.

But as the Americans invaded Iraq, things were heating up in Afghanistan. The enemy attacked Khost and Orgun-e. A Pave Hawk helicopter, attempting to evacuate and save the life of a ten-year-old Afghan boy, crashed and killed all six aboard. Harriers were diverted to provide air cover as rescue teams flew to the crash site. The ASOC was pushing for the Harriers to engage unidentified vehicles approaching the crash site with warning shots. Cooler heads prevailed and further tragedy was averted. But as we tried to save lives, Taliban insurgents gave no quarter. They executed a Red Cross worker near Tarin Kowt because he was helping the villagers construct a well.

The execution of the unarmed worker sickened me and hardened my resolve.

A few days later, the Taliban set an ambush near Kandahar that killed two Americans. They followed up with attacks on Shkin, Gardez, Spin Boldak, and International Security Assistance Force (ISAF) headquarters in Kabul. They were even taking shots at us at Bagram. Grouper had reported being fired upon while in the landing pattern, though he was unsure where the fire had come from. As winter thawed, the enemy raised the stakes. A spokesperson at Bagram explained that the recent attacks were the result of a "surge in enemy activity after the U.S. and Britain invaded Iraq earlier this month."*

The Nightmares responded as the grunts called us in to bomb suspected enemy locations. The CO dropped a thousand-pound LGB on what he termed "bushes" near Shkin, while Yap and Toby both dropped bombs near Spin Boldak on an enemy cave complex. Everyone was fighting for flight time, as it seemed the chance to drop a bomb was higher than ever.

Yet it was the coolness of Jolly and Dano on separate occasions that went unnoticed. Both had exercised restraint when the situation on the ground remained unclear and the weather poor. Dano was

* Todd Pitman, "Rebels in Afghanistan Step Up Attacks," Associated Press Newswire, March 31, 2003, http://www .afghanistannewscenter.com/news/2003/april/apr12003 .html.

Deployment day: October 7, 2002. Author's eleven-month-old son, Caleb, spends a few last minutes with Dad. Both wear earplugs to counter the noise being made by Harriers preparing to launch.

Navy Lieutenant Joe Primeaux, the squadron chaplain, and Lieutenant Colonel Jim "Grouper" Dixon, the squadron commanding officer, at the unveiling of the sign designating the Marine Camp as Camp Teufel-Hunden, or "Devil Dogs," a nickname the Germans gave the Marines in World War I.

Mosque and open market in Kabul, where the author and several Marines made a supply run. A few days after the author took this picture, two American soldiers and their Afghan interpreter were ambushed here.

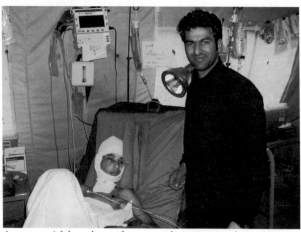

A young Afghan boy after a tracheotomy, and Dr. Nasser, who became a good friend of the author during his visits to the hospital. Afghan children who had accidentally stepped on old Soviet mines were frequent patients in the American field hospital. Many of them lost limbs or more.

Dr. Hamed, patient, and author on Christmas Day, 2002.

Marines and author after a mission. The AV-8B's Litening targeting pod, precision bombs, and powerful Gatling gun earned the Nightmares notoriety as premier hunters, especially at night.

Charismatic Sergeant Walcott in formation with the Marines showing off his new acquisition. Old British guns, leftovers from the Great Game, were a favorite souvenir. Some Marines bought more than one.

Bazaar gun seller.

Bagram's bazaar, where guns were the hottest-selling item.

LEFT: Major Andrew "AJ" Heino, the author's roommate, posing in a fur coat he bought for his brother at Bagram's bazaar. RIGHT: Captain Joe "Stern" Bertagna was lucky and able to walk away from this crash, after the AV-8B left the runway at night during high winds. Stern was returning from a mission in Asadabad in which he bombed insurgents who were shelling the American base. Bagram's fickle weather also claimed an F-16 and C-130 in 2002.

Stern over the Hindu Kush—an endless panorama of snow-covered peaks. Stern was later awarded the Distinguished Flying Cross for supporting American soldiers when their convoy was ambushed near Shkin.

LEFT: Captain Mike "Yap" Trapp placing a pin in the map following a mission. Each pin denoted one mission. Blue and green pins denoted reconaissance and escort missions. Red pins were where we had dropped bombs. There were few red pins.

BELOW: Captain Jarret "Stroker" Stricker tanking at sunrise at the end of dawn patrol. The storm in the background is on the border near Khost.

The author, Playboy 33 (U.S. Air Force Tech Sergeant Celio "Cee-J" Castiblanco), Playboy 10 (Craig), and wingman Captain Mike "Yap" Trapp pose after trading stories about the fight near Dae Chopan. Yap and I were awarded the Distinguished Flying Cross two years after a mission in which we supported Playboy 33 and Special Forces Team ODA 2056, who had been ambushed at Abdullah Kalay near Dae Chopan.

The Marines of ordnance crew, where camaraderie ran high.

The author and wingman returning home at the end of dawn patrol. Dawn Patrol missions, flown from slightly after midnight until shortly after sunrise, became grueling over time and took their toll on the author.

Captain Aaron "Boss" Haug and his Harrier breaking to the west over the Hindu Kush.

even mad at himself for not dropping. Back in January, he had confided in me. "XO, I just couldn't guarantee that the clouds wouldn't affect my lase. I had the cleared-hot but the LGB might have gone stupid." Dano had been right. No one was dying on the ground and the bomb could wait until the weather cleared or until someone brought a Joint Direct Attack Munition (JDAM). Everyone wanted to drop ordnance, especially since opportunities were limited. But the maturity to not drop when doubt existed was overlooked by most. It just didn't receive the notoriety of someone who dropped bombs.

I headed back to my hooch to get dressed. I was thinking too much. It was my affliction. For the last five months, I had flown mostly at night on the vampire schedule, but every now and then, I was thrown a bone—a day flight. It was both a blessing and a curse. It was great to see Afghanistan in colors other than the monochromatic green of the NVGs. On the other hand, the day flights threw my circadian rhythm out of balance. The constant mixing of day and night flights made it difficult to establish a reliable sleep pattern and marked the beginning of a serious battle with insomnia.

25

CHINESE WHISPERS AND FRIENDLY FIRE

The meetings had gone well, or so I rationalized. I was doing that a lot now—rationalizing. The first meeting had taken forty-five minutes, the AOM an hour. I didn't see the need for the meetings, but I was doing my best to swim with the current, not against it.

"Joliet 61, this is Tombstone. New mission. Advise when ready to copy."

I had broken one of my commandments and was thinking about work in the cockpit. *Done, never again.* After pausing a few seconds to ensure Stern was ready to copy, I answered the request. "Go ahead, Tombstone. Joliet standing by to copy."

"Joliet 61, proceed to grid four-two-sierra. Break. Yankee-echo-three-zero-five. Break. Zero-niner-one. Contact Striker 27 on Brown."

I punched the grid into the Harrier's computer. It showed near the Pakistani border, high in the Kunar valley next to Bari Kowt.

I keyed the back radio and called my wingman. "Stern, I show grid bearing zero-one-zero for a hundred and fifty."

"I concur," our new pilot answered.

"Tombstone, Joliet 61, copy all. Proceeding as directed," I told the ASOC, the ground agency at Bagram who directed our CAS missions before launch.

I knew what Stern was thinking in his cockpit. We were heading to a TIC—an ambush. He was wondering if we were going to drop. I wondered what the damage was. Had we lost anyone?

Twenty minutes after taking off, we arrived overhead the Bari Kowt safe house. Bari Kowt, located near Chitral, Pakistan, stood at the gateway to big mountains where peaks reach 26,000 feet. The sun was low in the west, creating long shadows across the valley. Striker 27 briefed us on the situation. One of their vehicles had struck a land mine. Looking through my targeting pod, I picked up the Toyota Hilux resting on its back, flipped over in the middle of the narrow dirt road. The medevac bird, "Viper," was picking up two casualties. Only one made it.

Due to the location of Bari Kowt, a few miles from the Pakistani border, it was difficult to hold directly overhead. Higher headquarters was constantly reminding us "not to fly into Pakistan." Stern and I held in a north-south track paralleling the border, offset five miles to the west. Striker called with a request.

"Joliet, can you give me a low pass. Break. We're

pretty vulnerable down here. Break. I need to send a message."

"Roger, Striker. Understand one, low 'show of force' pass. Please confirm."

"Roger. Striker 27 requests show of force, low pass."

"Roger, Striker. Stand by. We need approval from K-mart." I thought about just doing the pass anyway, but I felt it was better to work within the system, even with insipid rules.

Stern and I tried to reach Tombstone and Vice-squad on the radio without success. We were too far north—off the grid. Not only did higher headquarters not have a radar picture of what was happening, they had no capability to communicate with us, either. Frustrated with the situation, I pushed Stern south over Jalalabad to reach Tombstone or a tanker while I remained over Bari Kowt and the ambush site.

I continued to advise Stern of the ground situation while he kept me apprised of whom he could reach. Stern relayed the request to a tanker coming on station in southern Afghanistan. The tanker crew relayed the request to the radar facility in Kandahar, where someone got on a computer and sent it via secret Internet to the CAOC in Qatar. When the message finally reached K-mart, they inquired back, "Who is low on gas and why is Striker resetting the force?"

Our command and control was a bad game of

"Chinese whispers," where children sit in a circle and whisper a phrase to each other in turns. Simple sentences become discombobulated—contorted and thus utterly meaningless and ridiculously confusing. In our case, "Striker requests a show of force, low pass" became "Striker resets the force and is low on gas."

When we heard the response, Stern and I didn't understand why K-mart wanted to know our gas and what force had been reset. But we provided our fuel state and asked for the update on Striker's request. "What request?" responded the CAOC via the Internet, back to the radar facility at Kandahar, to the operator who called the tanker, who called Stern, who called me. "Goddamn it!" I yelled, banging my fists against the canopy. I was losing it. Finally, Striker's simple request was relayed correctly and approved, but the whole process took an hour.

It was maddening operating the way we did because higher headquarters, the CAOC, tied the hands of those fighting the war. I don't know what K-mart actually did for us by reviewing and approving the forward air controllers' request for a show-of-force pass. They provided no margin of safety, no clearance of fires, no intel update. I believe it gave someone purpose—status. Someone who wasn't on the front lines.

I told Stern to remain high cover as I rolled my airplane over on its back and pulled my nose toward the ground. The vast horizon disappeared, replaced with the detail of small mud buildings and farmer fields, no doubt some of them opium. The speed released pent-up endorphins and cured some of my madness. Everything was relative and speed up high had no reference points. Down low, next to the ground, every knot was sex.

As I blew through the valley, tiny mud huts blurred beneath me. To my right and left, the high valley walls looked down upon me. The Kunar valley was a chasm, and I was at the bottom of it shooting through like a bullet. As the valley opened, I pulled back on my stick and converted my airspeed for altitude. Nothing but sky filled my canopy as I stood the jet on its tail. Now, at the end of my mission and low on gas, the Harrier revealed its brute strength.

"Thanks, Joliet. That's just what I needed. We'll sleep better tonight."

"Roger, Striker. Sorry we got to go, but we're bingo."

"Rog, Joliet. Striker out."

Out of fuel, Stern and I began the flight back to Bagram. As we set up for our descent at the south initial, Stern called out some ground fire below us.

Skirmishes between local warlords were a common sight around Bagram. The spokesperson for Bagram Air Base had stated back in February, "There are two sub-unit commanders who both operate north of the base and they are in dispute over who owes who money and who should have access to the profits generated by some scrap metal. They are attempting to settle it with mortars."* These weren't subunit commanders working for the Americans. They were warlords with their own agendas. But the military couldn't say "warlord" because it might give people back home the wrong impression of what we were doing.

After landing, Stern and I shed our flight gear and headed to the Harrier ready room. AJ and Jolly were discussing tactics with the A-10 pilots around the map in the middle of the room. Our intel officer was waiting. Stern began the debrief, relaying the story of ground fire at the north end of the base. The A-10 commander, Lieutenant Colonel Billy Smith, cut him off. "No shit. Do you think they were shooting at you?"

Stern didn't bite. "No, sir. But they were unloading on each other."

"Grouper, is this your new guy?" Billy asked.

"Yeah. Captain Bertagna, meet Lieutenant Colonel Smith, the commander of the A-10s based here," Grouper said.

"Pleased to meet you, sir," Stern said, leaning over and shaking hands.

Billy turned back to Grouper. "Hey, Grouper, didn't one of your guys report getting shot at while they were in the pattern the other day?"

"Yeah, that was me. But I couldn't tell where it was coming from."

* "Afghan Factions Clash Over Scrap Metal Near U.S. Base," Reuters, February 27, 2003.

"Well, Grouper, you'll be happy to know, Tower has solved the riddle. They briefed us today where the rounds were coming from. Thought you got the word."

Grouper looked surprised. "No, where?"

"The Marine camp." The deadpan answer froze the room. Finally, Grouper laughed and we all joined in, some nervously.

After going to chow, I walked back to camp with Captain Jarret "Stroker" Stricker, our other new pilot. In the cool light of evening, Stroker gave me his uninhibited thoughts.

"Sir." He paused, unsure whether to continue. "Sir, this isn't like I thought it would be. Everyone lies around and sleeps all day."

I thought about the vampire cave in which we lived, where sleep was revered above all. Sleep during the day so as to hunt at night. Since Stroker had just arrived, he was on the day schedule, but we'd bring him over to nights soon enough. But Stroker was right. I was in combat—in the ring—and it wasn't what I expected. I thought about the self-generating crisis managers: the power brokers on Bagram who flexed their muscles, creating unnecessary requirements, because it made them seem important. I thought of the meetings, the inefficiency—insipid, onerous meetings, where little was accomplished. I thought about our intel, our strategy. What was it?

"Yeah, Stroker, you're right. We sleep a lot."

26

MISTAKES

The U.S. attacks against the Taliban near Spin Boldak continued. But we failed to learn the lessons of fighting a counterinsurgency. We were big, cumbersome, and continually taking too much time to get the "right force" in place. By contrast, the enemy had fought this type of war since the Soviets invaded in 1980—a war that wasn't much different from those against the British during the mid to late 1800s or perhaps against Alexander some two thousand years ago. The enemy knew how to attack, run, hide, and fight on their terms while frustrating ours.

What the military spokespersons at Bagram pitched in press releases differed sharply from the thoughts of their Afghan counterparts. The former was always optimistic and encouraging while the latter gave a more realistic assessment. The *New York Times* ran an article on April 4, 2003, that received little notice back home because of the attention focused on Iraq.

[D]espite the 35,000 pounds of ordnance dropped on the area [near Spin Boldak] and hundreds of Afghan soldiers surrounding them, the rebel leaders managed to break out and make a run for the border with Pakistan, said Gen. Abdul Razzaq, the Afghan military chief of the border region. . . . The battle, the latest in a series of clashes in recent weeks in which American Special Forces have had to call in airstrikes, was a stark reminder that the fighting is not over here, a year and a half after American forces first moved against the Taliban and al Qaeda in October 2001.*

That was not the message, official or otherwise, emanating from CJTF-180 headquarters. Nevertheless, I carried on. I had my own problems. After taping the heavy plastic tarp on the outside of the tent, I completed my patchwork inside, above my rack. I layered the plastic twice. *That had to hold. You'll get some good sleep tonight, Zak. Nothing is going to tear that down.*

Despite moving to the day schedule, I struggled to kick my vampire routine. I had become so accustomed to racking out late that when I went to bed early, I tossed and turned for hours, staring at my ceiling and the alarm clock, watching the minutes tick by and another hour pass.

* Carlotta Gall, "A Nation at War; U.S. Gunships Hit Taliban Camp; Most Fighters Escape," *New York Times*, April 4, 2003.

I acquiesced early to the urge and took one of the small pills that sometimes worked and sometimes didn't. Lying in my rack, I ignored the knock on the door. After a second knock, I heard the door push open and the footsteps of two men. They were pilots. I lay still, feigning sleep. I listened to them move to the far side of the room. AJ was awake, playing his video games. I listened as the pilots told their story. Through the whispers, the excitement in their voices gushed forth. One pilot chuckled as he described the video. It was the rush—the high after the game, when one basked in the success of the win. As the pilots left, I heard AJ walk over. He didn't hesitate to shake my rack. "Zak, wake up."

"I'm awake. What's up?"

AJ recounted the story I had already heard. He delivered it with the same zeal the two pilots had. As he finished, I felt the zolpidem's effects begin. I gave in and let go.

"Major Franzak, Major Franzak, wake up, wake up." Someone was grabbing me—shaking me. *What the fuck is going on? Am I dreaming?* A light shined in my eyes. I rolled over. Hands pulled me back. Hands holding the light. I came to my senses. Sergeant Tompkins from the operations department held the flashlight.

"Sir, the CO needs to see you immediately. There has been an accident."

"What's up, Sergeant Tompkins?" I asked in a semi-lucid state.

"Sir, there has been an accident. There are some civilian casualties. It appears we might have caused it. The CO wants to see you immediately."

I looked at my watch. I had been asleep for two hours. I got up slowly. My feet felt the cold floor. Tompkins remained in the doorway. He sensed I might fall back into my rack. He waited.

I pulled on my flight suit and jacket, grabbed my pistol, and swung it over my shoulder. Tompkins held open the door and led me down the steps. I walked around to the other side of our tent, knocked on the door, and went in. Grouper sat behind his desk typing a message. He told me to sit down.

"Zak, it looks like we dropped on some civilians. We don't know how many casualties there are, but there are some deaths. I need you to begin a formal investigation. This most likely will go to the highest levels, so make sure to follow the correct procedures. Don't hide anything. Work with the facts. You copy?"

"Yes, sir," I said. "You OK?"

"Yeah, I'm OK. The aircrew and Doc are waiting for you. They don't know it yet, but I need to ground the pilots. Just until things clear up. I'll tell them."

"Yes, sir. No problem. Anything else?"

Grouper shook his head. "No. That's it."

The discussion and direction had been short. I stepped back into the night and found Doc Marra and the two pilots waiting near the LSS vehicle. There was a cold mist hanging over the camp, almost a fog. In the darkness, the pilots' shadowy figures were barely discernible. It was creepy. The four of us climbed into the back of the truck. No one spoke. Tompkins drove slowly down Disney Drive to the Harrier ready room located in the base of the tower.

Once we arrived at the control tower, Doc took blood and urine samples from both pilots. Once he was done, I asked each pilot to write a statement regarding the incident. As they wrote, I sipped my coffee, studying them. Gone was the excitement and laughter that had accompanied their story a few hours earlier. A serious look—part sadness, part fear—bore heavily on each face. Doubt had replaced the confidence and swagger of earlier. I collected the targeting pod and HUD camera tapes from both pilots. I reviewed them before sealing them in a bag. The bomb had hit exactly where the pilot had designated the target. A small mud building disappeared in a fireball as the thousand-pound precision-guided bomb slammed into it.

The following day, officials took statements from the JTAC and ground commander. They explained that the Harrier pilots had confirmed the location of the target with the IR strobe on the Litening pod. After determining the correct target was identified, they cleared the Harrier pilots for release and the bomb hit the intended target.

The pilots had made no errors. Both pilots had done everything by the book: careful, methodic, but deadly. Regardless, the result was tragic. The event raised concerns back home, requiring the chairman of the U.S. Joint Chiefs of Staff, General Richard Myers, to issue an apology. It was the worst mistake in Afghanistan since the June 2002 accidental bombing of an Afghan wedding party in which forty-eight civilians died.

The number of casualties grew throughout the night and the following day. Finally, a factual figure emerged. Eleven Afghan civilians, eight to twenty-three years of age, most of them children, had died. Seven of them were girls. No one knew if any enemy had been killed. One press release stated, "The bomb missed the intended target and landed on the house."* That was not the truth. The bomb hit exactly where the pilot had designated, where the JTAC wanted it, where the enemy had fled.

The enemy spared no quarter as they waged their war, running into homes of innocent civilians, using them as human shields. The incident was a cold reminder of the threats we faced and the reality of war. Eleven innocent civilians, many of them children, killed in a matter of seconds.

The CO held a formation to set the facts straight with the Marines. He explained that the two pilots had done nothing wrong, but a mistake had been made on the ground, resulting in the tragic deaths. Then Grouper said something I didn't expect. He

* Todd Pitman, "Eleven Afghan Civilians Killed in Accidental US Bombing near Pakistan Border," Associated Press, April 9, 2003.

said that he had set a bad example concerning our mission—that his "casual attitude" may have prompted others to think too lightly of the consequences of our actions. He admonished himself in front of us, reminding us of the horrors of war. Then he dismissed us. As Grouper walked away, I found new respect for a man I had once hated.

The lawyers and staff officers from the CAOC arrived a few days later. The air force two-star had sent them. These were the boys from K-mart who directed our actions and those of every other air asset in the CENTCOM AOR. They were sent to help us review the current rules of engagement (ROE). All of us were familiar with the ROE. We lived with them every day, both in the air and on the ground. Nevertheless, the general thought we needed a refresher. What we received was far different from what I expected.

The lawyers and staff officers from the CAOC were nice people. They were just trying to do their jobs, but they became a source of frustration when they opened the floor for questions. One pilot complained about supporting ground forces next to the Pakistani border without being able to fly into Pakistan. "How can we effectively support our ground forces when we can't fly over them—provide a CAP on top of them?"

The lawyers had an easy answer. All we needed to do was request the airspace. "Just contact the CAOC, who will call 'Nitro,' the American embassy in Pakistan, and within minutes, you will be cleared

into a five-mile zone of Pakistani airspace." Simple—
no problem—guaranteed!

"What if no one is on station to relay our request to K-mart?" one of the younger pilots asked.
The lawyers conversed back and forth. Then one of
them spoke, but his logic went in circles. After a few
minutes, someone else interrupted and took over. Ten
minutes later, amid much confusion and discussion,
the joint answer was that we would always be able to
get ahold of the CAOC. I thought of my mission near
Bari Kowt a few weeks earlier.

Then someone asked why the JTACs couldn't give
their position to us. The rule, imposed by the CAOC,
was intended to protect the JTACs on the ground due
to a mistake a JTAC had made early in the war. During the opening months of the Afghanistan campaign,
a JTAC called in an air strike on a Taliban position
near Kandahar. The JTAC mistakenly relayed his own
position to the aircraft as the target. When the bomb
was released, it landed on the friendly position, killing several. To fix the problem, the CAOC ordered
that JTACs be prohibited from providing their exact
location to pilots in a grid or lat-long format. Thus,
to cure the problem, higher headquarters cut off their
own head and those who worked for them. We were
trying to protect ourselves from ourselves because of
our own stupidity. I later learned that when ground
forces needed immediate close air support, they
tossed this restriction out the window—JTACs provided us their exact location and then referenced the

enemy location from there. It was a matter of life and death and they preferred the former.

But the lawyers didn't have a suitable answer as to why the rule was in place. As they put it, "It just is." Because of the mistake of one, the CAOC created insipid rules that confused and hindered operations. It was one more indicator of how ridiculously out of touch the CAOC was regarding the war in Afghanistan. I was glad when the lawyers left.

27

BURNOUT

Rain drummed on the roof in a soft pitter-patter. It brought the smell of dust back down to earth. The smell was strong. I felt sorry for the two pilots— innocent blood on their hands and they had done no wrong. The investigation was completed quickly, but we never saw the results. No one ever spoke about it. It was taboo to mention it. The pilots had left shortly after the tragedy, along with twenty other Marines. Now that we were staying a full year, Grouper wanted to rotate crews home for a break. He sent the two pilots home first.

It was chance, probability, the only god I knew in Afghanistan. It could have been any one of us who had dropped. I turned my headlamp on and grabbed a book from the box that had arrived a month ago. We all needed something to help us. AJ had bought a TV set and PlayStation. He played Grand Theft Auto addictively. Many pilots had taken to an online computer game in which they fought each other as World

War II infantry or built medieval armies that took over the world. I took to books.

I had finished Daniel Boorstin's *The Creators* and Marcus Aurelius's *Meditations*. Now I had the poetry. I always found comfort in the poets: Emily and Ezra, T.S. and e.e., Robert and the suicide sisters. They were friends. I found an old favorite and began.

> *Because I could not stop for Death,*
> *He kindly stopped for me . . .*

I finished the poem and listened to the rain. I turned off my headlamp. *What is it like to kill someone—to take away all they ever were and are going to be? What happens to you? What happens when you learn there's a mistake? What if it's a child? Are there nightmares? Does it make a difference if you don't see their eyes? What time is it? How long have I been lying here?*

Despite moving to the day schedule, my body never made the circadian adjustment. After flying on the vampire schedule for five months, my body refused to sleep at night. I lay there for hours, watching the numbers on my clock change. As dawn approached and the light seeped under my door, sleep finally came. But it was a fool's sleep because I awoke four hours later, as the Afghanistan sun soaked our tent in heat.

I pursued anything to subdue my villain. Work out late. Work out twice. Force myself to get up early.

Avoid a big meal before bed. Read. Read some more. I began reading the dictionary, which fact AJ shared with the other pilots, much to my dismay. It brought on relentless hazing. I tried counting sheep at night. But every time I counted sheep, I thought how stupid it was and talked myself out of any benefit it might bring. I even tried meditation. Nothing worked. But I had the zolpidem, which I took with increasing frequency. I began to wonder if I was forming a habit. The effects of the sleeping pills diminished as my body became familiar with their tricks. In desperation, I took more. Sometimes they worked; sometimes they didn't.

Eventually I quit fighting the insomnia and read all night or walked over to the admin shop and went through the day's paperwork. I got five hours of sleep one night, three the next night, and then perhaps one hour the following night. Then I crashed hard the following day. I couldn't predict when I would sleep and when I wouldn't. I was walking a high wire—blind.

I rose and grabbed my bottle of zolpidem. I was using them a lot but didn't give a damn. I just wanted sleep. I opened the lid and shook two pills into the palm of my hand. I tossed them down with a swig of water. I was slowly slipping. There were signs—some subtle, some obvious—but I ignored the warnings, even the ones I wrote before me.

Tuesday, 22 April 2003: 1430 Zulu. I am so tired. I experienced a pain today that I never have before. Being so tired and wanting to sleep but not being able to. It causes me alarm to think that maybe I really am losing it. I've been forced to stay awake for several days before, the most memorable being Recon School when I hallucinated. But this is different. This is a pain that could be an effective torture. Trying to sleep—knowing that you are so tired, you need to sleep, but not being able to sleep. It's outright maddening.

While I struggled to sleep, the war in Afghanistan took on a casual, familiar role to the Nightmares. The missions were the same. The terrain was the same. The dry heat of Afghanistan slowed life to a crawl. Hours blended into days, days into weeks, and weeks into months. Every day was Monday. The only recognition of time came in the seasons and stars. And when the seasons changed from freezing cold to unbelievably hot, so too did the stars.

My celestial friend, Orion, disappeared. Scorpius now rose in the southern night sky. The sinister constellation's red supergiant, Antares, replaced the cool blue twinkle of Orion's Rigel. In old Arabic, Antares was Kalb al Akrab—"the scorpion's heart." Scorpius reminded me there was no respite from the Afghanistan heat, even at night.

In May, President George W. Bush announced "the end of major combat operations" in Iraq, a hasty assessment that many failed to acknowledge. Nevertheless, there was a sense of jealousy within the

Nightmares. Although we had been in combat longer, we hadn't experienced the excitement our brethren had in Iraq. Now they were heading home to victory parades while we were stuck in Afghanistan for another six months.

There was talk of sending a Harrier squadron to relieve us, but it was wishful thinking that ignored the realities of logistics. It was much easier to keep us in place instead of swapping us out, and that is what the generals decided to do. As our friends returned home to the premature celebrations of victory in Iraq, we remained in Afghanistan in what appeared to some a forgotten war.

28

ON EDGE

"I don't give a shit, Doc. Here's the deal. Don't get me wrong, but you're going home. You're going home next week, with the chaplain and some of the other Marines. You're not coming back. You've done a great job here, but you're leaving and being replaced. Well, I'm not and neither is new guy here." I pointed to Stroker, who sat quietly. "But Stroker here is new, just like Stern, and they both got the new-guy attitude. That's great. We need it. But everyone else—Toby, Dano, Jolly, Yap, Boss— they've been here awhile. And we're all staying another six fucking months. And we got a fucking job to do. And I'm not going to stand by and watch some of us do the job half-ass. It's fucking simple, Doc."

"Sir, we're not arguing with your need to make sure things get done. It's what happened this morning," Stroker said. "There are reports from the officers that your temper is out of control. Perhaps you need a break. Maybe you should go home and take some leave."

As Stroker talked, I replayed the morning's events. I had flown with Wiz. Tombstone had sent us south to a grid near Shkin to work with Hardrock 18. After orbiting for twenty minutes and not raising anyone on the radio, we flew back to Bagram, where we contacted Tombstone. They sent us back to the same grid but gave us a new frequency. We arrived over Shkin a second time, but still were unable to contact anyone. So again we proceeded back to Bagram, where we could talk to Tombstone. Tombstone then realized they had passed the wrong two-letter identifier for the grid. Tombstone gave us the new grid and sent us southwest, this time toward Ghazni. Once there, we finally reached Hardrock 18. He wanted us overhead because his unit was sweeping a town. But he couldn't give us his location because he didn't have a GPS. He tried to talk me onto his position by referencing the "three small hills" just to his north. I looked down from my vantage and saw three hundred small hills. It was then that I lost it.

I yelled over the radio, losing all composure. My mind raced. "How the fuck can I support you if you don't know where you fucking are?" I beat my fists against the canopy while I screamed into the radio. Wiz was silent, embarrassed that his flight lead—the executive officer of the squadron—had lost it. He said nothing in the debrief, either. His eyes told me where he was. He had found Stroker or Doc afterward and they had found me. I thought about the incompetence of Tombstone, K-mart, CJTF-180 headquarters. Everyone was fucked-up. How were we ever going to win this war? I waited until Stroker finished.

"I don't need a fucking break. What I need is for shit to get done around here without me or the CO coming around and asking three or four times if what needs to get done is done. We're fighting a fucking war. But when fitreps or awards are due, then we fucking turn them in on time. I'm fucking tired of chasing shit down. I'm fucking tired of incompetence. I'm tired of wrong grids and excuses." My rage prevented any objective view. I was becoming what I loathed. Stroker and Doc remained cautious, sensing the danger. "Look, I don't mind if you take this to the CO. In fact, please do. I'm fucking pissed. You can tell him I think everyone is fucked-up. And then I'll go tell him why everyone is fucked-up."

"Why don't you come off the flight schedule for a little bit, maybe a day or two?" Doc asked.

"Fuck that. I already said I don't need a fucking break. I'm OK. I just want everyone else to do their job. What else do you guys need? I got some paperwork I need to do."

Stroker and Doc looked at each other and shook their heads.

"I'm glad we had this talk. Really. I'm not being sarcastic," I added. "I got some things off my chest. Can I go now?"

Doc looked at our new safety officer, Stroker, and asked, "You got anything else you want to add?" Stroker shook his head and sighed.

"Nope."

Doc looked back to me. "OK, sir. Thanks for talking to us. Take it easy, will you?"

"Yes, thanks." I stood up, left the medical office, and walked to the S-1 shop. It was only 11 A.M., yet the sun's rays burned. I opened the door and went to my desk. There was a letter next to my computer. It was from Kevin H., my new childhood friend in New Jersey. I put the letter aside to enjoy later. I opened Microsoft Outlook and saw an e-mail from the MAG-13 adjutant, who was in Kuwait with the rest of the 3rd Marine Aircraft Wing. They were packing up and heading home. I wondered what the news was. I clicked on the e-mail and read:

Major Franzak,

I need you to submit all of your squadron's pilots for air medals immediately. I also need you to submit your CO for an end of tour award. I need the awards submitted within 48 hours.

Captain X.

"Motherfucker!" I screamed aloud. The Marines inside the S-1 building grew silent. They knew the consequences. The female captain didn't even sign the request with the common military acknowledgment of "Very Respectfully," or "V/R," or even "Respectfully," or simply "R/." She could have at least signed it "Semper Fi." I burst into the CO's quarters with a printed copy of the e-mail.

"Sir, MAG-13 has lost it. Read this disrespectful piece of shit from that bitch," I stammered, throwing all tact out the window.

"Hold on, Zak. What do you have?" Grouper sat in his large chair, with a book in his hands.

I held out the e-mail. "Sir, perhaps they're done fighting their war, but the last time I checked we're still fighting ours. Just because they are submitting all of their pilots for awards, doesn't mean that we need to be doing the same thing. It's fucking ridiculous. We've got another six months of flying missions before we begin thinking about awards."

"It's OK, Zak. I know," Grouper responded calmly. He read the e-mail I had handed him. Looking back up, he grinned. "The adjutant is a piece of work, isn't she?" Grouper didn't give me time to answer before continuing. "What do you need to comply with the request? The MAG CO is pretty fond of his adjutant, so I wouldn't go pissing on any trees."

"Sir, I can get it done, but why the rush? Why not wait until we go home? It's stupid. I'm going to call the MAG XO and ask what's all the hoopla about."

"Fine with me, Zak. But keep your cool," Grouper stated, bending his head forward and looking over his bifocals. I got the message.

I called the MAG XO on the phone. Despite the

slight delay between Afghanistan and the Persian Gulf, our connection was good. I asked him what was going on. Were things chaotic? Why the rush?

Wolfman began. "No, Zak, things are pretty slow here. We're packing up. I'm not sure what the rush is regarding the awards. I wasn't aware. I should be, but I wasn't. My only advice is that several of us have tried to rein in the adjutant, but she has a special relationship with the MAG CO."

I knew that Lieutenant Colonel Clyde "Wolfman" Woltman wasn't hinting of anything improper.

"Sir, will you please do me a favor?" I asked. Can you tell the adj I'm working on her request and will complete it within a day or two? Everything but the CO's award. That will take a few weeks at least."

"OK, Zak. No problem."

I hung up the phone and headed to Ops to grab each pilot's logbook. I had a dozen awards to write.

Forty-eight hours later, I completed my task. I asked Staff Sergeant McCosar to double-check my work and then I sent the twelve awards via several e-mails to the MAG-13 adjutant. A day later, I received a response.

> Major Franzak, where are the awards? I have not received anything and I need the awards ASAP. Please complete this task or I will have to raise the issue with my superior. Also, we only have two air medals here due to all of the ones we've passed out to the MAG pilots. Do

you have any there? I sure hope so because the
only air medals I know of are back home in
Yuma.

                                    Captain X.

My rage boiled but there was no way to reach the gist of arrogance and stupidity. *What were they thinking?* We didn't pack up air medals for our deployment. It wasn't on our list of things to bring. I asked Sergeant McCosar to send the documents a second time while I added a personal note: "We don't have any fucking air medals, nor do I care." I never heard from her again.

A week after I submitted the awards, the first Marine Corps general arrived, Lieutenant General Earl Hailston, commander of Marine forces in the CENT-COM AOR. After overseeing the invasion in Iraq, he was heading back to the United States. But he wanted to stop in and let us know that we weren't forgotten. He was a nice fellow. He talked to the Marines, who asked him questions about Operation Iraqi Freedom. But a few Marines asked other questions: "General, is another squadron going to replace us?" After a two-day visit, he left and we continued our combat patrols.

A week later another Marine Corps general arrived. This time it was the 3rd Marine Aircraft Wing commander, Major General James Amos, our ultimate boss back home. Again, like the previous general, he wanted to tell us thanks, pump us up, and let us know we were doing a "great job" and an "important one" at that. And he gave us our air medals. I never saw it coming. The urgency to submit the awards was so the general could present them to us. I didn't think it was his idea, but it didn't matter. Because the boys in Iraq had finished their war, were heading home and being put in for their air medals, someone didn't want us to feel left out. Each air medal read the same. I had written them that way so that no pilot was viewed better than anyone else—we were a team.

I stood at attention in a long line of pilots. As the general pinned on my air medal, I thought not only of the irony—that I had written the award I was receiving—but of the ostentatious way in which it was presented, like it was special. I just didn't get it.

29

SLIP SLIDING AWAY

I unzipped my flight suit and let it fall to the floor. I pulled my boxers down over my boots. Her hand felt warm. I hoped I wouldn't get hard. She was pretty, but I tried not to think about it. It had been a long time. She pushed and prodded the skin and muscles of my inner left thigh. Then I felt her grab my scrotum and push my testicle upward.

"Turn your head to the side and cough. OK, again." She pushed back her stool and peeled the plastic gloves from her hand, tossing them into the garbage can. Navy lieutenant Michelle Kreisberg had replaced Doc Marra the previous week. Like Tim, Michelle was young, healthy, and intelligent. Unlike Tim, she was a "she" and attractive.

"Sir, I can't feel anything. I don't think you have a hernia. It's possible there might be a strain, but I don't think there is a tear in the peritoneum. You say you run six to eight miles a day."

"The pair-a-what?" I asked.

"The peritoneum. It's the membrane, the lining of the abdominal cavity. The pain you are experiencing is probably from a strain—maybe overtraining. How many miles a day are you running?"

"I don't know. It depends. Sometimes six, sometimes more." I pulled up my boxers and zipped up my flight suit.

"Sir, no PT for two weeks. Then we'll see if the pain is still there."

"No PT for two weeks. I can't do that. I'll go crazy."

"Sir, if you want to get better, then no PT." Lieutenant Kreisberg looked at me with a serious eye. There wasn't a smile.

"OK, no PT." I swung my pistol over my shoulder and added, "On another note, Doc, I need some more no-go pills." With my prescription filled, I walked out of the hospital and back onto Disney Drive. The smell was still with me—that pungent, sickly sweet smell of the hospital.

"Hey, get out of the road, you dumbass." The sound of a horn blared as the green truck sped by, leaving me in a cloud of dust.

"Hey, you assholes. Give me a ride or I'll schedule you all for double duty," I yelled back. Twenty yards past me, the truck skidded to a stop and waited. I jogged up to it, grabbed the tailgate, and jumped into the back. AJ was driving the truck full of squadron pilots to chow.

"Hey, it's Dr. Jekyll, or is it Mr. Hyde?"

I looked at Dano and asked, "What do you mean?"

"Sir, it's just we don't know who you are sometimes. It's hard to tell when you're joking and when you aren't."

I sat down on the bench next to JC. "Dano, it's not important you know. Only that I know." I regretted the Pattonesque line, a vague attempt to cover my crumbling character. The truck bounced down the potholed road. The pilots, who had been joking and smiling before I jumped into the vehicle, now remained silent.

After dinner, I called Katie and my parents. They were visiting each other back home. I wanted to thank them for the most recent package, especially the fans. Their voices replayed in my mind. It was my mom's words. Innocent words of love that sank like a knife into my chest, slowly, eliciting pain for which they were not intended. "Michael, he's so big now. He can walk and talk. He's changed so much." The last words hurt the most. The call was over. It was done. I rolled over and looked at the clock—22:52. I closed my eyes and tried not to think of home.

It was strange, wasn't it? Why had I stayed? It was them, wasn't it? People like AJ and Dano. There was Tex, Butts, and Gila and then there were those who were no longer here. Wicky. Why was it that the best—the pure or innocent—were taken? But I remembered them—most of them. There was always something about each of them that I remembered most. With Wicky it was the waterfall.

I had jumped first. Then she had jumped. Then they all followed. Even Mello. Then I found the ledge that wasn't quite clear. You couldn't jump standing from it or you'd hit the rocks at the edge of the pool. You had to run. But you couldn't slip or you'd make a mess of it. You had to run, then jump, and then you could make the pool. But you had to run fast and jump far—without doubt—then you'd find the pool. That dark pool of cold water. And then someone ran and jumped from the ledge—maybe it was me who ran. Then more of us ran and jumped and did it again, but not everyone. It was the young—the bulletproof. Mostly the captains. But Mello had run and jumped. Then I ran and dove. No one had dove. I didn't want to dive, but I had thought about it. That was the problem. Once I had thought of it, I couldn't back away from it, because I knew I was backing away from something that I was scared of, and I couldn't do that, so I ran and dove. Then I came back and drank a beer with Wicky. Yes, she understood the waterfall.

I looked at the clock—01:25. I flicked on my light and grabbed the bottle of no-go pills.

Try not to think so much. Just relax. But it was them, wasn't it? All of them. Rip, Pops, Gator,

Wicky, and all the others. God, can I remember them all? There was Jake, he had been the first. They say he just flew into the ground, never pulled out of the dive. Then Wheels and Biscuit. Don't forget JJ. Beav and Davey at the same time. Somewhere in there it happened to Palmatier, my A-4 skipper. God he was nice. There was Lefty, Bull, and McDonald. What was McDonald's call sign? So many faces, but it was the close ones that stayed with me now. What was it with Rip? We had roomed together at SERE school . . . Oh shit; it was when he whipped his cock out during Sinbad's lecture as the "attention getter." He swung that huge piece of meat around, windmilling it like a club. Goddamn that was funny. And when he went, his wife gave birth a few weeks later. That was a bummer . . .

What about Pops? It had to be the 1v1 flight out of Kadena. The quick turn, where I let him win the first one to build his confidence and then showed him Mello's tricks on the second hop. He didn't know what to say. Mello had done that to me. Damn, Mello was good . . . What about Gator? It was how he wore that flight suit, with his sleeves always pulled up above his elbows. It was like a little man trying to be bigger. And the shorts. Those really bad corduroy low-cut shorts. I can still hear Hawk calling out at the squadron BBQ, "Hey, Gator.

The seventies are calling. They want their shorts back." Fucking Hawk. Now, that's a character. I'm glad he's still around. Goddamn, Gator was a good pilot. Fucking the best. No, Mello was better, but Gator was good.

I looked at the clock—03:42.

What mattered? Did any of this matter? Yes, it had to. Something had to matter, even if I didn't understand the purpose. Remember the boat, when you first stepped off the helo onto the massive aircraft carrier. That big, tall, black petty officer took you under his wing— Tony—Tony Thomas. Yeah, that was his name. Remember when he asked if you were superstitious? You said, "No," and they said "Good." And then they showed you your rack. It was on the bottom of the tier of three under the two wire in a room with 150 other sailors. Then you found out the next day that the previous resident had committed suicide. He just "flipped," they said—something about not being able to handle it. Handle it? Handle what?

And then you—then I, it is me, why am I talking to myself like I'm two people—then I found the poem. The poem about wanting to melt the ship into razor blades. He had scratched it into the metal on the rack above him. No one else had seen it. They couldn't have because one had to lie in his rack to read it. And no one had lain there but me, after him. He hid it. He had written it and I had found it. But I found it after it was too late. Or was I? Maybe he was writing to me. Then I learned he had cut his wrists with razor blades. What was he thinking? How does it get that bad?

Damn, I'm not going to sleep tonight. Fuck. It's like being drunk and then thinking about not coming, then getting worried about not coming. Then you can't come because you're thinking about it. That's how it is with this sleep. I just need to quit thinking about it . . . What if I beat off? If I beat off, I can probably still get a few hours of sleep. I'll have to go to the outhouse so that AJ doesn't hear me, unless he's asleep. Fuck, this is stupid. Quit thinking about it.

As I walked back from the outhouse and into the hooch, my eyes turned to the clock—05:15. I lay back down. *Now what?* I tried not to look at the clock, but it didn't matter. It wasn't long before the light of day began to creep underneath the door. I had lost again. I lay there listening to the beat of my heart, a drum that beat slow but loud. A quiet, deafening sound.

"Zak, get up. Let's go to the bazaar."

I rolled over, trying to ignore AJ. I looked at the clock—09:03. I had at least slept two hours. If I stayed in bed, I risked not breaking the cycle. I had to force the adjustment. Besides, the heat was coming. It was unavoidable now. Soon the tent would be an oven. "All right. Get the CO's truck or the Paddles vehicle. I don't want to walk."

As AJ drove I sat quietly in the passenger seat. "I hope the influx of newbies hasn't raised the prices. I saw the perfect gift for my bro." AJ spoke in an up-beat tone.

"AJ, do you know what hell is?" Out of the corner of my eye, I saw AJ turn his head. I didn't look at him. "I think hell would be immortality. Never dying. Always being alive after everyone is gone. After the sun has gone cold, wanting to die, to sleep, but not being able to. That would be hell."

"Zak, you think too much."

AJ spun the vehicle into the large parking lot full of other vehicles at the south end of the base. We got out of the truck. The bright sun reflected off the light tan dirt and stung my eyes. We walked over to a long line of tables and open booths that held an endless supply of pirated DVDs, CDs, knives, rugs, cheap jewelry, lapis rocks, rugs, and guns. Lots of rugs and guns.

Guns were the biggest-selling item at the bazaar. Old British rifles, leftovers from the "Great Game." The guns had been passed down from generation to generation of Pashtun fighters, and now they were being sold back to the infidels who brought them here. Some of the guns were single-shot, bolt-action Lee-Enfield rifles, the British army's standard rifle, introduced in 1895. The same guns provided by the CIA to the mujahideen in the beginning of the covert war against the Russians.*

Many of the Marines bought the old British rifles as souvenirs. Some bought two. Buyers favored the older, more exotic weapons with inscribed dates, pre-1900. But the Afghans were experts at modifying the dates and then antiquing them to look authentic. It was hard to tell what was authentic and what wasn't.

"Hey, Zak. What do you think about this?" AJ held up a large black fur coat.

"Yeah, that's great, AJ. How much?" I asked.

AJ turned to the vendor and asked how much. In broken but comprehensible English the old, weathered Pashtun man sitting cross-legged on the ground responded, "One hundred dollar."

"Fifty dollar," AJ retorted.

The old Pashtun looked down and shook his head. "One hundred dollar."

AJ, not letting up, quickly answered, "Seventy-five dollar."

The weathered Pashtun said nothing. AJ stared back. Then the Afghan spoke. "Seventy-five dollar."

AJ whipped out seventy-five bucks, paid the man, and claimed the knee-length fur coat. "Just don't ever have it dry-cleaned, AJ. The hair will probably fall out," I said as we walked off.

* Steve Coll, *Ghost Wars* (New York: Penguin, 2004), pp. 58, 66, 583.

"My bro is going to love it."

AJ's brother, Dave Heino, was a Special Forces officer who had arrived in Afghanistan several months earlier. The two brothers traded stories about the Afghanistan frontier, one from the ground, the other from the air. I thought it interesting that two brothers would meet at such an unlikely place, but the war brought unique things.

"Looks real good, OPSO. You'll pick up some chicks with that. You're pimpin'," called a voice from behind us. I turned around and saw First Lieutenant Johnson, our intel officer, standing with Yap. Yap held two British rifles in his hands.

"Going hunting, Yap?" I asked.

"Yeah. I'm going to get the fuckers who got us yesterday."

"What?"

First Lieutenant Johnson stepped in. "Sir, the mission you and Wiz supported yesterday. Well, we had seven casualties. Five wounded, two dead. Fucking Ass-crack-a-stan."

"I hadn't heard. That sucks." I turned to AJ. "Hey, let's go. I don't feel good. I think I'm coming down with something."

As we drove back to camp, I watched the billowing clouds in the distance. They were dark, fat, purple clouds that rolled over one another. There was a chance I would make it. I decided that my promise was null and void given the recent news. The anger throbbed in my temples. We always arrived after the damage, when it was too late to do anything except look for revenge. I had been there, again, like before, Shkin. I was there with Wiz working with Hardrock 11, Hardrock 17, and Playboy 20. I heard their anger—desperation in their voices as Wiz and I scoured the hills. The F-16s were stacked on top of us. The Predators above them. The A-10s worked below us with the Apache gunships. All of us were doing the same thing we had done before, over and over again—hunt for the elusive enemy as it made its way back across the border. I pushed our fuel until there was no more time to give. We didn't find them. No one did. That was yesterday.

As I stripped off my flight suit and put on my running shorts, AJ prodded me. "I thought you said you didn't feel well."

"I don't." I grabbed my pistol. "I think a run might clear my head."

I took my usual route along the perimeter road next to wrecked Russian MiGs, T-62s, and APCs. I crossed the ditch and passed the second guard tower. As I reached the other side of the base, the dark clouds opened up. First it was just a few sprinkles, but then buckets came and with them bolts of lightning.

I tossed my pistol back and forth between my hands, counting the seconds between the flashes of light and the cracks of thunder—twenty seconds, sixteen seconds, eleven seconds. I picked up my pace. The storm's wrath increased. Eight seconds between flash and crack. I thought about taking cover, but there was nowhere to hide. Only open plains of minefields surrounded me.

It was appropriate. I had sought the showdown and God had answered. As the sheets of rain stung my skin, I no longer cared. I ignored the thunderbolts that cracked and broke the air in two. The loudness rang in my ears. I yelled but the storm smothered my voice. God had me in His sights. My arrogance and misplaced anger had finally pushed Him over the edge. His patience with me was through. I held the pistol tight in my hand, wondering when the lightning would strike. But I continued to run.

Then something inexplicable happened. I stopped. I turned and faced the stinging rain and looked across the Shomali plains, past the mud homes toward the towering peaks of the Hindu Kush. I imagined the river that my brother had once shared with me high in the sacred country, north of Taos. Suddenly I was thousands of miles away on the other side of the world, high in the Sangre de Cristo Mountains, where the Rio Costilla runs big and swift, and wild cutthroats swim in its blood. I was home. I closed my eyes and let the rain wash me clean.

The storm passed and the rain let up. I walked back to camp trying to savor the moment. As I approached the gate, two Marines standing guard eyed me. The younger of them spoke first. "Sir, are you all right?"

"Yeah, I'm fine," I lied. "Just went for a little run . . . in the rain."

The older Marine, standing with his M-16 cradled in his arms, let out a low, approving groan: "Urrrrrrh."

Nobody said anything as I walked back to my hooch. They looked at me, until I looked back. Then they looked away. When I entered my tent, I saw the wet wall above my rack. My improved patchwork had failed. I looked at the dark, wet wood, where the water had soaked through. It had run down the wall to the shelf, where it pooled and then overflowed onto my cot, soaking my sleeping bag, watering the fertile ground where the seeds of insanity were slowly growing.

30

SHAHI KOT VALLEY

"Gentlemen, you're supporting Operation Dragon Fury tonight. The 505th, part of the 82nd Airborne Division, is putting a bunch of guys on the ground in the Shahi Kot valley trying to round up some al Qaeda. Our guys are going to move out from Gardez and sweep east. Task Force Nibbio, the Italians operating out of FOB Salerno near Khost, are going to set up blocking positions in the passes to prevent the enemy from escaping." Jolly finished and handed me a folder with all the mission data.

"How long has the op been going on?" I asked.

"They went in this morning," Jolly said, before turning around to answer the phone ringing in the background.

Over the last month, I had flown missions with Stroker and Boss escorting convoys through the Gardez–Khost pass. The enemy was ambushing our convoys when air wasn't on station. Ground headquarters saw the enemy action and made a noticeable change in our strategy. We began bigger, more aggressive operations—"named operations." Instead of hunting individuals, we moved to control the terrain.

We knew Shahi Kot. Shahi Kot was where navy SEAL Neil Roberts and the soldiers and airmen who tried to rescue him lost their lives during the battle of Takur Ghar. To honor the fallen comrade, the ridge where Roberts lost his life was now called "Roberts Ridge." I was tired of seeing Afghanistan geography named after Americans.

The air slipped beneath my wings, pressing me up toward the heavens. I was glad to be free of the demons that haunted me below, especially the ones in my cot. I was alone in my cocoon—the center seat of the planetarium. I glanced upward and saw Vega at its zenith, highlighting the summer triangle. I searched for satellites. It gave me peace. Plath was right.

> *The night was only a sort of carbon paper,*
> *Blueblack, with the much-poked periods of*
> *stars*
> *Letting in the light, peephole after*
> *peephole . . .*
> *A bonewhite light, like death . . .*

But between my contemplations of the universe and time, I was what I was—a hunter. A hunter whose skills had dulled because he no longer practiced the intricate art of dive-bombing and gun firing.

It was all show. I knew that now. I also had discovered a man inside me I didn't like. A man focused on hate. I wanted blood—revenge. The towers, Flight 93, Sergeant Checo, the flights over Shkin where we never found anything: they had groomed it. I kept the hate in a safe place, where I fed it slowly, keeping it alive, waiting to release it—waiting for the chance. I thought of myself as a veiled vigilante, waiting to ride the pale green horse of death.

"Joliet 61, Warlord."

"Warlord, this is Joliet 61. Go ahead," I answered.

"Joliet 61, new mission. Proceed to whiskey, alpha, two-five-zero, niner-niner-five. Contact Hardrock 16 on Brown. How copy?"

Shit. Shkin! I knew it as soon as I heard the grid coordinates. "Joliet 61, copy all. Switching. Flight push Brown on the left," I responded while punching the data into the plane's computer. AJ and I established contact with Hardrock 16, who was en route from the safe house to the ambush site. We focused our targeting pods on the roads and searched for the enemy. We pulled our throttles back to conserve fuel. It was night and the chances of getting popped at altitude were minimal.

While I was looking out the left side of my cockpit, a bright flash suddenly appeared below and in front of me. I stared at the burning light that hung in the air. It wasn't moving. *Constant bearing—decreasing range. SAM!* I froze. After all my years of training, I froze. A second or two passed before

I hit the expendables switch and ejected decoy flares in the missile's wake. I yanked the stick to the right and pulled down in a beleaguered attempt at a break-turn. Because of my slow speed, the jet behaved like a fat cow being led to slaughter. I then realized I had put out the wrong expendables program—a pre-emptive program, not the one to defeat an airborne missile. I thumbed inboard on the decoy switch and showered the night sky with flares. I reversed back to gain sight of the missile.

It was still there in the same location, hanging in the sky. Why hadn't it closed? What was it? The racing of my heart and breath subsided slowly. Ten seconds later, I realized my mistake. It was an illumination round fired from the artillery at the Shkin FOB. My anger overrode all embarrassment. I was the tactics guru, the former MAWTS-1 instructor, the senior aviator of the squadron with all the experience and qualifications. I provided the instruction to the pilots. Yet, in a few seconds, I proved my value—I froze. Then when I did do something, I did the wrong things. I employed the wrong expendables plan. I didn't jettison my ordnance. I didn't maneuver my jet effectively. And I didn't call it out over the radio to warn AJ of the threat.

"Hardrock 16, Joliet 61. You guys firing arty down there?" I asked.

"Joliet 61, it appears so. Sorry about that. I never got the call. Can you guys hold to the north above the thirty-two forty line?"

AJ and I moved to the north and held. Our gas burned down as we waited to be called in. There was no sense telling AJ about my mistake until we landed. I didn't feel like searching anymore. I knew how it would end. I had been privy to it too many times. Except tonight I had realized my own incompetence. There was no one left to blame. For all my disgruntlement, the cause lay within. We orbited another hour until AJ finally used the word I wanted to hear. *Bingo.*

31

BONK

I lay naked on my rack, sweating despite the two fans blowing on me. Across from me, AJ slept in his cool sarcophagus. The air conditioner had arrived a few days ago. As with his other amenities, the TV and PlayStation, AJ had ordered them and had them shipped to Afghanistan. Because the Marines didn't have air-conditioning, I didn't want to buy anything they weren't issued. I was both stubborn and stupid.

AJ had installed the air conditioner the day before, when the sun blistered the hut. But AJ's air conditioner didn't have the power to cool the whole hooch. So he set it up for himself. He installed it in the cutout window and positioned it so it blew directly onto his rack. He then tacked lines on both sides of his rack that ran across the room, three feet above his cot. He draped sheets and extra blankets across the lines and completed his coffin. A cold box—a mausoleum in which he escaped with his earplugs and his night visor. And he slept. I heard his snores against the purr of the AC that fed cold air into his sanctuary, while I lay restless in the tent's suffocating heat. Two feet separated our racks, yet the difference in temperatures was that of heaven and hell.

I was no longer on days. I wasn't on nights, either. I wasn't flying with one person; I was flying with several—Boss, Stern, Stroker, JC, and Yap. A day flight one day, a night flight the next. Then two day flights followed by three night flights. There was no rhythm to my schedule but I refused to ask for favors. I took whatever Ops scheduled me. I thought pulling rank was a crutch of the weak.

I had reinjured myself and was convinced I had a hernia despite the prognosis of three doctors. Nevertheless, their direction was the same as Lieutenant Kreisberg's: "Lay off the PT." I had lost my last vestige as I followed their strict orders of not running. I also quit taking the zolpidem. It no longer worked. We had four months to go. I was hanging on. My last flight with Yap had convinced me that our strategy was doomed. We were too incompetent.

Yap and I had been escorting C-130s out of FOB Salerno the day before. The enemy was constantly shooting at the heavy, slow cargo aircraft, so they tasked the Harriers as escorts to protect the C-130s as they flew in and out of the hotly contested Khost Pocket. As Yap and I took the last of our gas at the tanker and prepared to pick up the next C-130, Warlord called us on the radio. Salerno was under attack.

The enemy had been sighted and a raid team was giving chase. Our timing couldn't have been better. A chance at revenge. A chance to fix something before the damage was done. Yap and I had a full load of gas and were only ten minutes from Salerno. As I threw the throttle into the corner, with Yap in trail, Warlord switched us to Salerno Tower. We were only five minutes out now. But Salerno Tower informed us there was a problem. The raid force chasing the enemy was Italian. No Americans or JTACs had accompanied the Italians as they gave pursuit. Salerno Tower said they couldn't understand what the Italians were calling for on the radio. The Americans didn't speak Italian and the Italians didn't speak English.

I thought I had seen it all in the Afghanistan AOR, but I hadn't. Yap and I landed and didn't bother to debrief. What was the point? As Yap poked a pin into the map denoting the mission we had just flown, Gunny Rodenkirk pulled me aside. "Hey, sir. We've been flying a lot lately, and well . . . do you think we're making a difference?"

That was yesterday. As I lay in my rack, I wondered why Rodenkirk had asked me that. Was it something in my body language or just coincidence? I told him honestly, "I don't know anymore."

The purr of AJ's AC kicked on again as my fans oscillated back and forth, blowing hot air onto me. I rolled over and imagined myself fly-fishing the cold waters of northern New Mexico.

The sleep came in fits, as the heat kept waking me. When I met Yap for the brief, I wasn't sure I was going to make it. I thought about canceling, but Yap brewed some coffee and forced me to drink several cups. I dreaded the upcoming dawn patrol mission.

Captain Mike "Yap" Trapp was a talkative former enlisted Marine who had previously served as an intelligence analyst. Yap was the kind of pilot I liked. He took to the books, studying the threat, memorizing the enemy radar frequencies and capabilities as well as the SAM systems and threat aircraft. He viewed the job as I did. It wasn't about being a jet jock—it was about being an attack pilot.

I briefed the sortie and felt better as the java kicked in. We launched and proceeded east toward Jalalabad and the Kunar valley. Looking south toward Tora Bora and Khost, huge billowing cumulonimbus rose upward, giant cotton balls stacked on top of each other. Every few seconds they lit up and glowed with bright flashes of light. The summertime light shows during the Afghanistan nights took on a rare, spooky beauty through the green glow of the NVGs. One second there was nothing but blackness, then the sky lit up as bolts of lightning arced across the clouds, illuminating the goliaths. I felt trivial as God flexed his muscles.

"Sir, it's a good thing we're not down there," my wingman stated.

I keyed the mike back. "Yeah, no shit. Khost is getting hammered."

It was a beautiful sight, though the grunts underneath the storm didn't feel that way. It was a perspective only pilots had from their warm, dry cockpits, looking God in the eye. Our fascination with the storm was interrupted by a call on the radio.

"Nightmare 31, this is Warlord."

"Warlord, this is Nightmare. Send your traffic."

"Nightmare 31, contact Hardrock 02 on TAD 61. Shadow requests an update."

"Roger, Warlord. Nightmares copy. Flight push TAD 61 on the right."

The CAOC had shuffled call signs for most players the previous week. Perhaps they were tired of being called "K-mart." The CAOC was now "Shadow." When AJ learned of the upcoming reshuffling of call signs, he requested that the Harriers be given the call sign we used back home. To my surprise, the CAOC approved the request and "Joliet" was changed to "Nightmare."

Yap and I established contact with Hardrock 02, who was colocated with Playboy 42 near the Khyber Pass. They were overlooking one of hundreds of spider lines used by al Qaeda to infiltrate from Pakistan. The enemy had set up more than a dozen training camps in the lawless Northwest Frontier province of Pakistan and had recently begun sending their operatives through to attack the Asadabad FOB. In response, we initiated "Operation Unified Resolve." Although it was planned as a joint operation with Pakistan, the Pakistani military had little power in this region. This was hard-line Pashtun country.

"Nightmare 11, Playboy 42."

"Go ahead, Playboy, this is Nightmare," I answered.

"Can you guys check out Nawa Pass, north of our position. Grid yankee, delta, zero-zero-one. Break. Four-five-zero. How copy, over?"

"Roger, we'll keep you apprised."

As we flew north, I aimed my targeting pod down on Nawa Pass. The enemy was now using the same route that Alexander the Great had taken some 2,300 years earlier. To the east, the lights of Peshawar's urban sprawl spread across the landscape. By contrast, the nighttime landscape of Afghanistan was a black void. I looked north and picked up a few faint fires that burned on the mountain slopes in the Kunar valley. Kuchis—nomadic herdsmen camping out for the night.

We were now in the third hour of dawn patrol. I hated the early morning hours before sunrise. The coffee had worn off. I no longer had the go pills. *If I could just see the first glimpse of light on the eastern horizon, I'd be all right.* Everything had become so monotonous. The missions were the same. The landscape was the same. The people never changed. Then it happened.

The smell of Piñon and Juniper. The shade of a tall Ponderosa Pine. Mayflies dancing on invisible Ferris wheels, while caddis scurried a millimeter above the water. The feel of the cold stream on my hands as I let the fish swim free. Where am I? Am I

*dreaming? I'm in my airplane. I'm dreaming of fly-
ing. Or am I flying?*

Ten seconds, possibly thirty seconds, maybe longer were missing. I really didn't know how long it
lasted, since there was no way to measure the lapse.
But there was no denying what had happened. As I
came to, a cold chill shot through my body—fear. I
realized where I was and what might have been. I let
out a loud, damning scream while my fists pounded
the canopy. I grabbed the pen attached to my knee-
board and stabbed it into my right knee. I did it
again. I needed to feel pain—any pain. I bit down
on my lip. Hard. Harder. I tasted the blood. I had
just made an unforgivable error and had somehow
emerged unscathed. Cold thoughts of death remained
as I tried to play off my mistake.

"Nightmare 32, how's it going over there?" I
called to Yap. I did not care to divulge my angst.

Yap responded immediately, breaking the night's
monotony. "Not seeing much. Just a few assorted
fires and no vehicles. How about you?"

"Same, Nightmare 32. Hey, I'm feeling a little
groggy up here. Do you mind if we chat for a while?
Can you tell me a story or a joke or something about
your family?" My request sounded corny, cheap,
void of any masculinity.

There was a long pause. Yap was unsure how to
respond. "Uh, sure, Nightmare 31." A longer pause
followed. "Did you hear about the American, the En-
glishman, and the Frenchman who were flying over

the Hindu Kush in an old beat-up DC-3?" Yap talked and brought me around while I placed dip after dip of Skoal inside my lower lip. The gum line on my lower jaw rubbed raw and bled before the purple and pink hues of dawn finally came.

After landing, I found the CO next to the maintenance hangar talking with some Marines. "Sir, can I get a word with you?" I asked.

"Sure, Zak. Go ahead."

"In private, sir."

Grouper turned and led me to the back of the hangar.

"Sir, I've got a problem. I'm not getting any sleep. I'm tired all the time and I'm fighting it in the cockpit. I can't fucking sleep and it's killing me. I need to come off the flight schedule for a few days and try to get over this thing."

Grouper stared at me with a puzzled look. "Sure, Zak. You OK?" he asked, cocking his head sideways in an inquisitive glance.

I dropped my head in shame and stared at my brown boots covered in dust. "Honestly, sir, I don't know."

"OK, Zak," he said, dismissing me. "Go rack out. I'll talk to you later."

I headed to my tent, my body aching of defeat. I was angry with myself. I never quit. I hated quitters. They were losers. But I had met my limits. Like in my first marathon, I bonked. And when I did, I bonked hard.

32

SWIMMING POOLS AND FIREWORKS

My body wanted more sleep, but my mind, after twelve hours of Daliesque dreams, desired something else—something normal, reality, a tangible action to remind itself it was alive. A shower and shave seemed a simple, doable compromise. I rose, grabbed my Dopp kit, and shuffled awkwardly to the shower. The razor pulled the hard, dry stubble off my face in long, painful scrapes. My trembling hand slipped and the blade nicked my chin. I felt the sting and paused. The red sliver grew. I dipped the razor in the stainless steel bowl of warm water, one of eight sinks in our communal shower, and rinsed it clean. Setting it down, I faced the mirror.

The blood oozed from the cut. I stared trancelike, mesmerized by the color. Despite my attempts to blot it, the claret sap quickly returned. I tore the corner off a paper towel and pressed it hard against my skin. Leaning over to examine the cut closely in the mirror, my gaze shifted to my eyes. They looked hollow. My torso drew back, surprised by the stranger in front of it. Wanting to look away, I stopped and forced myself to look—to stare into the bloodshot eyes before me. I did not like what I saw. I had to change. It wasn't going to be easy.

I picked up the bowl of water and carefully carried it to the corner, where I dumped the contents into a large barrel labeled BROWN WATER. Above the waste container, AJ's handmade sign still hung prominently: CHOSIN RESERVOIR SUCKS, a reference to the famous Marine battle fought some fifty years earlier and a small jab at what the Marine Corps had issued us for bathing. Most Marines believed the dingy showers were relics of another forgotten war—the Korean War. They looked that old, like part of the M*A*S*H movie set.

Dejected by what I had become, I returned to my rack and updated my journal. It bothered me that I had folded—quit. That I could no longer handle the pace. Someone else now had to pick up my slack. I grabbed my logbook and searched for clues.

Why had "I" failed? Me, the experienced officer, the competent tactician, the former MAWTS instructor, the runner, the triathlete, the 300 PFT machine, the Recon graduate, top 10 percent from OCS, honor grad at Airborne School and the Basic School, the iron-willed Marine who never quit. Was I the weak link? Was my ego so big that I couldn't see my weakness? Or was my weakness my ego?

The logic and reasoning in me wanted to explain it all away—to uncover the fault quickly as if it were some simple oversight in a mathematical formula that when corrected instantly transformed me into who I wanted to be.

Part of the problem I discovered in my logbooks. The rest of the elusive answer would come in time.

For the first five months of our deployment, I was on nights—the vampire schedule. Then, in mid-March, I came off nights and began two months of day sorties. In May I returned to nights but flew day missions as well. My circadian rhythm twisted into a Gordian knot as I never knew whether a day or night mission lay before me. By the end of June, my ninth month in-country, the mind-eating insomnia won and I bonked. As in that first marathon, I had believed myself stronger than I was.

Throughout the deployment I hadn't asked any favors from Ops, but I needed one now. I told AJ that I needed three days off followed by a week of day missions. If there weren't any day missions, it was better to leave me off the schedule. I needed to establish some regular sleep patterns. AJ's response: "No problem, Zak."

For three days, I did nothing other than sleep, eat, and read. As I slept, a catharsis took place. I dreamed of home—Katie, Caleb, the Sangre de Cristos and its rivers—the things I loved. During periods of consciousness, my mind churned on the person I was and the man I was not. My priorities and anger had been misplaced. A truce with God was in order. Maybe he wasn't all-powerful or all-knowing. Maybe he was doing the best he could given the circumstances. I wished that Joe was still around. He would be good to talk to, but he had gone home in May. His replacement was a youthful evangelist whose self-righteousness chided me. I needed to resolve the crisis myself.

It was early July. The air conditioners finally arrived, much to the relief of every Marine, especially those on night crew, who had to sleep during the hottest part of the day. Every tent got AC. I worshipped mine. Back home, block parties, barbecues, bikinis, and fireworks were heating up Americans' backyards, and we in Bagram decided to do the same. Base contracting had completed our headquarters building in June, which in reality was a large morale, welfare, and recreation (MWR) facility. Grouper had planned it that way despite the resistance from senior army officials. Because base contracting wouldn't build an MWR facility for the Marines—they deemed it non-mission-essential—Grouper and Wiz renamed the proposed project "Marine Headquarters Building." Base contracting then approved the project and built the building.

Once construction was complete, the Marines made the final additions, installing the TV sets, Ping-Pong table, foosball table, library, Internet computers, couches, chairs, Xboxes, and PlayStations. We then moved our operations department and intel shop from the base of the tower to the Marine Camp, placing them in the back of the headquarters building. Outside the headquarters building, in the center of the Marine camp, was the recently completed, greatest morale booster in Bagram—the pool. Other than the showers and outhouses, the Marine Camp looked little like it had when we arrived.

An American patriot had sent us a large aboveground swimming pool as gratitude for our service. Grouper wanted to go first-class with the pool, installing it in the ground and surrounding it with a large concrete deck. Unfortunately, base officials opposed the idea. They didn't want the Marines to have a pool because no one else had one, but Grouper ignored them. We offered a deal to our neighboring engineer unit. If they helped install our pool, they could visit and use it at their leisure. Using their heavy equipment, they dug a giant hole, installed our pool, and then helped us pour the concrete deck and build a wooden gazebo. When the base commander found out what we had done, he was furious, but it was too late.

To celebrate the grand opening of Devil Dog pool, we commissioned it on the greatest of all birthdays— the Fourth of July. Our resident chef, Corporal Young, and several staff NCOs cooked up a barbecue. Except for the absence of alcohol and fireworks (which came later), it was one of the best parties in Bagram. The Marines found their playful youth and everyone forgot we were fighting a war.

The pool wasn't heated, but it didn't need to be.

It was so damn hot, it felt great to jump into that cold, clear water. Lounge chairs were scrounged up. Inflatable pool mattresses were acquired. A volleyball pool kit even turned up. Once the pool opened, the Marines extended invitations to a select group of soldiers on Bagram—young, pretty females. The Devil Dog swimming pool became the hottest ticket inside Bagram's wire.

I finished my swim and grabbed a Coke from the fridge. Pulling a chair behind the wooden bar in our newly commissioned headquarters building, I plugged a set of headphones into the corner TV. I didn't want to bother the other Marines reading books, playing video games, or just relaxing—Marines who had no interest in what I had patiently waited all day for. It was the first mountain stage of the Tour de France. We all needed heroes and mine was a cancer survivor named Armstrong. Sipping my cold Coke and watching the riders duel, I transported myself miles from my physical location.

As the peloton began the final climb, I felt a tap on my shoulder. I turned around to see a tall, young Marine with a reputation of a prankster standing behind me. I removed my headphones. "Sir, I don't mean to bother you, but I think we're under attack," the Marine stated calmly.

I tuned my ears to the sounds around me. It was silent except for the jabber of Marines playing Ping-Pong. No sirens or loudspeaker warnings. I stood up to survey the rest of the building. Two Marines were playing Ping-Pong. Another Marine was reading a book in the library. Two Marines were on the computers. A small group of Marines were watching a movie in our makeshift theater. No one else showed any concern. "What do you mean, Lance Corporal Miley?" I asked.

"Sir, I think a rocket or mortar attack is taking place."

I paused and listened again but still didn't hear anything strange. I sensed a practical joke and decided to play along. "Roger that, Devil Dog. Probably ought to let the MPs know. Run down to the guard shack and ask them what's going on."

"Yes, sir," Miley responded, bounding away.

I returned to my hidden sanctuary, placing the headphones over my ears. I wasn't in the mood for games. Nevertheless, after ten minutes my curiosity stirred. I rose to see if Lance Corporal Miley had returned. The view startled me. The building was empty. "Aw shit!" I exclaimed, throwing off my headphones. Nobody other than Miley knew I was behind the counter, hidden in the corner. I ran outside into a night that was silent and dark. In the distance, the sound of pounding feet on gravel alerted me to an approaching figure. He ran by without pausing. "Hey, what's up?" I called out to the fleeting figure.

"Sir, there's been an attack. There was an explosion on the flight line," yelled the Marine over his shoulder. He then disappeared in the darkness.

I ran down to the flight line and found several Marines still working inside the hangar. Most had cleared out. I directed the remaining Marines to get their flak jackets and helmets and to proceed to the bunker. I told them I'd join them shortly. After the Marines left, I walked over to the avionics shop, where I knew there was a TV. It was still on. I changed the channel to the Tour de France and sat down. I figured the attack was probably over. That's how it usually happened.

The next day military officials issued a press release stating that a "suspected rocket attack occurred near the perimeter of Bagram air base . . . but there were no casualties or damage."* I don't know how they came up with "suspected." The enemy rocket flew directly over the Marine camp before exploding on the taxiway fifty yards in front of the Harriers. It was a lucky shot that almost found its target—a jet, the hangar, or worse, the Marine camp. Gunny Ewell, who was returning from chow, ducked when the rocket buzzed overhead. He laconically summed up the attack for me with a simple observation: "Sir, it was kinda scary."

As air force personnel hastily repaired the cratered taxiway the following morning, I headed to Bagram's force protection office with hopes of locating a recording of the attack. A high-performance EO/IR

* "Suspected Rocket Attack Near Afghan Base," Reuters, July 12, 2003.

camera suspended a thousand feet above Bagram by a small blimp provided constant surveillance for the base. The eye in the sky was supposed to deter attacks. As the soldiers searched through the recorded tapes, I watched the operator work the camera.

"Hey, Sergeant. Can you show me the Marine camp?" I asked. I was curious about how well the camera compared to our targeting pod.

"Sure, sir," the operator responded. As he zoomed in on our swimming pool, the burly sergeant murmured, "There she is—the blonde." Realizing his faux pas in the presence of an unknown entity, the sergeant looked back at me, unsure how to proceed. I smiled and winked. He then began a lengthy description of the women who frequented our pool (he had nicknames for all of them) and the glories of the female anatomy. I thought of Katie. We had three months left. Like the last three miles of a marathon, they now seemed doable.

33

SILENCE OF THE LAMBS AND KUH-E BANDAKA

The month of July brandished a cruel heat wave made more miserable by howling dry winds. The winds forced us to cancel sorties and roll them into GCAS on a regular basis. The air force, ensuring that no mission dedicated to support the army went unnoticed even if it never took off, tracked and reported our GCAS missions on a systematic basis—missions that never left the ground. Whereas XCAS ("airborne" on-call close air support) was a glorified version of flying around waiting for something to happen, GCAS ("ground" close air support—an alert condition that launched only when necessary) was a glorified version of sitting around hoping something didn't happen. Despite the weather and cancellations, the Marines' morale remained high. They could see the finish line and so could I.

The piles of paperwork that encompassed my duties as executive officer never subsided. I had led men my whole life. Now I led none. I was in charge of no one and no one thing. I was a sounding board for squadron policy who often disagreed with the delivery. I was a figurehead in a dispensable position searching for footing. Unhappy with myself, I set about to change. First, I quit worrying about all the things I couldn't control—all the things I believed we were doing wrong at the operational and strategic level. Second, I dedicated myself to helping those I could: Marines applying for promotion, officer programs, and those who wanted to raise their PFT score. I also realized my sole purpose in Afghanistan was supporting the lowly infantryman, the grunts I never saw but whose voices I knew well. Nothing else mattered.

As the summer wore on, our ground campaign shifted its focus inward and away from the Pakistani border. After operations Dragon Fury and Haven Denial, the 82nd Airborne Division, working alongside the Afghan National Army, launched Operation Warrior Sweep in the Zormat and Ayubkhel valleys. Launched on faulty intelligence, the operation failed to engage Taliban or al Qaeda operatives, though soldiers uncovered several large weapons caches. Caches with newly minted heavy-caliber weapons and MANPADS—handheld, IR, surface-to-air missiles.

Stroker and I were now paired together. The winds were calm and predicted to remain that way for the next forty-eight hours. It was a short hiatus from the shamals that plagued Bagram during the summer. When the shamals came, a wall of brown dust several miles wide and a thousand feet high engulfed Bagram, blocking out sunlight and turning bright afternoons into eerie evening scenes.

Stroker and I launched in the early morning darkness under a waning gibbous moon—dawn patrol. We proceeded south and began our circuit, checking out the safe houses below. A call from Warlord broke the night's silence. "Nightmare 31, this is Warlord with a request."

"Warlord, Nightmare 31. Send your traffic," I answered.

"Nightmare 31, Scorcher is on station and has some targets for you to check out. They would like to work with you on a discreet. Are you able?"

"Warlord, Nightmare 31 affirmative."

"Roger that, Nightmare. Contact Scorcher on Mauve 12."

"Nightmare 31, roger. Nightmare 31 flight, push Mauve 12 on the left," I announced to both Warlord and my wingman.

I punched in the new frequency and checked in the flight before contacting Scorcher. Scorcher was a new asset in the Afghanistan AOR—a J-STARS aircraft. It had been used in the Iraq War. Now that the major fighting in Iraq was thought to be over (that was the presumption in July 2003), the J-STARS arrived in Afghanistan with the return of the tankers and AWACS.

Like the large AWACS airplane, the J-STARS was a modified Boeing 707 commercial airframe redesignated as an E-8 Joint Surveillance Target Attack Radar System (J-STARS). While the AWACS tracked airborne targets, the $250 million J-STARS flew with a large crew that tracked ground targets. The crew in the J-STARS could track most ground targets as long as they were moving, though they couldn't discriminate the type of targets they were tracking. The J-STARS was designed to detect Soviet tanks pouring through the Fulda Gap into Western Europe at the beginning of World War III. Its application in the Afghanistan AOR was both questionable and unproven.

"Scorcher, Nightmare 31 up Mauve 12."

"Nightmare 31, this is Scorcher. I have you loud and clear. I have some work for you. Advise when ready to copy."

After pausing five seconds to ensure Stroker was ready to copy the information, I responded, "Scorcher, send it."

"Nightmare, I have several targets moving very slowly near the town of Zormat."

We had lost several soldiers at Zormat the previous week, resulting in a crackdown on that area. I acknowledged the call. "Roger, Scorcher. Standing by to copy grid."

"Nightmare, targets are located at whiskey, bravo, zero-five-zero, break. Niner-two-five. How copy?" the J-STARS controller asked.

I waited a few seconds to hear if Stroker had missed any part of the transmission. Silence was consent. After a short pause, I answered, "Solid copy, Scorcher."

I punched the grid into my jet's INS and commanded my targeting pod to stare at the designation. The target bore 140 degrees for thirty miles. I pushed the flight southeast toward the target area and set up a wagon-wheel orbit above the suspicious location. Nine months earlier, my blood would have sparked with an infusion of adrenaline, but I knew the game now. I wasn't expecting a lot, but I played along.

"Nightmare 32, what you got down there?" I queried my wingman.

"Nothing, 31," answered Stroker, who had the disadvantage of having only NVGs.

I looked over the canopy rail at the barren ground below, empty rural countryside. Slightly to the northwest sat a small town with a few twinkling lights. Inside my cockpit, the infrared image from my targeting pod revealed nothing. I zoomed out and spotted something to the east. I slewed the pod to the suspect image. The heat signature coming off the target was clear, though it didn't conform to any shape I was familiar with, vehicle or human. The target appeared as a small crowd. I looked back over the canopy railing to where the targeting pod was pointing but didn't see anything unusual through the NVGs. Regardless, the warm IR images in my targeting pod were unmistakable. Something was down there and it appeared to be moving slowly northwest toward Zormat.

"Nightmare 32, I've located Scorcher's target. Advise when ready to copy," I said, alerting Stroker.

"Go ahead, 31."

"North thirty-three, twenty-one-point-five-seven-zero, break. East zero-six-nine, zero-four-point-three-six-one. How copy?"

"Solid copy, 31," Stroker answered.

"Scorcher, this is Nightmare 31. We have several unidentified targets in the vicinity of north thirty-three, twenty-one-point-five-seven-zero, east zero-six-nine, zero-four-point-three-six-one. Break. Nightmares will continue to track," I stated, updating the J-STARS crew over the primary radio.

"Roger that, Nightmare. Scorcher will pass the information to Shadow."

Great. Fucking new guys. Our observations were now being passed directly to the CAOC in Qatar. It wasn't that I wanted to keep higher headquarters in the dark, but there wasn't a need to invite micromanagement. Some senior officer, sipping coffee, standing the midnight watch in a large air-conditioned building, just got his morning excitement. These were the same people who worked among rows of computers, surrounded by giant TV screens that portrayed live Predator video to UAV crack addicts—officers who stared at TV screens waiting for something to happen. Apparently it was addictive. Dano had given me the report after a trip to the CAOC a few months earlier. He had gone to open a better line of communication with higher headquarters, to advise them on things they could do to help us fight the war more effectively. He returned dismayed. His analysis was simple: "They sit around and watch live Predator video. Even when the UAVs are parked in the hangars, they watch the TV screens as if hoping for something. They watch live video of hangar doors. Doors that don't move. Occasionally maintenance personnel walk in front of the Predators' cameras and break the monotony of nothing. It's like they don't know what else to do."

I now expected a never-ending request for updates.

Stroker and I rotated back and forth to the tanker, leaving one jet overhead to track the target. The IR blob on my targeting pod was amorphous in nature, a giant amoeba changing its shape as it moved along the terrain. Perhaps a band of insurgents low-crawling in a ravine, hiding from someone—maybe us, the hunters.

Scorcher continued to ask for updates, prompted by Shadow, the CAOC back in Qatar. We had been tracking the targets' movements for two hours when the sky lightened in the east. We removed the goggles as the eastern sky turned orange, rendering the NVGs useless. After the sun rose, I switched my targeting pod's sensor from infrared to high-resolution daylight camera, which provided better clarity and target recognition. Viewing the target through the daylight camera, I began laughing. I should have known. Before I could say anything, Scorcher called us on the radio.

"Nightmare 31, Scorcher. I show a new target that bears one-nine-zero for ten miles from current target."

I looked to the south and spotted a vehicle moving north on a small dirt road approaching the area we were now holding above.

"Scorcher, Nightmare 31 has a tally. Will keep you apprised." I knew the CAOC was interested in what was going on. Stroker and I had been tracking this target for over two hours under the direction of the J-STARS aircraft. It was daylight now. Game over. The CAOC was expecting an update, and I gave it to them.

"Scorcher, Nightmare 31. New target is now moving at a high rate of speed closing on first target." My voice had emphasis. I was stirring the pot.

"Roger," responded Scorcher.

"Scorcher, target is a vehicle. Break. A truck. Break. The truck has now stopped at initial target location. Break. Two men are getting out of the truck. Break. Scorcher, two men are now resupplying the target. Over."

Scorcher, who was relaying the information back to the CAOC, was running with my story. "Say again, Nightmare, about resupplying the target."

"Roger, Scorcher. I repeat. Two adult males are now *re-sup-ply-ing* the target." Thirty seconds later, enough time so that I knew my previous transmission had been relayed to the CAOC, I resumed. "Scorcher, the men are throwing hay to the target."

"Nightmare 31, this is Scorcher. Say again, over."

"Scorcher, I repeat. Two adult males are throwing hay to the target." After another thirty seconds, I added, "Scorcher, the target is eating the hay. I repeat, the target is eating the hay."

There wasn't a response. No more requests for updates. Just silence. I imagined that Stroker was laughing but I didn't know. He too saw what was going on. We had spent the last two and a half hours tracking a herd of animals under the direction of a $250 million strategic asset. It was part of our absurd strategy of using the tools sent to fight the war rather than the ones we needed.

"Scorcher, the target is a flock of sheep," I stated, in case there was any confusion on the other end. I continued to provide updates on the target to Scorcher, who by the tone of their voice didn't think it was funny. Their reply was simply "Roger," but I didn't care. I was making the best of it now. Whatever was thrown at me, I'd just roll with the punches. I was over my quixotic ways of fighting windmills. I adopted the approach of Sancho Panza, Don Quixote's faithful squire. Now I just laughed at our stupidity, viewing the war and its ironies in dark, sardonic humor.

After completing our assigned ATO period, we still had forty-five minutes of remaining fuel. With clear skies and the best visibility I had seen in months, I offered Stroker what I had offered only two other pilots. "Nightmare 32, you wanna check out the peaks?"

"Sure. Show me the way," Stroker answered.

"Warlord, Nightmares are complete with Scorcher. Break. We're going to check out the area up north on our way home."

"Warlord copies. You're cleared Colorado."

I drove east until picking up the nefarious Kunar valley, just north of the Khyber Pass. Turning northeast, I followed the valley until reaching its juncture with the Pakistani border. In the background stood the Tirich Mir massif, the King of Darkness, a rock wall jutting upward. Its peaks covered an area of a hundred square miles, an island in the sky, the highest peak rising to 25,289 feet. Unfortunately, it was in Pakistan. Otherwise I would have flown toward it.

I banked left and climbed from 20,000 to 24,000 feet, pointing my nose at Kuh-e Bandaka, the promontory overlooking the Hindu Kush in northeast Afghanistan. At 22,349 feet, Kuh-e Bandaka was imposing. I had visited it twice before, once with Boss in October and again with Stern in February. The other flight leads did not like to venture this far north. I did.

As we neared the peak, the RADALT tripped, causing Bitching Betty to sing, "altitude, altitude," in her soft, disarming voice. It was her way of telling me I was less than 2,000 feet above the ground even though I was cruising at 24,000 feet. Stroker didn't say anything. He didn't need to. I knew he was thinking the same thing I was. The Montana mountain man was spotting lines and routes on the vertical faces and glaciers below. Since my last visit, the snows had retreated, revealing dark blue mountain lakes in the alpine valleys. The lakes reflected the color of the precious stones, lapis lazuli, mined high in the Hindu Kush, a pure, deep cobalt blue.

After circling Kuh-e Bandaka three times, I pointed the jet southwest toward home. Picking up the steep contours of the Panjshir valley to the south, I followed it back toward Bagram. I worked my targeting pod down the valley, scanning the thousands of tiny rock homes camouflaged in the mountainside cliffs. I rolled my Harrier up on a wing to get a better view of the past, passing beneath me. This was Massoud's land. Over the centuries, the valley's inhabitants had survived and flourished, isolated from the development of the civilized world. I remembered what Cow had said before we deployed: "How do you bomb someone back to the Stone Age when they are a stone's throw from it?"

Soaring above, I thought of the history below. In 329 B.C., Alexander and his army marched up the Panjshir valley before striking north through Khawak Pass toward Samarkand. The first-century Roman historian Quintus Curtius Rufus described the people and the landscape Alexander and his men encountered deep within the Hindu Kush:

Their huts they build of brick from the foundations up and because the country is devoid of timber (even the mountain range is bare), they employ the same brickwork right to the top of their buildings. . . . In fact, the snow cover is so thick on the ground and so hardened with ice and almost permanent frost that no trace is to be found even of birds or any other animal of the wild. The overcast daylight, which would be accurately called a shadow of the sky, resembles night and hangs so close to the earth that nearby objects are barely visible.*

Looking down from my Harrier, some 2,300 years later, I could see that little had changed in the Panjshir valley, and for that matter, in Afghanistan.

* Quoted in Stephen Tanner, *Afghanistan: A Military History from Alexander the Great to the Fall of the Taliban* (Cambridge, Mass.: Da Capo, 2002), p. 38.

34

EJECT

The magazine's pages were worn and torn. Some were missing. The cover had long since departed. The well-used magazine had been handed down and across the ranks and at some point it had been handed up, since I now had it. The lieutenant had lent it to me. It was property one never truly owned on a deployment to a war zone. It just traveled along, lent, traded, and shared by those lucky enough to encounter it. The magazine was a strange change from my poetry books and historical biographies. But it wasn't words that captivated me.

For the first time since my arrival in Afghanistan, I actually had *real* privacy. AJ had gone home a few days before for two weeks of leave. The hooch was mine. I listened as the winds gusted and beat the canvas tarp against the wooden walls. At least it wasn't raining.

My thoughts returned to the pictures in front of me. My nerves tingled and my heart quickened. It had been a long time. *And what was it about two women? I could lock the door and take care of business in a few minutes. The pressure gone, the stress removed, the anxiety displaced. What was wrong with that anyway?* Trying not to think about it, it seemed impossible to avoid, as if I were only delaying the inevitable.

A banging on my door instantly crushed my dreams. The door flew open, revealing a short, husky Marine in the darkness. He saw me lying in the rack, holding the magazine. "Sir, I think there's been an accident. I heard Captain Trapp yell 'Eject, eject, eject!' over the radio. He was waving Captain Bertagna." Sergeant Tompkins gasped for air. It was obvious he had sprinted to my hooch from Ops.

"Where's the skipper?" I shot back.

"Sir, he's having dinner with his old boss, the new CENTCOM commander, somewhere on the south side of the base. We tried calling him on his radio, but he didn't answer."

"OK, give me a minute," I said, tossing the magazine on the floor. Sergeant Tompkins looked at it and then turned away, allowing me to rise and adjust myself without further embarrassment. I was grateful that the interruption had not happened five minutes later. That ignominious call sign had already been bestowed on another in our squadron. I grabbed my pistol and pulled the door closed behind me. Despite my desire to run, I walked across the Marine camp to our headquarters building. I didn't need to fan the flames. I assumed the worst. *If we had crashed a jet, had we lost a pilot?*

As I stepped into the Ops shop, the officers and Marines paused and looked at me, as if I knew something they didn't. Jolly stood on the far side of the room, the mishap binder open in front of him. "Well, Jolly, do we have a mishap?" I asked.

"Don't know, XO. Yap was waving Stern when we heard Yap call 'Eject' over the radio," Jolly answered in direct, unemotional terms.

"Is Stern OK? What about the jet?"

"We don't know. We think Stern is OK. Yap said that he rode the jet into a minefield. Boss is still airborne. They are trying to figure out if the runway is clear."

"How much gas does Boss have?" I asked.

"Ten to fifteen minutes."

"Are you going through the mishap steps for notification?"

"Yes, sir."

"OK, let's assume we got a class A. Make the call to the safety center. Prep the OPREP-3, Navy Blue message, but don't send it out. I'll head out to Yap and check on Stern and the jet. Let's let Yap get Boss down, then we'll figure out where we are. Oh yeah, I assume you've already got someone looking for the CO, but if not, designate a Marine and find him." I turned toward Sergeant Tompkins. "You're with me. You're driving. Get keys for a vehicle and a set of NODs."

Sergeant Tompkins returned thirty seconds later holding keys and PVS-7 night-vision goggles. "Sir, do you want to drive?"

"You drive. I'll tell you where to go using the NODs," I answered.

Sergeant Tompkins drove blindly in the night as I directed his turns and stops across the darkened airfield. Within a minute, we pulled up next to Yap, who was standing next to Stern. "You all right?" I asked, leaning out my window. Stern stood expressionless. He was looking at the jet resting awkwardly on its wing. Its landing gear had been sheared off, crumpled beneath the flattened beast. "Hey, Stern, are you OK?" I asked again.

"Yeah, I think so. It just didn't want to stay on the runway. I tried as best as I could, but it kept veering to the right. So I shut off the motor when I heard the eject call and I just rode it out."

As the senior member of the squadron mishap board, I knew what lay before me. I grabbed the radio. "Ops, this is the XO. You up?"

"Go ahead, XO," answered Jolly.

"You can send out the Navy Blue. We definitely got a class A."

The C-130 pulled slowly into the Bagram taxi apron and parked in front of the tower. The pilots cut the motors and the back ramp dropped. I followed a group of thirty soldiers and seven Marines onto the aircraft. They were going home for one reason or another, some on leave, others for good, having completed their rotation. I was going with them, or at least part of the way. I needed a break. Warning signs had appeared again—impatience, insomnia, indifference. This time I heeded them. "Just three days out of this hellhole," I had told the CO. Grinning at my choice of words, he promptly approved my request. My refuge was Manas Air Base in Bishkek, Kyrgyzstan.

The C-130's props provided a soothing yet strange vibration as the cargo aircraft taxied out. I was accustomed to the whine and shake of the Rolls-Royce Pegasus in my Harrier. As we lifted off, soldiers near the small circular windows twisted their bodies around to glimpse a god's-eye view of their home, something I had seen hundreds of times. They were smiling. I closed my eyes and contemplated the recent past.

I had spent the previous week working endless hours on the mishap. But I was done with it now. Ripper had it. Major Tony "Ripper" Nerad had arrived the day before, assigned by the general to complete the investigation. Because it was a class A mishap, the senior member had to come from outside the squadron. I was glad about that. And though I didn't have to think about the mishap anymore, I did.

I felt bad for Stern. He was grounded until the investigation was complete. That would take several months, since the engineers had to analyze the damaged jet's nosewheel steering box. Only then would the mishap board make its final recommendations. Stern knew he was under the microscope—the caustic scrutiny that follows a crash, the analysis by many under tranquil conditions unencumbered by time as they determine what one should or should not have done in fractions of a second.

Stern had confided his story to me the day after the accident. He knew he was lucky to be alive. The jet had left the runway at high speed before smacking into a large dirt mound and stopping. Had the jet flipped or hit a mine, the investigation would have taken a different course, as it had with Rip, Pops, Gator, and so many others.

"XO, the winds were bad, so I opted to put the section on alert," Stern began. "But fifteen minutes later, the CAOC ordered us to launch because the enemy was shelling A-bad [Asadabad]. Boss and I showed up overhead and the weather was dog crap. Because of the blowing winds, visibility was shit. But I was still able to lase the target and bomb the enemy. I thought to myself, *At least our guys will sleep well tonight*. When I returned to Bagram, I knew the crosswinds were strong. I was looking out the side of my cockpit on the approach. On touchdown, the jet veered right due to a large gust. I tried to keep it on the runway, but every time I corrected left, the jet threatened to flip over. Once I left the runway, I shut down the motor and rode it out. I figured ejecting in those winds over the minefields was a death sentence."

It was chance. It could have been any one of us. Toby and Yap had grabbed me a week before the mishap and complained that the CO was flying when the winds were out of limits. The captains were upset by the appearance of a double standard, but all of us were pushing the envelope. July's heat and winds had been brutal. Despite having to cancel numerous missions, we were flying more in July than we had since our arrival in theater. The grunts needed us and we responded. The enemy had become more brazen in their attacks. They introduced a new weapon on the battlefield—an improvised explosive device (IED). The enemy no longer relied on simply planting Soviet mines in the roads. They were now making their own bombs and setting them off remotely with deadly accuracy. Ambushes became more common and began occurring during daylight.

A few days before the mishap, Stern and Wiz were supporting a ground convoy near Shkin. Insurgents attacked the convoy when Stern and Wiz refueled at the tanker. They returned overhead to hear the JTAC screaming over the radio, "We've been hit and have casualties! We need help!" With the soldiers hiding under their vehicles unable to provide a reliable GPS location, Stern did the only thing he could—he dove his jet to the deck and skimmed down the road until he spotted a small group of vehicles. The ecstatic JTAC screamed over the radio, "We are off your left wing—the enemy is off your right." Stern pulled up, rolled in, and engaged the enemy with his gun.

The attack stopped. Stern and Wiz remained on station until the medevac bird arrived and successfully evacuated the wounded. The next day Stern and Wiz visited their comrades in the hospital—soldiers who thanked the Harrier pilots for their lives.

Four days later, the mishap occurred when Stern crashed his jet after taking all the precautions one could. He was also returning from another mission in which he saved more lives. As Stern said, "All the tactical success of my last few missions came to an end when I took aircraft zero-four off the runway. Not everyone treats you the same after you've crashed an airplane. I had gained a lot of valuable experience and confidence after the ambush-strafing mission only to crash a jet ninety-six hours later. Talk about going from hero to zero."

35

VALHALLA AND A RETURN TO HELL

I awoke as the C-130 touched down in Bishkek. Stepping off the airplane into a cool breeze, I felt as though I had ascended from hell to heaven. Tall green fir trees swayed around me. After checking into an open-bay barracks and placing my bags on a lower bunk in the corner, I discovered "Valhalla," a pub aptly named by the local fighter pilots. My venture there seemed appropriate. In Viking mythology, Valhalla was home for dead warriors—brave souls who had fought gallantly but lost. I ordered a bottle of wine and drank several glasses before pulling out my journal:

I left Bagram this morning to get away for a few days. I'm tired, buzzed, and feeling strange. The world is different. It is more different than I remember. There are colors here—green and blue. People without guns. Civilian clothes. As I sit here drinking my glass of wine, I can't help but make the simplest observations. I look at the trees. They appear alive and healthy. They literally sway in the breeze, a joyous, playful dance. The pink clouds, long wispy feathers that float high, contrast softly against the blue sky. Like Afghanistan, there are big mountains here. Beautiful, big mountains. . . . There is green; there is life. It is now clear to me how barren and destitute Afghanistan is.

Bagram is hell. Afghanistan is the most desolate place on earth. That is clearer to me now. I close my eyes and I am there. It is a harsh, barren landscape and everything there reflects that nature. The trees that are alive do not appear so. They look like they are struggling for life. They do not appear healthy. Their branches and leaves are few. They are dirty, covered with dust. They do not sway in gentle breezes. They stand dormant in the oppressive heat or bend greatly in the strong winds that scar and disfigure them.

Life in Afghanistan is like the trees. It is harsh. It is not joyous and I no longer see the beauty that I once did.

I closed my journal as the sun slipped below the horizon. I savored the Merlot in tranquility as the coolness of evening set upon me. I felt I was in the most beautiful place in the world. Finally I walked to another club, where a younger, livelier crowd played pool, threw darts, and danced. A cacophony of languages engulfed me—German, French, Danish, Dutch,

Spanish, and Italian. Tight skirts, jeans, and halter tops accentuated female curves that swirled around me. My eyes desired the sweetness, but my heart resided in another place. I would be home soon. Stumbling back to my barracks, I flopped down on the steel bunk bed and its mattress. A mattress! I was in heaven. A bed never felt so good.

I stepped off the C-130 into Afghanistan's merciless heat and winds, later noting it in my journal as a "return to hell." I immediately sought Grouper to let him know I was back after a three-day escape. He was surprised to see me, believing I might have vacationed longer. I checked in with AJ, who had returned from two weeks in the States with his family. He wore a huge smile. I asked how things were going. Everything was the same. Nothing was new. Everyone was just waiting for September so we could go home. The strong winds were forecasted to continue for several days, so I called on a friend, accepting an offer he had proposed a month earlier.

I had met Wayne, a Naval Criminal Investigative Service agent, and Walid, a former mujahideen commander turned translator, in July. They worked at the Bagram Collection Point (BCP), where hundreds of suspected Taliban and al Qaeda persons under control (PUCs) were interrogated. Wayne had offered to give me a tour of the BCP when I found some free time.

Wayne greeted me as though we had known each

other for years. He introduced me to Sergeant Doug, who appeared to be in his early twenties. Wayne informed me that Sergeant Doug was going to interrogate a PUC later that morning. Wayne would give me a tour of the facility, and then we could watch the interrogation, something I had specifically requested.

I didn't know then what I know now, and it bothers me. During the time I was in Bagram, several Afghan prisoners were killed—tortured to death at the Bagram Collection Point. It happened in December 2002. It would happen again after I left. Perhaps some of the people killed were evil. Perhaps some of them were not, merely pawns in a game between more powerful players. Regardless, the blood stains our hands. At first, the American military denied the allegations, but after an investigation by the *New York Times*, the military confessed to the homicides in 2005. In one case, a prisoner named Mr. Diliwar, who had been chained to the ceiling and then beaten by "multiple soldiers," died after a few days of interrogation. The medical examiner stated in the official army report that "even if he [Mr. Diliwar] had survived, both legs would have had to be amputated."* But all this was unknown to me when I began my tour of the BCP in August 2003.

Wayne escorted me into the building, where I removed my gun and name tag, leaving them at the security desk. The BCP was located in one of the few

---

* Douglas Jehl, "Army Details Scale of Prisoner Abuse in an Afghan Jail," *New York Times*, March 12, 2005.

standing concrete buildings on Bagram. After coalition forces took over the base in 2002, the building, a former Soviet jet engine repair facility, was converted to a detention facility for Afghan prisoners under American control. Wayne took me upstairs to a catwalk that surrounded the interior of the building. Many of the guards were women. American flags hung prominently from the ceiling and on the walls. There was an American flag displayed in every room. I looked down from my perch to the prisoners below. There were several hundred of them, all in orange jumpsuits with three-digit numbers displayed across their backs. They were crowded into six large pens made from chain-link fence, each topped with barbed wire. There were approximately fifty PUCs to each large holding cell. Everything was transparent. Guards who walked the catwalks looked down on the prisoners and saw everything. Inside the open cells were old men and teenagers, some who looked like boys. It was not the enemy I expected to see. Many of them prayed aloud. Others sat in silence on the hard cement floor. Occasionally a guard ran up to the fence and shouted at a prisoner, telling him to quit looking around and not to talk to anyone.

We moved on to the solitary confinement cells, where hard-core prisoners were held. I peered through the windows and saw middle-aged men. They looked hardened, their faces chiseled. Their bodies were wiry but muscular, a sinewy appearance. They had dark hair and beards. Some of them had long beards, others short beards. None of them looked toward me. Instead they prayed.

Wayne led me to where Sergeant Doug was going to conduct his interrogation. After ten minutes of waiting, two soldiers brought a PUC into the small room. Dressed in an orange jumpsuit with shackles around his legs and hands, headphones over his ears, and taped-over goggles covering his eyes, the prisoner moved slowly with the aid of his escorts. Once seated, the guards removed the headphones and goggles and the interrogation began. The shackles remained on. The man was a Tajik, accused of being a driver for the Taliban. After fifteen minutes of the interrogation, I told Wayne I had seen enough. It was boring. He escorted me outside and we returned to his office.

"Zak, you know it's hard as hell to interrogate these guys," Wayne stated.

"What do you mean?" I asked.

"Well, our guys in the field bring these guys in, but they don't document exactly what they were detained for—they don't document the evidence. We're guessing in some cases, hoping they indict themselves. And there are so many of them." Wayne paused, looking at me to see if I was following. "Every time they go into the box, they get stronger and we get weaker. We need to break them early or we won't get them."

"What's up with all the old guys?" I asked.

"Zak, I'm gonna be honest with you." Wayne was from New York. He was in his mid-forties and had seen his fair share of things both on the street and in Afghanistan. His heavy New York accent gave greater punch to his words. "A lot of these guys just get swept up at the wrong place at the wrong time. Sometimes it's the result of a feud with a neighbor who turns them in as a Taliban sympathizer just to get rid of them. I'm going to tell you a story that occurred a few weeks ago."

Wayne stood up, poured us both some coffee, then sat back down. "We were interrogating this older Pashtun man from Zabul. It was fucking hot. You know. You live here. Well, during the interview the PUC kept looking down to a small fan in the corner of the room. The interrogator was having a hard time keeping the PUC on topic. Finally the PUC staring at the small white fan said in Pashto, 'That thing is amazing. What is it?' Clearly the old man had never seen a fan before. Ever! The young interrogator, now realizing he had something, ran with it. He was intent on showing the PUC how powerful the United States was and that it was impossible to resist the interrogation."

Wayne had me now. I moved forward and spilled the hot coffee on my flight suit. Stunning myself, I set the cup on the table. Wayne waited, then proceeded. "The young interrogator leans forward in his chair and tells the translator to tell the PUC, 'You know, we've put men on the moon.' The Afghan translator does as he's told and translates the interrogator's words to the PUC. The PUC just sits there without any facial expression and then responds with a slight nodding of the head, saying in Pashto, 'Sure. OK.' "

I sat back and gave Wayne a quizzical look. "I don't get it. What happened?" I asked.

Wayne laughed. "Zak, the old Pashtun didn't believe the interrogator or the translator. He just agreed with them to avoid any kind of hassle. It was over his head. Shit, 'men on the moon'? Hell, the old man hadn't even seen a fan before. There was no way he could believe men on the moon." Wayne rolled his eyes, shaking his head back and forth. "Sometimes I'm not so sure we're doing this right."

36

THEY KNEW WE WERE COMING

By the eleventh month, the rhythm of operations had become comfortable, and that was dangerous. But it wasn't only complacency we fought. There were other battles. Mine were sown from within. Perhaps it was my nature. Rhythm makes efficiency, and efficiency creates space, and space allows thought. And thought, when unencumbered by action, with too much time for its own good, grows like an unkempt vine that can swallow a person whole.

I sat in the large pillowed chair that AJ and I had acquired when we first moved into our new hooch, my journal and pen in hand. While the grunts clamored in their modern-day foxholes—outposts overlooking the Khyber Pass, the Korengal, Shkin—I read and wrote comfortably in a discarded air force cushioned rocker. I was updating my journal, or, to put it more accurately, I was philosophizing.

For as long as I could remember, I had been intrigued with the adventures of warriors and their bravery. I saw them as good men, noble, serving a higher station. I had studied well the history of war, schooling myself on the great captains, but it was the aviators who enthralled me—Richthofen and Rickenbacker; Bong, Boyington, and Boelcke; Foss, Yeager, Hartmann, and Galland. Those who survived to rise in rank forever remained operators, always on the front lines in battle. Their stories captivated me. Near-death escapes. Harrowing crashes. Their courage in the face of seemingly unconquerable odds. But one had to be careful what one wished for.

I had been in combat for eleven months, had flown over one hundred combat missions, and had over three hundred combat hours. Yet I had not dropped a bomb. Clearly, not what I expected. Though I didn't mind not having fired a weapon, I questioned my service. *Was I making a difference?* It was the intangibles one had to believe in for consolation. But intangibles were squishy. They lacked substance and created doubt because one *never really knew*.

A knock on the door broke my meditations. "Come in," I called out. Jolly pushed through the door and stepped into our wooden hut. His face bore concern, his brow furrowed.

"XO, you got to see this," he began.

I set aside my journal and pen, expecting something good. "What is it, Jolly?" I asked, looking up with a smile.

"Sir, we just got a high-side e-mail from the MAR-

CENT staff," Jolly answered slowly, tauntingly, shaking his head back and forth. He was referring to the Marine Corps Central Command. "They want *us* to review a force request for six AV-8Bs from September through December."

"No shit—"

Before I could finish, AJ was up from his desk in front of both Jolly and me. He started spewing forth.

"What the fuck do those assholes want? Are you sure it was through December, Jolly?"

Jolly turned toward AJ, who stood akimbo, his lips drawn tight over clinched teeth. Jolly resumed. "Yes, sir. It was through December and it was for six Harriers. Read the writing on the wall. Christmas in Bagram—again!"

"Fuck!" AJ yelled, stampeding out of the tent. Jolly turned and followed him, the door closing behind them. I reached down, picked up my journal, and read my latest entry. *AJ was right. I think too much.*

AJ went straight to the operations department and read the e-mail. He then typed out a detailed response asking politely what was going on. He also noted that we had been in combat for eleven months while every other Harrier squadron had served less than six months in Iraq. AJ pushed SEND and the electronic bits of ones and zeros that coded the e-mail into undecipherable garbage unless properly decoded went on its way—to higher headquarters. It was the equivalent of loading a shotgun with both barrels, sighting in, and firing.

The e-mail wasn't received well at MARCENT headquarters. Grouper, who hadn't seen the e-mail before AJ sent it, was upset, and rightly so. It was the CO's prerogative to respond to these issues and no one else's. AJ knew he was wrong, but that didn't stop him from speaking out. The "I don't give a shit" factor was directly proportional to the amount of time spent in a combat zone. As AJ's e-mail stirred the pot, I found Yap to discuss our upcoming mission. We were scheduled to support an air assault in the Gayan valley in a few hours.

While the temperatures of August soared without reprieve, so too did the action. The 82nd Airborne continued its large-scale operations, coordinating their efforts with Special Forces teams deployed throughout the area. The focus was our lines of communication, the roads between Bagram and the eastern FOBs: Gardez, Salerno, Khost, Orgun-e, and Shkin. Roads that were often mined in the narrow mountain passes where ambushes were common.

The Gayan valley was notorious bad-guy country infested by al Qaeda as they infiltrated from their sanctuary in Pakistan. The most notorious ratlines originated in Wana, part of the tribal areas and the source of many foreign fighters entering Afghanistan. Located twenty miles southeast of our FOB at Orgun-e, the Gayan valley stretched twenty miles in length. Bordered by Lwara in the north and Shkin in the south, the Gayan was a wicked area controlled by hard-line Taliban sympathizers.

With visibility only a few miles, Yap and I took off into Bagram's summertime scud layer, a product of smoke from burning shit and the fine, talcumlike soil of Afghanistan whipped up by frequent shamals. The dust hung in the atmosphere, taking days to return to earth. The two combined for an obnoxious haze that stung the eyes.

We proceeded east until reaching the Pakistani border, setting our CAP at 24,000 feet above the valley. Yap's jet didn't have a targeting pod, but he always carried a set of binoculars. I had no idea how critical those binoculars would become. I directed Yap into a counter-rotating CAP so that one jet was always "hot," pointed toward the targeting area. Taking turns refueling at the tanker, Yap and I traded updates, I through my targeting pod, Yap using his binoculars.

Tiny mud compounds, dirt roads, and a haphazard scattering of crop fields in various sizes and shapes marked the valley below. No doubt some of them were *Papaver somniferum*, opium poppy. The village appeared like any bucolic setting on a hot summer day—sleepy. It was a ghost town. Everyone was either gone or inside their adobe homes seeking shelter from the relentless sun.

Three compounds had been identified as suspect locations. I worked my targeting pod over each but scanned the nearby countryside as well. The homes, fields, and roads sat idle. No people, no animals, nothing. We had arrived on station an hour before the insert to provide an update to the helos before they landed. Specifically, they wanted to know if the LZs would be "hot." We had been holding forty-five minutes when the ground suddenly stirred below.

One man, then another appeared in the center garden of the northern compound. A boy emerged from the northern compound and ran south to the center compound. Another boy emerged and ran from the center compound to the southern compound. All three compounds were now swarming. Then I heard the call. "Nightmare 11, this is Warlord. The package is airborne."

"Roger, Warlord. Nightmares copy." The helicopters at Orgun-e were lifting off. The frantic pace below picked up. It was as though someone had stuck a stick into a seemingly dormant anthill. Children climbed the mud walls and positioned themselves on the corners of the compound, looking outward. They were watching and waiting for something—us. Men with shovels worked frantically in the gardens. Doors flew open. Women in burkas shuttled quickly back and forth, appearing and then disappearing from sight. Men ran wildly about, all doing something with a purpose. What before had appeared as an abandoned settlement was now a seething, active hive. Then something strange happened.

As I passed overhead, the ants scurried away, hiding under trees or in shadows next to tall walls. I had been spotted. Once clear of the target area, the bustle returned. The people emerged from their cloaked settings and resumed their feverish activity, but the 32x magnification of my targeting pod allowed me an unprecedented view even when I wasn't directly overhead.

"Nightmare 11, this is Hardrock 01. Airborne as fragged. We're ten minutes out."

"Roger, Hardrock. Nightmare has a solid copy. Be advised. Your surprise party has been canceled," I responded.

"Say again, Nightmare."

"Hardrock, your surprise party has been canceled. They know we're coming. Expect a hot zone."

Ten minutes later the helos began their approaches to their respective landing zones. Six CH-47s set down simultaneously, dropping their ramps in unison. Out poured soldiers like ants infiltrating a neighboring colony. They swarmed toward the compounds in organized groups, moving in leaps and bounds so that one element always provided cover for the next element. They reached the compounds and entered with relative ease. The second wave of helicopters began their approach. Then we picked up a distress call. Five miles to the south, Foxtrot 13, a Special Forces team, had been hit.

Yap and I watched the AH-64 Apaches dip their noses and speed hastily away. Because the TIC was only five miles southwest of the Gayan valley, Yap and I adjusted our CAP so that we could cover both the helo assault and the TIC in the south. The Apaches circled a small knoll while a Black Hawk landed and discharged the quick reaction force (QRF). Soon the QRF team leader reported they had found several caves hidden under the sparse vegetation, but no enemy. I was now well accustomed to the fact that the enemy possessed magical powers. They could disappear easily, even in the middle of the day when surrounded by four hundred men.

I knew we were going to drop. I felt it in my gut. I was an arrow drawn deep in the bow. The bow's string was incapable of doing anything else other than letting me seek the revenge I had long since harbored. But it didn't happen. The enemy vanished as quickly as they appeared—an apparition that transformed itself like the Afghanistan shamals, appearing out of nowhere, wreaking havoc, and then disappearing without a trace.

Yap and I remained on station taking turns hitting the tanker, so that one was always overhead—circling, waiting. We even extended our ATO period forty minutes, but the time came to return the jets for the next launch. After landing and exiting our cockpits, Yap and I just looked at each other, stunned, amazed with the enemy's seemingly endless bag of tricks—the desolate, poor, austere foe that at first glance was so easy to underestimate. We theorized what happened.

As we held overhead, the town slept. But when the Chinooks, Black Hawks, and Apaches lifted off from Orgun-e, the word went out. How the enemy communicated something that quickly, to the minute if not to the second, remains a mystery. We guessed the enemy used cellular or satellite phones to communicate. Maybe they had a source in the Orgun-e FOB or someone outside watching the action and warning of the coming invasion. It's difficult to hide a four-hundred-man air assault.

The enemy may have never known we were heading to the Gayan, but maybe they didn't need to. Perhaps every outlying enemy sanctuary was notified that some sixteen helos had lifted off out of Orgun-e at 1300 hours and were heading southeast. Regardless, one thing was clear: they knew we were coming, and it wasn't Afghan versions of Ozzie and Harriet living in that valley. There were some bad people down there.

37

UNLIKELY BUT POSSIBLE

A few days after my mission over the Gayan valley, the visitors arrived. The assistant wing commander, a one-star general, came to motivate the Marines. We held a formation, after which the general asked the Marines to gather around so he could talk to them personally. He told us what a "great job" we were doing and that we were giving a "great name" to the Harrier, which had always been "unfairly criticized" by the press. The general was a nice man but he came across as a deflated basketball—no bounce. Then he dropped the bomb. He told the Marines that there was a force request for six Harriers in Afghanistan through December, but he added it was unlikely the Marines from VMA-513 would fill it—"unlikely but possible." At least he told the truth.

I looked around the crowd. There wasn't one Marine who believed him. The Marines no longer trusted the senior leadership. It was etched in their faces. When the general opened the floor to ques-

tions, every question challenged the supposition that
we'd be going home in a month and not staying in
Bagram through December. From my seat it appeared
funny, then uncomfortable, and then embarrassing.

"General, why won't they send an air force squadron to replace us?" a young corporal asked.

"Well, we're looking at that. We're looking to see
who can replace the Nightmares," the General responded confidently.

"General, why would they keep one Harrier
squadron deployed for fifteen months when none
of the other Harrier squadrons have been deployed
more than six months?" a lance corporal followed.

"Well, that's why I said, we're looking at that,"
the general answered curtly.

The general continued taking questions and the
Marines kept addressing the same topic: "When will
we be going home?" Each Marine seemed unsatis-
fied with the previous answers. It wasn't just the junior enlisted. The staff NCOs followed the same line
of questioning. The "I don't give a shit" factor was
once again directly proportional to the amount of
time spent in a combat zone. The officers kept silent,
watched, and listened. I was enjoying the bludgeon-
ing when I saw the CO get fidgety. What was he to
do? He wanted to stop the Marines from pursuing
a line of questioning that appeared more like a hundred prosecutors badgering a feeble witness. But the
CO didn't want to embarrass the general by inter-
rupting the line of questioning he was allowing.

With each answer the general tightened the noose around his neck, to the point of getting frustrated at the Marines, snapping at them. The gallows door swung open and the rope pulled taut, though it appeared the general didn't know it. It was as if the fall didn't break his neck. I watched him gasp and choke while his feet kicked in the air, his body swinging awkwardly back and forth, his voice rambling on, pitching higher as if his words would forgo his fate. An uneasy feeling settled upon me: fontrum, that uncomfortable emotion when someone embarrasses themselves so much, you become embarrassed for them. Finally it ended. *Thank God.*

The general left the next day. He had only been the messenger. Higher levels were arguing whether the Harriers stayed in Afghanistan. It appeared to us a game of chicken between the air force and Marine Corps. As time went on without a definitive answer, we knew we'd be the losers since we were already in place.

Before the general left, one of his accompanying staff left me a gift. Lieutenant Colonel Michael "Curly" Kozik, a bald-headed former Harrier pilot whom I had known and worked with over the years, had traveled from Iraq to visit his Harrier brethren in Afghanistan. Back in our hooch, Curly reached into his helmet bag and pulled out a gallon of Jim Beam. He handed it to me, smiled, and flicked his eyebrows with an innuendo that we should open it. I stood dumbstruck. Except for my three-day escape to

Kyrgyzstan, I hadn't drunk any booze since arriving in theater some eleven months earlier. Curly said that despite the restrictions in Iraq, most pilots there had their own stash and regular "cocktail" hours. I was better off living in ignorance.

But Grouper had specifically endorsed the "no booze" policy of Bagram, something most other units ignored. AJ and I respected the CO's decision though we both wished otherwise. I placed the bottle underneath my rack and told the CO about it the next day, lest someone else tell him first. He smiled and politely told me, "Keep it there—unopened."

After the general's departure, the CO and Boss were directed to support a SEAL team near Lwara. The target was near the safe house we had abandoned in December. Even though we had left, al Qaeda and Taliban hadn't. The SEAL team, emplaced to provide an overwatch on the ratlines coming from the tribal areas, reported Pakistani border guards were aiding the enemy. Having tracked several militants to a small outpost near the border (militants who had just attacked FOB Orgun-e), the SEALS cleared the Harriers on the target. Grouper rolled in and squeezed the trigger. The GAU-12 Gatling gun burped out a hundred rounds in a two-second burst.

Reviewing Grouper's tape in Bagram after the mission, the gun runs appeared flawless. The outpost, a shack on top of a hill, ignited in a hail of bullets. Men scrambled out of the shack, tripping over each other, pushing each other down as they literally jumped off the side of the mountain trying to save their own lives.

Boss was unable to line up on the target following Grouper's attack, so Grouper rolled in again, squeezing off another hundred rounds, peppering the shack once more. Malice, the SEAL team, now wanted the Harriers to bomb what was left of the small outpost, though it was unlikely anything in the tiny shack was still alive. But if the guys on the ground wanted it, we provided it.

Grouper designated what was left of the small outpost with his targeting pod and then pushed the bomb "pickle" button releasing the thousand-pound laser-guided bomb toward its destiny below. But Grouper made a mistake. Out of habit when he pulled off target, Grouper "safed" his master arm switch, which effectively killed the laser and caused the LGB to go stupid. The bomb landed harmlessly in an empty wadi short of the target. Grouper was honest about his mistake, since it was impossible to hide it when he showed us the tape. Then someone noticed something else. "Sir, you dropped without a cleared hot." It was true. Grouper had committed a cardinal sin in the attack community. Fortunately, no friendlies were hurt and the result was only slight embarrassment and the cost of one keg of beer at the next squadron party.

They were simple mistakes, which might have been prevented had we been allowed to train realistically. After eleven months of not dropping a bomb, it was no surprise that some pilots, even the most senior and experienced ones, made simple mistakes when asked to do something in which they were no longer proficient. Thankfully, those mistakes didn't hurt anyone, but that wasn't the end of it.

We received the news that afternoon. The Pakistani government lodged an official protest against the United States, saying the attacks resulted in the deaths of two Pakistani guards and injury to a third. A Pakistani official stated, "It was due to some misunderstanding," while the U.S. Central Command added, "The incident resulted in the unfortunate and unintended engagement of Pakistani security forces in the area."*

Once again I failed to understand the political correctness of our leadership. *What misunderstanding and unintended engagement?* The SEALs didn't have any misunderstanding. There was a legitimate target, it had been properly identified, and then "intentionally" engaged. And to my satisfaction "killed." Nevertheless, an official investigation was initiated. Since I was junior to the CO, I was prevented from conducting the investigation, much to my relief. It was assigned to an air force colonel who quickly surmised the Harrier pilots had acted appropriately.

Two days later, AJ and JC dropped near Khost. A Special Forces team on patrol came under mortar fire

---

* Bradley Graham, "U.S. Forces Kill Two Pakistani Border Guards," *Washington Post*, August 12, 2003.

and requested assistance. AJ and JC had just taken off and were immediately directed to the area. AJ later described the situation as "kind of crazy." AJ established contact with the JTAC, who then tried to talk AJ onto the target. But AJ couldn't understand the JTAC's directions or description of the target. Finally the JTAC, frustrated and under fire, directed AJ, "Fire over there!"

"Fire over where?" AJ responded. AJ demanded a grid and finally received one. Then he bombed the grid, which he described as a collection of "trees and bushes." JC did the same. Fortunately, the enemy broke contact and the Special Forces team withdrew to the safety of Khost.

Reports the next day stated that one hundred suspected neo-Taliban and al Qaeda fighters had attacked an Afghan army outpost near Khost.* Fifteen enemy and five Afghan soldiers were killed. One enemy attacker was captured. It was suspected that five of the fifteen killed and the one captured were Arabs—foreign fighters, al Qaeda. As the scorching heat wave of August continued, it appeared to me an omen. And I feared its sign of things to come.

---

* Kimberly McCloud, "Twenty Killed in Attack on Afghan Border Post," *Afghanistan Report*, August 14, 2003.

38

AMBUSH AT ABDULLAH KALAY

The wind blew hard for three days as a front struggled through. Then the rains came. They were strong but brief, and once again my roof leaked, but I no longer cared. I conceded defeat and discovered an inner peace as I watched the rain seep through my ill-fated repair and run down my wall. While the rain fell, I sat in my chair, updated my journal, and thought. It was my mission over the Gayan that bothered me. Filled with hate, wanting blood, revenge, but unable to get it. Now the storm was cleansing me, again.

I decided I no longer wanted to drop. In fact, I hoped I wouldn't. It seemed silly at this point. It was wrong and selfish and I knew it, but I just wanted to go home. I longed for Katie and Caleb. I wanted to be a father again—present, loving, comforting, anonymous. Nevertheless, I had my role as XO and I did my best to carry it through, "acting," as one former CO had previously emphasized. I didn't see the value then, but it seemed appropriate now. The storm finally passed and purged the putrid funk that hung over Bagram like a mildewed drape. A deep blue sky and unrivaled visibility called to me. This was flying weather and there was always solace airborne.

"XO, here are the freaks," Yap stated, handing me the assigned frequencies for the upcoming mission. "It's supposed to be the French FAC 'Disney' and a couple of Germans." The mission was a training sortie in the Big Cat range, the "official" training range for pilots in Afghanistan in which pilot training was anything but. We could have accomplished the same amount of training on the ground since it was more of a comm drill than anything else. I didn't care for Big Cat sorties, but flying was flying and that was the mission we were given.

"Thanks, Yap," I said, taking the sheet of paper. "I tell you what: I let you lead the last sortie. I'll take this one. Let's brief in twenty, if that's OK with you."

"Sure, sir. I need to push out a quick e-mail regarding our after-action report. I'll meet you in Ops." Yap turned and walked away, while I gathered the maps, cards, and notes and prepared for our brief.

"Nightmare 63, Tombstone. TIC in progress. Grid, four-two, sierra, break. Tango, bravo, break. Four-eight-eight, break. Zero-seven-eight, break. Contact Playboy 33 on TAD 33 or TAD 68. How copy, over?"

I waited a few seconds to see if Yap missed anything. When he didn't respond, I acknowledged, "Solid copy." Yap and I plugged the information into our jet's navigation systems and confirmed the target location as we taxied out. "Nightmare 63, alpha check. Two-two-zero for two hundred miles?" I queried my wingman.

"Nightmare 64, concur," answered Yap.

The target was located in southern Afghanistan, in the rocky, dry, inhospitable part of the Hindu Kush. Maybe we weren't heading to the Big Cat after all. I reviewed the brief in my head and was glad that I had covered real mission contingencies. After taking off, Warlord harangued us on guard frequency, telling us to contact them immediately. Once clear of Bagram, I switched the flight to Warlord. "Warlord, this is Nightmare 63. Send your traffic."

"Nightmare 63, this is Warlord. Contact Boar 63 on TAD 61. They are currently working with Playboy 33. TIC in progress."

"Roger, Warlord. Solid copy. We got the grid from Tombstone. Break. Request you reposition our tanker to the Perseus track."

"Roger, Nightmare. We'll pass the request to Shadow."

Even the large AWACS was only a pawn. The boys in Qatar called all the shots. The Poseidon track was 150 miles from the target area, while the Perseus track was a hundred miles farther south and thus closer to the TIC. In the event things were happening, we'd have to travel a long way to refuel, wasting precious minutes of support. While I waited for Warlord's response regarding my request, I called for the flight to switch to TAD 61 on the back radio. "Boar 63, Nightmare 63, you up this push?"

"Nightmare 63, this is Boar 63, affirmative. Go ahead."

"Boar, Warlord directed Nightmares to contact you this push. They said you were working with Playboy 33 on a TIC. Send us an update when able."

"Nightmare, this is Boar. We're currently working with Hardrock in the vicinity of Shkin. Negative on Playboy. Negative TIC."

"Roger, Boar. Thanks. Nightmares, push tactical on the right." I paused a few seconds and then continued. "Well, Yap, what do you think?"

"Sir, it's not surprising Warlord is clueless. Let's push south to our grid and see if we can raise Playboy on TAD 68."

"Yap, you're going to make a good flight lead."

"Sir, the way you've beat me up, it's only fair."

"Touché."

Yap and I flew down the eastern side of the Hindu Kush making calls in the blind to Playboy 33, but there was no answer. I looked west at the parched, boulder-strewn land, void of vegetation, where every living thing competed for the scant water that appeared only in the valleys. I thought to myself of the hellish existence below. *How does one survive in such a godforsaken land?*

Thirty minutes later, as we approached the target

area, Playboy 33 responded. The JTAC quickly gave us an update. He was part of a thirteen-man Special Forces team that had split into three elements. His element consisted of himself and one other soldier. He was pinned down taking fire from the west, but his concern lay elsewhere. The headquarters element was several thousand meters to the north, while a third element, Mustang 56, was pinned down in the southwest. Each element was reporting fire from a different direction. Playboy directed me to contact Mustang 56, whose situation appeared worse. Yap and I worked with what we had.

"Mustang 56, this is Nightmare 63. How copy?"

"This is Mustang 56, over. Say again your last. We're taking fire, over."

I knew immediately I was talking to a soldier unfamiliar with close air support operations. I leaned forward, hoping to help him. "Roger that, Mustang 56. This is Nightmare 63, a section of AV-8s. We're loaded with six hundred rounds of twenty-five mike-mike and several LGBs. We have forty minutes on-station time before we need a drink. Talk me onto your position or the enemy."

"Uh, Nightmare, we're being shot at, over. Nightmare, they're firing at us from the west and north. Break. From the high ground, over. How copy, over?"

I slowed down the conversation, trying to ease the burden below. "Mustang 56, this is Nightmare. Roger, copy all. Break. Can—you—give—me—a—grid?"

"Uh, Nightmare, this is Mustang, unable grid. I don't have a map, over. I can't keep my head up long enough to give you a talk-on. Break. We're getting hit pretty hard down here, over. Nightmare, we're in a valley, shit, get down, get down—"

Mustang's voice ceased, but the transmission key held down by the soldier below allowed us to hear the flurry of gunfire. A few seconds later, the voice returned.

"Nightmare, this is Mustang 56. We're receiving some pretty heavy fire here, over. The enemy is on a ridgeline to the west. Grid eight-zero-zero-one-zero-zero." The grid later proved wildly inaccurate.

"Solid copy, Mustang. I read back, eight-zero-zero. Break. One-zero-zero. Talk my eyes onto the enemy," I said, hoping to reassure him things were going to be OK. "I can use my gun once I get my eyes on the target. Work with me, Mustang." I circled the grid as the cacophony of machine-gun fire and explosions rang in the background of Mustang 56's broken, stammering voice. Then it happened.

I couldn't see it, but I knew. Yap knew because he heard it. The tanker crew monitoring our comms knew. All of us airborne knew, but Playboy 33 and the commander of the Special Forces team did not. Their radios masked by the terrain could not hear Mustang 56—the fear, the panic, a din of gunfire as Mustang 56 held down the mike key. There was the word *Nightmare,* the only coherent word, then cussing, screaming. Then silence.

There was no stopping or slowing of time. There was no anger, sadness, or hope. There was no thinking or debate. There was no fear, except that of failure, and it ruled large. Emotion carried me forward. I rolled my aircraft upside down and pulled sharply on the stick until I was in a steep dive pointing at the ground below. My heart raced while I struggled to swallow. Suddenly my throat was parched. I was afraid—afraid of failing as I had seen done so many times before, only now I was here, first. I was terrified they were dying on my watch. While I couldn't see their death, I felt it. I knew. Nose down and gaining speed, I keyed the mike and tried to make a supporting call. "Mustang 56, stay with me. Don't lose me now. Call visual my position—" I choked on my own words.

The call went unanswered but I had begun the dive so there was no reason to stop it now. *Come on, stay with me. See me. Come on, I know you see me. Call visual, Goddamn it, call visual! I'm right here . . . Come on, c'mon, c'mon . . .* I kept repeating the words to myself as I flipped my expendables switch, punching out a string of burning flares. My jet zipped through the narrow valley as a stream of flares came off my back end. I was scraping rocks. Steep ridgelines flanked my right and left sides as I snaked low in the valley, yanking back and forth on the stick to avoid a predictable flight path.

Nothing. No radio calls. Perhaps it was already over. I was too late.

At the north end of the valley the ridgeline to my east and west pinched together. A prominent peak rose vertically in front of me. I pulled back on the stick and climbed the mountainside, keeping a few hundred feet between me and the granite. Once I cleared the mountain peak, I flipped the jet back to the south and again dove my airplane into the valley. My left thumb pumped the expendables switch, jettisoning the flares, highlighting my position for miles. At the south end of the valley, I yanked back on the stick and shot like a rocket upward to 20,000 feet, converting the 500 knots of airspeed to the safety of altitude. "Mustang 56, this is Nightmare. Are you there?" Nothing. I paused in sadness, alone.

"Nightmare, this is Mustang. The enemy has stopped firing. We're withdrawing to the east. Thanks for your help."

I didn't know whether to laugh or cry. Breathing a sigh of relief, I now wanted the enemy, but it wasn't blood or revenge. This was different. "Roger that, Mustang. Where is the enemy?"

"Uh, Nightmare, we're withdrawing. You're cleared to RTB. Contact Playboy."

Somewhat confused, I realized that Mustang 56 and his team had gotten the break they needed. They were leaving as fast as they could. "Roger, Mustang 56. Break, break. Playboy 33, this is Nightmare 63. How copy, over?"

"Nightmare, this is Playboy, go ahead."

"Playboy 33, Nightmare has provided a show-of-force pass. It appears the enemy has broken contact. Break. Mustang 56 is withdrawing to your position. Break. Would you like us to remain on station? Over." I was even beginning to talk like a grunt on the radio.

"Nightmare, this is Playboy. That's a big affirmative. Remain overhead!"

"Roger that, Playboy," I acknowledged. Yap and I held overhead as Playboy talked us onto his position. After thirty minutes, we needed gas. "Playboy, we're going to cycle aircraft to the tanker and keep one of us overhead for support. How copy?"

"Solid copy, Nightmare," Playboy answered.

"Nightmare 64, you got TAC lead while I get a drink."

"Roger, 63. I got the TAC lead," Yap assured me.

I had flown with Captain Mike "Yap" Trapp over fifty times but I never realized how lucky I was to have him as my wingman until then. He did all the things a good wingman does. He kept quiet, listened, and backed me up. He also used his binoculars to point out things I couldn't see. The same guy who kept me awake—and alive—over the Khyber Pass was now backing my every move. Scheduled for Big Cat training, I weighed the irony. *This is turning out to be one hell of a training mission.*

Shadow had approved our request to reposition the tanker in the Perseus track. But then something strange happened. The tanker crew, who had been monitoring our comms, repositioned themselves overhead on their own initiative. They had left the Perseus track, some sixty miles to the east, and positioned themselves over the fight below. I doubted they informed Warlord or Shadow of their decision, but I didn't ask.

At my twelve o'clock, ten miles in front and turning back toward me, was Shell 01, as if they were reading my mind. I didn't say anything but my gratitude ran deep. We were in this together. As I slipped into the basket, I asked Shell to relay the situation to Warlord and Shadow. When I departed the tanker, I needed only to spiral down a few thousand feet to the CAP we had set up over Playboy. I relieved Yap, who then got his gas.

After Yap returned, we made several low show-of-force passes in the valley. Two of the three elements were together withdrawing to the north, to the safety of their vehicles, radios, and heavy weapons. Things appeared calm as we all caught our breaths. An hour went by, then another, as Yap and I watched Playboy 33 and his team struggle through the rocky valley. Then things heated up. "Nightmare, this is Playboy 33. We're taking fire again. How copy?"

"Playboy 33, this is Nightmare 63. I got you Lima Charlie."

"Nightmare. We got guys flanking us to our west with sporadic automatic fire and the occasional RPG. Break. I'm going to reposition myself up the eastern ridge so that I can direct you onto the enemy. How copy?"

Hell, who is this guy? The voice below radiated confidence. It oozed through the radio. "Roger that, Playboy. Nightmare standing by," I answered. Yap and I maintained our orbit over Playboy 33 and his team. It wasn't creative, but it didn't need to be. We kept our counter-rotating CAP so that one of us could attack while the other maintained high cover. It also allowed us to view the ground from different perspectives at all times. Perhaps one of us would catch a flash of the enemy, a mistake, a reflection off a gun or something that gave them away.

"Nightmare, this is Playboy. I have a modified nine-line; advise when ready to copy."

I waited the normal five seconds and didn't hear anything from Yap, after which I responded, "Nightmares ready to copy."

Playboy commenced the attack brief. "Nightmare, nine-line to follow. Lines one through three, n.a. Line four: seven thousand four hundred. Troops in defilade. Grid, tango, bravo, eight-five-seven-one-zero-two. Break. Talk on. Southeast, two thousand. Remain overhead. Advise when ready for remarks."

Playboy provided all the information necessary to attack the enemy but kept solely to the basics. The target was at an altitude of 7,400 feet at grid TB 857-104. The nearest friendly position, Playboy 33 and his team, was located two thousand meters to the southeast. "Nightmares, copy all. Standing by for talk-on."

"Nightmare, enemy is located along a north-south-running ridge to our west. Break. They are firing from different locations. I want you to engage the enemy that is near the small ridge that runs east off the bigger ridge and down toward my location. I want you to light up that small ridge with your gun. How copy, over?"

"Solid copy, Playboy. Tally target area."

"Roger, advise when rolling in."

"Stand by. Nightmare 63 is positioning to the north for a north-to-south run." I pushed to the north to allow for a longer attack run while double-checking I had selected the gun and that the master arm switch was armed. I designated the target with my targeting pod and ensured it was recording the action as I climbed to gain more altitude and, more important, more time. I pulled the jet hard to the left, rolling it upside down. Then I settled my nose on the target. My left hand pushed the throttle forward. Every nerve within me focused on steadying the tiny concentric circle, the pipper, on the target. "Night-mare 63, in from the northeast, wings level."

"Nightmare 63, with friendlies in sight, you're cleared hot."

Ohhhh shit. I didn't have the friendlies in sight. I knew where Playboy was, but there was no possible way I could see him. "Seeing" and "knowing" are two different things and the direction was "friend-lies in sight." I expected the abort, but I had lined up long and deep to ensure nothing was rushed. I had at least fifteen seconds of tracking time. I keyed the radio. "Negative, Playboy 33. I do not have friendlies in sight. I know where you are, but I can't see you. Target is off my nose." I unkeyed the mike and steadied the pipper. I waited and listened, hoping the geometry of my dive would convince Playboy I had the correct target.

"Roger, cleared hot."

Time stopped. This was for real. Before, someone else was dying and I was a witness. Now death was a trigger squeeze away—from me. I thought for half a second, which at the time seemed an eternity. *What do I do?* Instincts took over. Thirteen years of flying jets, two thousand Harrier flight hours, teaching the same thing over and over again—how to kill. My right index finger tensed. I felt the jet dip and twist left as I held the trigger down.

The five-barreled GAU-12 Gatling gun let fly a shower of steel. A hundred and fifty high-explosive incendiary (HEI) rounds spewed from the nose of my Harrier. I watched the deadly rope of red tracers arc outward from my jet to the ground below. I released the trigger and pulled back on the stick. My left thumb hit the expendables switch, stringing out a line of flares behind me. The jet bucked and rocked awkwardly, threatening to depart.

Shit. Misfire. I'm going to have to eject over this piece-of-shit valley. My mind raced in fear. It had happened many times before—the gun jamming, misfiring, double-feeding a round, exploding, and damaging the Harrier's fickle motor. A student of mine had lost sight in his left eye and his flight status following an ejection after the Harrier's gun had misfired. Like the Harrier itself, the GAU-12 cannon wasn't as reliable as advertised. My fear ceased when I sorted out my cockpit. I realized the Harrier's nozzles were 20 degrees down. The recoil from the gun was so strong it knocked my jet exhaust lever aft. My left hand threw the nozzle lever forward and the jet's erratic behavior stopped.

"Good hits, Nightmare 63. Good hits. Shift your fire to the southwest four hundred meters."

A sense of relief settled over me as I knew we were beginning the deliberate process of killing the enemy like a surgeon cutting out a malignant tumor. "Roger, stand by for Nightmare 64. Nightmare 63, off southwest, blind, press," I stated as my ship rocketed upward.

Yap was on the other side of the circle watching everything, ready to attack. We had flown together so much, we thought as one. "Nightmare 64, tally lead's hits. Visual 63. In from the east, wings level," Yap called out in perfect tempo.

Playboy responded, "Nightmare 64, from lead's hits southwest four hundred. Cleared hot."

I yanked the nose of my jet back east to provide high cover for Yap's gun run. As Yap sank low in the valley, a torch of yellow fire belched from the bottom of his Harrier. Transfixed by the flame, I stared awestruck in disbelief. *Ho-ly shit! This—this isn't training.*

"Nightmare 64 off west, blind," Yap called out

as he pulled his Harrier upward, letting me know his attack was complete but that he didn't have me in sight.

"Good hits, 64. Good hits." Playboy continued to work us on the target, shifting our fires in deliberate moves of a hundred meters this way, then two hundred that way. One attack after another, we soaked the ridge with lead until our guns smoldered empty. The enemy fire stopped and the Special Forces team continued their retreat.

Yap and I took turns cycling back and forth to the tanker, always leaving one of us overhead. After another hour, the SOF team arrived at the top of the valley and the safety of their vehicles. The commander now wanted us to bomb the ridgeline and the caves in it. They fired their .50-cal to mark the target but the rounds were hard to see. Yap put down a rocket but it was north of where they wanted the bombs. Finally, Playboy 33 passed us a modified nine-line target description and cleared us for the attack. I set the section up for a northeast-to-southwest attack, with Yap flying high cover. I designated the target with the laser and waited. Yap confirmed "good sparkle" and Playboy delivered an emphatic "cleared hot."

I pressed the pickle button and felt my aircraft shudder as the thousand-pound bomb released from my left wing. I drove straight ahead watching the targeting pod video on my right TV screen, but nothing happened. I turned and looked over my shoulder. The bomb had gone off, but well short of the target. Yap later told me that he watched the LGB come off slick, the guidance fins failing to open as the bomb fell stupid to the ground below. I was glad my tape proved the laser had remained on and that I had not turned the master arm off. I was learning from the mistakes of others. Sometimes even the most expensive weapons failed. We circled back around as I prepared to lase the target for Yap.

We began our run the same as before. Yap called "good sparkle," acknowledging that his jet had picked up the laser energy emitting from my targeting pod. With a "cleared hot" from Playboy, Yap released his bomb. Twenty seconds later, I watched a puff of dust bloom where the laser was pointing. A perfect hit, but no explosion. *Dud.* I couldn't believe our luck.

Over the previous hour, Shell 01 had relayed our situation to Warlord, who then passed the updates to Shadow. As a result, our relief had arrived, a section of Danish F-16s who had vexed our last attack with their interfering calls. Despite their impatience, I gladly gave them the lead. Yap and I checked out with Playboy and began the flight home.

A little more than six hours after we began a training mission, Yap and I landed uneventfully back in Bagram—out of bombs, out of bullets, almost out of gas, and definitely out of breath. I filled out the paperwork for the flight and then debriefed our intel section on everything that had happened. Physically and emotionally exhausted, I flopped down on my rack and thought about it all. I thought for a long time.

39

PRAYERS AND PROMISES

In the coming days we read about the battle on the Internet, comparing the press releases and news-wires with our classified intel updates. The chance engagement between Special Forces ODA team 2056 and the enemy developed into something bigger—a slaughter. Harriers, Hogs, Bones out of Diego Garcia, Dutch and Danish F-16s from Bishkek, and AC-130 gunships from undisclosed locations all joined the fray, but Yap and I were the first. Initial reports stated fourteen enemy fighters were killed. The number was soon revised to thirty, then fifty, then to "about 124."* Eventually Lieutenant General John Vines, commander of the 82nd Airborne, stated as many as two hundred enemy fighters had been killed since the operation began on August 25. Colonel Rodney Davis added, "The operation has resulted in

* Agence France-Presse, "Two US Soldiers Wounded in Afghanistan, US Confirms 124 Militants Dead," *Afghanistan News Center*, September 8, 2003.

more enemy killed in action than any operation in a year."*

It was strange. After eleven months of combat, the crux came (or so I thought) when I least expected it. The emotions following the mission were strong and difficult to untangle, not because of the killing, but because of the saving. I asked myself, *Who knows? Who knows besides Yap and me what happened?* They were selfish thoughts, since I wanted some assurance that I had done good. I soon found an answer, an ironic one given my beliefs.

As I updated my journal, writing those questions before me, the answer appeared. *I know. Yap knows. The guys on the ground know, both good and bad. And God knows. Nothing else matters.* My belief in God was agnostic at best, but I found comfort in the answer. For a short period, I debated who was good and bad and the relativity of each depending on where one stood. But it passed quickly. I then moved on and didn't think about that flight again—for a very long time. I became adamant about thinking forward and not of the past.

In the next forty-eight hours, I exercised heavily, read frequently, sent letters to an elementary school in Indiana and their second-grade class, endorsed a sergeant for an officer program, prepared an after-action report on a Harrier squadron's yearlong de-

*Dana Priest, "U.S. Raises Total of Dead Rebels in Recent Afghan Battles to 200," *Washington Post*, September 8, 2003.

ployment to Afghanistan, wrote two awards, and waited impatiently for my next flight. I did everything to keep my mind occupied and unable to dwell on the past or debate the future.

Two days after my mission with Yap, Ops scheduled me with Stroker. I asked what the mission was. The answer: Big Cat. Perhaps the schedule writers felt I hadn't served my penance. But flying was flying and the skies were again blue. Another storm had passed though something different tugged at me. Shadows were a tad longer and the air had a crisp feel. Fall was nearing.

"Disney, Nightmare 63. Airborne as fragged, capped at base plus ten in the Big Cat," I said, circling overhead, Stroker swept down my right wing. It was my fourth time on three different frequencies trying to raise the FACs we were scheduled to support. I turned and looked at Stroker. He shrugged. His visor up, I saw his eyes smile. The Montana cowboy couldn't hide his youthful features. I looked away and down at the dry plains below. There were no vehicles. Maybe the FACs were a no-show. "Tombstone, this is Nightmare 63. Still no joy with Rocky or Disney in the Big Cat. Break. Can we be rerolled to XCAS in the Gatling Echo?" We were supposed to begin a push near Spin Boldak in the coming days. Getting sight of the terrain before a mission always eased the stress.

"Nightmare 63, this is Tombstone. Copy all. Stand by," the ground controller responded. I waited patiently, hoping for a change. The voice behind a desk returned. "Nightmare 63, developing TIC. Grid to follow. Whiskey, bravo, two-eight-zero, zero-four-zero. Contact Warlord on Magenta." As soon as I heard "whiskey-bravo," I knew where we were going—Shkin.

"Tombstone, Nightmares solid copy. Flight, push Magenta on the left." I waited to ensure Stroker had punched in the new frequency before continuing. "Warlord, Nightmare 63."

"Nightmare 63, Warlord. Contact Lightning 21 on TAD 120. Proceed to 'Boulder,' one-zero-eight, for one hundred."

"Warlord, Nightmare 63. Solid copy." I did the math, comparing the bull's-eye call to the grid given. They matched. I looked southeast and saw the puffies. It was early afternoon. As the temperatures rose, the clouds would build. There was a chance—a small chance—we might be influenced by the weather. Realizing I hadn't briefed a plan for low-altitude attacks, I keyed the radio. "Nightmare 64, this is 63."

"Six-three, go ahead," Stroker answered.

"In case we have to go low today, we will do standard, same-side, low-altitude attacks with action at ten miles, pops at four, topping at three for ten-degree strafing runs. How copy?"

"Nightmare 64, solid copy. Same-side attacks, action at ten, popping at four, ten-degree gun runs."

With the clouds building and the target located next to the Pakistani border, I decided to request a preclearance for Pakistani airspace in case we needed it. I had never requested the airspace, but the CAOC lawyers and watch officers had assured us it wasn't a problem. We needed only to request it. "Warlord, Nightmare 63."

"Go ahead, Nightmare."

"Warlord. Clouds are building in the local area and may obscure the target. Request Shadow contact Nitro for authorization to use the five-mile buffer zone in Pakistani airspace. How copy?"

"Solid copy, Nightmare. Stand by for update."

As I waited for the answer, I wondered, *What am I missing?* I checked my weapons, then my sensors: targeting pod, FLIR, laser spot tracker, radar warning receiver. They seemed OK. I looked behind me, checking my six. Just sky. I pulled out my map (I still carried a pocket-sized one in my g-suit) and looked at it. I didn't even know why I was looking at it, except I felt I had to. Then I realized it was me. I quietly acknowledged it was all right to be on edge.

"Nightmare 63, this is Warlord." Only five minutes had passed. I was impressed with the CAOC's ability to process the request that fast.

"Go ahead, Warlord."

"Nightmare, Shadow says the request is denied."

Those muthafuckers. I had actually bought into the line sold to us by higher headquarters. How naïve I was. While I didn't know all the intricacies, I knew we were the tip of the spear, looking for the best ways to support the grunts. If things got hot, we wouldn't have time for a request. The fact that we had been turned down within five minutes led me to believe my request hadn't been routed far, if at all. I visualized the watch officer in the CAOC, sitting in the padded chair, staring at the Predator video, sipping coffee, being told of my request . . .

Knock it off. Focus. You have a mission. I trimmed the stick and looked south. The plains rolled out before me, a few peaks, my destination on the horizon—Shkin. I looked at the clouds. There were more now. As we neared Shkin, I reached Lightning 21 on TAD 120, giving him the usual information: number of aircraft, weapons and sensors, time on station, and current location.

"Roger, Nightmare, copy all. Lightning 21 and six pax traveling in two vehicles, en route to grid whiskey, bravo, two-eight-zero, zero-four-zero. Break." There was a long pause before Lightning continued, his breath winded, heavy. "Nightmare, we got a small problem down here." My curiosity was piqued with the unusual statement conveyed in a casual tone. I waited. "Nightmare, our current route is mined. We need to take the eastern route, next to the border. Break. This is definitely bad-guy area. Can you scan the hills to our east?"

"Roger, Lightning. We're visual your position and will scan the hills," I answered, not identifying that the JTAC's request was a difficult assignment. The targeting pod was great for zooming in on suspected enemy locations, but it was the equivalent of searching through a soda straw. I slewed the pod east, on the road next to the hills, looking for ambush sites and potential IEDs. But from my vantage I couldn't see the turned dirt, the trash out of place, the wires that weren't supposed to be there. I did my best. "Lightning, turn in the road two hundred meters ahead. Cluster of trees on your right next to a small building. Looks empty. Small road coming up on your left."

It was a typical mission. Hanging tight over a ground convoy and waiting. The enemy stayed away when they heard us. An hour passed and we needed gas. "Lightning 21, Nightmare 63. We need to get a drink within the next fifteen or we'll be bingo."

"Solid copy, Nightmare. Can you give me another ten and then refuel? It's eerie quiet down here."

"Affirmative, Lightning 21." I pulled the throttle back to conserve gas—hanging on the blades, we called it. My mind turned on his words "eerie quiet." I listened to the sounds in my world. The hum behind me, feeling its rumble. On the back radio, Warlord approved Shell's request to reposition to the Athena track. Shell had initiated it, not me, though I would have done so. But the fact that I didn't made me more appreciative. They were in it, just like us. Ten minutes passed. "Lightning 21, Nightmare 63. We need gas. We'll be back as soon as we can."

"Roger, Nightmare. Lightning copies." There seemed a heavy sigh in his voice.

"Lightning 21, we'll continue to monitor this push as we refuel," I added. Stroker and I turned west and began the climb to 24,000 feet. The clouds were building. They had been small and innocuous before, but they were growing now, as they did every afternoon between Khost and Shkin. A few had shades of gray but none were black. I was glad things were going smoothly. Lightning 21 would be at the grid soon. We'd confirm the enemy was gone. We'd hold for a little bit. Then we'd go home. I had done it so many times, I knew the outcome.

Stroker and I slid behind the tanker and effortlessly into our respective baskets. If there was one thing we had become experts in over the last year, it was in-flight refueling. We bobbed up and down in the baskets as the thermals jostled us around. The radio was quiet. Neither Lightning 21 nor Shell 02 said anything. Even Warlord was silent. As my fuel gauge rolled upward, I thought how lucky I was to be a Marine pilot. To soar where others couldn't. I was glad fall was coming. We'd be going home soon.

The radio crackled. "Nightmare, this is Lightning. We're taking fire! Lots of it. How copy, over?" A staccato of pops rang in the background. My eyes immediately sought my fuel state. I was six hundred pounds shy of topping off. I could do with what I had. My left hand inched the throttle backward and the Harrier slid aft, popping free of the right-side basket. Normally I would have asked permission to disengage, but that took seconds. Shell was listening. They understood.

As I popped free of the basket, I became a hunter.

My hands commenced a series of tasks they knew instinctively: reseating the refueling probe, putting the flaps in "auto," turning the expendables on, calling up the targeting pod, selecting the gun, slewing the pod toward the target area. My fingers and thumbs had been trained well. They accomplished the tasks in a few seconds, naturally, without thought. I looked at the master arm switch but decided to leave it off, at least for now.

I glanced left. Stroker was mimicking my actions. Neither of us had said anything, though we worked in unison. Then the helmeted figure with the gray oxygen mask and dark visor looked at me, his face and eyes hidden. I didn't think he was smiling. It was a ghostly creature, a stranger. Then I realized it was me, in a mirror—a pale rider of death.

I turned away, rolling my jet sharply to the right. The Harrier entered a nose-down slicing turn back to the east. Stroker fell in trail and then picked up combat spread on my south side. We were fifty miles due west, six minutes away. Ten seconds had passed since Lightning's call. "Lightning 21, Nightmares solid copy. Six minutes out. We're bustering." I pushed my throttle to the stop as the jet screamed downward from 24,000 feet. I stared at the clouds straight ahead, clouds over the target area. We had to go low.

As the jet descended and the speed increased, she began to shake. The Harrier didn't have sleek aerodynamic lines like an F-16 or F-18. Her fat, rounded edges created drag and supersonic air flows around her control surfaces. She began an uncomfortable "dutch roll" as we passed .85 mach, but I refused to pull power—seconds mattered. Then it happened. Only this time I had heard it before—forty-eight hours earlier to be exact. The calmness of Lightning 21's voice was gone.

"Nightmare, we're taking *heavy* fire. They're walking mortars onto our position. I repeat heavy—" The call came broken and garbled but understandable. The sound of gunfire and men yelling. A scream. Then silence. It was déjà vu. But there was one difference. One big difference. Two days earlier I had been directly above those I was supporting; thus my actions were immediate and without thought, because there was no time. Now there was distance—space—time, and with it came—thought.

"Five minutes out," I shouted back. "Hang on, we're coming." *Fuck. Please God. Not now. Please God, please not on my watch. Please God. Help me out this one time. Oh shit. Come on, God. Please keep them alive for a few minutes. Fuuuuuuck. Please, please, please . . .*

My profanity collided with my prayers in a psychotic banter as words swirled in my head, a visceral litany that only I heard—perhaps that of God, but I wasn't sure. My combative relationship with my maker took on a heightened sense of anxiety. As I flew east, all my missions over Shkin came back to me. All those times we lost and another American traveled home in a bag. I was mad at God but begged for help. *Just one time. Just this one time. I promise I'll go to church if you bail us out this one time.* I was trying to cut a deal without any bargaining power. My lips twisted on the words as the miles ticked off slowly. I checked my airspeed in the HUD—520 knots, close to 600 miles per hour. Still, I wasn't moving fast enough. "Four minutes out. Nightmares are coming. Hang on," I stated emphatically. There was no answer.

"Nightmare 64, blind." Stroker had lost sight of me in the descent. I hadn't pulled any power and thus gave him no margin to keep up. But there was no way to get his eyes back on me unless I turned or slowed down. Trying to regroup the section would cost time, grains of sand in an hourglass I wasn't sure we had.

"Nightmare 63, copy. Six-four, take high cover over the target," I directed. The flashing red warning light illuminated as Bitching Betty called out "altitude, altitude." I reset the radar altimeter to 180 feet and continued to lower myself down, slowly. The trees, bushes, and dirt rushed by, filling my peripheral vision with a mosaic of ill-defined lines and fuzzy colors, like some Impressionist painting, yet the canvas wet and moving, blurred in a slow-motion movie. My senses were alive. I could see, feel, hear everything at once, separating each synapse into its respective box. I centered my eyes on the small diamond in my HUD—the location of Lightning 21, less than a mile from the border.

I assessed my options. Flying straight ahead would put me into Pakistan. I didn't care about the lawyers, watch officers, border guards, or diplomats, but I did care about Lightning 21. Paralleling the border flowed with the terrain. I guessed that might work best. At eight miles I cut to the right and began my offset to the south. At four miles I pulled back on the stick and climbed. "Nightmare 63, popping from the south," I said, simultaneously flipping the master armament switch on. There was no response.

A few seconds later, I reached three thousand feet and rolled my jet upside down. I pulled the nose back down toward the target in a heavy g-turn. Upside down with dirt filling my canopy, I rolled the Harrier upright and steadied myself in a 10-degree dive. "Nightmare 63 in from the south, wings level." There was no answer.

I kept my pipper on the valley hoping for a "cleared hot," but I wasn't expecting one. I knew it was over. There had been no response since Lightning 21's desperation call. Those five minutes of prayers had been an eternity, but now I was overhead, putting out a string of flares, highlighting my position to those below. I pressed the attack to the deck, hoping my noise shook the earth. The Harrier bottomed out of the dive as I pulled hard on the stick to avoid a certain impact. Once climbing away, I jinked left, then right, and then back to the left, keeping an erratic, unpredictable flight path. Still there was no answer from Lightning. It was Shkin and I knew the outcome, but I continued the fight—alone.

"Nightmare 63, 64 has you visual. Two-mile trail." It was Stroker. At least he was here. With the clouds solid at 6,000 feet there was nowhere to climb and nowhere to hide, except laterally, so I exited to the west, away from the border. "Roger, 64. Six-three is exiting west," I said.

"Nightmare 63, Lightning 21. I have a modified nine-line. Advise when ready to copy."

The familiar voice was back. The panic gone. *Hot damn.* I again didn't know whether to laugh or cry. "Ready to copy," I answered quickly.

"Seven thousand five hundred. Whiskey, bravo, two-seven-niner, zero-zero-five. Illum on the deck. Northwest, one thousand," Lightning 21 stated in simple, direct terms. "Nightmare, we're putting together a fire mission. We'll have an illumination round on the deck in a few minutes."

"Roger, Nightmares standing by," I answered. Doubt consumed me. I had seen few artillery missions successfully fired over the previous year. Putting together an artillery mission took time. We advertised we could put fire missions together in minutes, but the sad reality was we were less competent at integrating fires than we claimed. I sensed we were wasting time, giving the enemy an out. I arced westward, scanning the border to the east while cross-checking my cockpit and targeting pod video.

"Nightmare 64, tally mark," Stroker called out.

I looked toward the target area and saw the burning flare. I couldn't believe it. The fire mission had taken only a few minutes. "Lightning 21, Nightmare 63 contact mark."

"Roger. Southeast three hundred," responded the JTAC.

Before I was stunned, but now we were approaching fantasy. The round was not only timely but also accurate. The amazing thing was that we weren't practicing this every day, so the fact that it came together so perfectly was either a testament to our skill or to luck. I believed the latter.

The illumination round burned in the small valley that I had attacked from the south on my first run. Not wanting to attack from the same direction twice, I pulled the jet's nose toward the mark and drove southeast. At four miles, I began my climb. Reaching my apex of 3,000 feet, I rolled inverted and pulled my nose back to the ground. The valley filled my canopy. Hanging upside down, I waited until the pipper was slightly above the target, then I flipped the jet upright. I steadied the pipper on a group of trees three hundred meters southeast of the burning flare. "Nightmare 63 in from the northwest. Wings level."

The ground grew bigger in my HUD as I dropped from 3,000 feet to 2,000 feet and then to 1,000 feet. I looked for faces. My right index finger rested softly on the trigger, waiting for the call. Nothing. I yanked the stick backward. Once climbing safely away, I began my off-target maneuvers.

"Cleared hot," Lightning 21 called out. But the call came too late.

"Nightmare 63, off east. Unable. Too late," I responded.

With gunfire in the background, Lightning 21 answered in an animated voice. "Roger, Nightmare. It is hard to tell if you are pointing at us or the enemy. They're pretty close. Recommend a west–east run, over."

"Lightning 21, Nightmare 63. Roger. Setting up for a west-to-east run." I continued jinking left and then right, scraping the tops of the hills before dropping down the backside of the ridge. I was in Pakistan now, but I didn't care. I flew north for a few miles before turning west, jumping back over the ridgeline and into Afghanistan. I picked up the valley but no longer saw the mark. The illum round had expired. I pulled my nose around, back to the east, and made my call. "Nightmare 63, one minute out."

"Roger, continue."

As I drilled toward the target, I realized how similar this was to training. The terrain, weather, comms, the JTAC, the jet. It was as if I were back in the ranges near Fallon, Nevada, or Yuma, Arizona, or Ruidoso, New Mexico. Except this wasn't training. Nose on the target, I commenced my pull earlier and climbed higher, opting for more time in the chute— more time for Lightning to sort out the attack, more time for a "cleared hot," though I wasn't enthused about more exposure. "Nightmare 63 popping," I said. I thumbed my expendables switch aft and the flares popped out behind me. I rolled inverted and pulled myself back toward earth.

"Visual, continue," called out Lightning 21. Perhaps the preemptive flares were helping.

I rolled upright and then steadied the pipper on the target, making what I hoped was my last call. "Nightmare 63 in from the west, wings level."

"Nightmare 63, can you positively identify the friendly position?"

I couldn't. I wished I could, but the human specks remained hidden. I knew they were somewhere to the northwest of my pipper, hunkered down, firing back. "Negative, Lightning 21. Target is off my nose. Wings level," I said. As I had done two days earlier, I hoped the geometry of my attack and my nose position alleviated confusion.

"Cleared hot."

I bumped the throttle forward, hit the expendables switch one more time, and then steadied the pipper as smoothly as I could on the target. *Brrrrrrraaaaaaat.* I held the trigger tightly. My distance to the target was closer than two days before. Thus I saw the effects instantly. The bullets kicked up a cloud of dirt punctuated by hundreds of tiny bright flashes: explosions from HEI rounds—death.

"Good hits, Nightmare. Good hits."

"Roger, egressing north. Stand by for dash two." I pulled up, jinking left in a long, hard turn to avoid ricochets. Once clear to the north, I continued my off-target maneuvers as my left thumb pumped out decoy flares.

Before Stroker answered, Lightning 21 called out,

"Nightmare 63, I want everything on that position. How copy over?"

The adrenaline surged through my body as I snapped my jet back to the west, looking for my wingman. We needed to join for the next attack. "Roger, Lightning. What do you want? A thousand-pound LGB or a five-hundred-pound LGB?" I asked for better clarification. The response was emphatic.

"I want it all!"

"Roger that, Lightning. Nightmares are going to conduct a west-east attack and drop the thousand-pounder, then circle back around and drop the five-hundred-pounder. Then we will both follow up with our guns and rockets till we are Winchester."

"Approved. Stand by for another fire mission. H-E will be on the deck in sixty seconds. Remain clear until the H-E is down. Will advise. Over."

"Roger, Lightning. Nightmares will remain clear to the west until the fire mission is complete," I said. Stroker joined as we set up for the precision attack. I looked back at the target area and the clouds hanging over it. The LGBs required at least ten seconds of "fall time" to work. They weren't low-altitude weapons like the gun. The attacks would have to be "level laydowns" below the overcast to ensure each bomb had enough time to track properly. While we assessed the cloud deck, the target area erupted in tiny dirt geysers. It was the H-E (high explosive) raining down.

"Nightmares, H-E is complete. Continue with your attack."

"Roger. Nightmares sixty seconds out." I checked the target designation as Stroker and I drilled east, our jets highlighted against the clouds. I hoped the H-E and my previous attack kept the enemy down as our vulnerable altitude hung us out before the enemy. "Nightmare 63, heading one-one-five, wings level," I said, double-, then triple-checking the master arm was on. The response was immediate.

"Cleared hot."

I selected "auto release." A vertical line appeared in my HUD. I dipped my wings left and right to keep it centered. A horizontal bar appeared at the top of my HUD, then slowly lowered itself. I pushed the bomb pickle button and waited. As the horizontal bar dropped farther and touched the top of the velocity vector, the aircraft shuddered.

Beep. The delivery tone signaled the release of the weapon as it fell free from its mother. My right wing dropped slightly from the release of the thousand-pound weapon. I retrimmed the aircraft and flew straight ahead, into Pakistan. I stared at the video on my right screen, ensuring it didn't jump, move, or skip, but that it stayed centered on the enemy. The screen erupted in violence as the bomb exploded.

"Shack. Good hit, Nightmare. Good hit. Can you put the next one down a hundred meters to the west?"

Shack? I couldn't believe the JTAC said "shack." It was a word used in training for a bull's-eye. I never expected to hear it in combat, but we all reverted to our training and the vernacular was part of it. I moved the designation a hundred meters farther west, though I thought it strange. The kill radius of the bomb was several times that, but if the grunts wanted it, we provided it. "Nightmares copy. One hundred meters west. Break, break. Nightmare 64, buddy-lase right. Same as before."

"Nightmare 64, copy. Buddy-lase right," Stroker acknowledged.

We swung our jets back toward the target and commenced another run. Sixty seconds later I heard the beep from Stroker's jet. I glanced outside, then back inside to the targeting pod video, then back outside looking for fire, then back inside, making sure the designation hadn't moved. I waited. Nothing. *Was it a dud?* Suddenly the valley erupted in a shower of dirt, smoke, and flame.

"Shack, shack. Great hit, Nightmare." The JTAC's animated voice enforced the elation. Ten minutes earlier the outcome was dubious. Now we were on top.

"Nightmare 63 ready to follow up with guns," I responded.

"Roger, Nightmare. Continue."

I pulled myself around in a tight circle and dropped into a 10-degree dive. "Nightmare 63 in from the west. Wings level."

"Cleared hot."

I waited until the valley filled my HUD, then I tightened my index finger. The jet kicked left and down. I held the trigger down until the last of my three hundred rounds had fired. I purposely let the pipper walk up the valley, raking it with HEI from the GAU-12 "Equalizer"—the Harrier's 25 mm Gatling gun. When she worked, she was beautiful. Smoke, dust, cordite filled the air above the valley. The gray cloud lifted upward, then drifted east into Pakistan. I wondered what it smelled like. "Good hits, Nightmare," Lightning called out. "Good hits."

"Roger, stand by for Nightmare 64. Nightmare 63 is Winchester." I was out of ammo but wanted Stroker to expend the rest of his gun and rockets on the remaining enemy.

"Negative, negative, Nightmare. We're leaving. We're getting out of here. Can you remain overhead and escort us back to Shkin?"

"No problem, Lightning," I answered. Stroker and I held low over the vehicles as they drove south.

Shell 02 had monitored our comms, relaying the progress back to Warlord, Tombstone, and Shadow. Reinforcements had arrived. Boar 63, a flight of two A-10s, had waited patiently to relieve us. Best of all, they had kept quiet as Stroker and I worked with Lightning. I was out of ammo and Stroker was almost out of ammo. We also had less gas than the fully loaded and armed A-10s. I asked Boar 63 if they were ready to assume the TAC lead. They answered "affirmative." I called Lightning on the radio and made my recommendation. "Lightning 21, this is Nightmare 63. We've got a section of Hogs, call sign

'Boar 63,' that are fully armed and have more play-time than we do. Recommend they take over your escort. How copy?"

"Solid copy, Nightmare. You're cleared to RTB. Break. One more thing." There was a slight pause in the transmission. "Nightmare 63, I think you really saved our ass with that first low pass. I can't thank you enough for that."

"Roger, Lightning. Glad to help. Good luck. Nightmares are bingo. Nightmares push Magenta on the left." As we flew home, dodging puffies, Lightning 21's words replayed themselves over and over in my head. I grasped my actions. I had done good. I smiled, but stopped myself there. I thought about the teamwork. My wingman, Stroker, had performed flawlessly. He had been as good as Yap, perhaps better. The tanker aircrew, Shell 02, had used their own initiative to reposition themselves to support us. The artillery unit put a fire mission together in minutes and delivered it accurately. And without a doubt, I couldn't forget Lightning 21. I could not imagine walking in his shoes, doing what he did under such duress. I was glad he was alive. But there was still someone else I needed to acknowledge—God.

I thanked Him for two things: the seconds he gave me and keeping the grunts alive in those seconds. I had come to hate and fear my missions over Shkin, a place where Americans left in body bags. But not this time. This time God had answered a Nightmare's prayer.

40

FINISHING LINE

I finished my run and then slipped through the hangar's back door, between ordnance and powerline. I avoided attention that way. The SNCOs guarded the other entrance. I was seeking the young Marines, alone, where I could test the waters of morale. The back entrance was where they hid. Several of them were playing cards, taking a break from the grind. Alice in Chains' "Them Bones" played in the background. The song's dark lyrics and discordant power guitar seemed a fitting theme for the Nightmares.

The Marines had spent the day packing boxes, preparing for the redeployment, though there was still no official word. The visitors who had arrived three days earlier had left the day before. Another general had promised we would be going home soon. There was more confidence in the delivery of the promise than the hem-hawing given by the one-star three weeks ago. Nevertheless, the Marines whispered, "I'll believe it when I see it."

"Hey, sir, what's up?" Lance Corporal Futrell said, seeing me hovering near the entrance.

"Not much. Just cooling off," I answered. I walked forward, sensing an invite. "Now that the general is gone, I see that your octagon death cage has returned," I said, pointing to the container where the junior enlisted placed the large, spooky-fast camel spiders they caught. They arranged fights between them. It could have been ordnance, but powerline had created the pastime.

"Yes, sir," Futrell answered, gauging me, unsure of my motives.

"I appreciate you guys hiding it when the general was here," I followed.

Futrell chose to change the topic. "So, sir, you're a lieutenant colonel now. When do you become a CO?" he asked, referencing my promotion the day before. I found the question strange, since I had never expected to stay that long in the Corps. It just happened.

"Lance Corporal, I'm never going to be a CO. I'm not a company man. I'm like you. I complain and make too many waves."

"Shittttttttttt, sir, I don't make waves," Futrell chuckled.

"Hey, sir, why you hanging out with powerline? I thought you said you was an ordie," called an unknown voice behind me. I turned and saw Lance Corporal Bushby approaching.

"Bushby, I'm neither powerline nor ordnance. I'm just a Marine."

"Shit, sir, don't be pulling that," Bushby said, shaking his head. "So, I gotta ask, sir. How does it feel?"

"How does what feel?"

"You know, sir."

"No—no, I don't know. You mean being a lieutenant colonel? If that's what you mean, I don't feel any different. Why, do I look or act different?"

"No, sir. I'm not talking about that. I'm talking about the missions the other day. How does it feel?"

"How does what feel?" I didn't know how to answer the question, nor did I want to think about it. "You dropped twice sir, back to back. We heard you really hit 'em, using the gun and all. Both times you came back with nothing on your jet. That gun kicks ass, don't it, sir?" Bushby said.

"Sir, Captain Moore says you were lucky," Futrell interjected. "He and the other pilots say that if you want to drop in Afghanistan, you got to be scheduled with the XO on a training mission."

I turned and asked Futrell, "Do you think I'm lucky?"

"No, sir, I don't think you are," Futrell answered. "I don't think any of us are lucky. I think we'll be spending Christmas here—again. That's what I think."

"XO, are you hassling my Marines?" Gunner Jim Inglis called out as he swaggered over from the ordnance shop. My cover was blown.

"Just one of them. He wants to know how I feel?

I told him he needs to see a shrink if he's worried about my emotions."

"Hey, Bushby. Leave the XO alone. You know he's touchy-feely," Jim added.

"Thanks, Gunner. I appreciate the vote of confidence."

"Sir, you got a second?" Jim followed.

"Sure." I turned and walked out the hangar's back door. It was dark now. The night was cool. I shivered in my running gear. I stopped near the tow tractors and electric carts wondering what Warrant Officer Inglis wanted. Gunner Inglis stuck out his hand, offering me something. It was wrapped in a white cloth. I took it and peeled the cloth back. It was a 25 mm shell casing.

"Sir, it's from your mission the other day. I had it polished and the bottom engraved with the date. Thought you'd like it as a souvenir."

A lump appeared in my throat. "Jim, I don't know what to say. It's beautiful. Thank you. Thank you very much."

"No, sir. Thank you." And with that Gunner Jim Inglis turned and walked away, leaving me in the evening's coolness.

It was September now. The days were still warm, but the heat of summer was gone. With my gift in hand, I turned and walked quietly back to my hooch, thinking as I always did. It was our intel that bothered me. The number of enemy combatants estimated in the Dai Chopan district, where Yap and I supported Playboy 33 and ODA 2056, had been no more than 50 when we began the operation. But after the initial firefight, intel kept raising the estimates, every day: 200, then 300, then 600, and eventually upwards of 1,000 Taliban fighters, considered "the largest concentration of militants seen since the regime fell in 2001."* I found it ironic because there hadn't been that many Taliban reported in southern Afghanistan, never mind one area. Who really knew how many enemy there were? I don't think we did. We didn't have people on the ground to give us those answers, so intel guessed.

I stopped at the blue porta-pottie next to my tent. I looked around. There was no one. It was quiet and I believed I could do it without being caught. I looked around again, paused, and listened. I heard no footsteps or voices. Sure that I was alone, I lay down on the hard gravel next to the Hesco wall, beside the outhouse. The Marines would think I was silly if they saw me. I didn't want to explain myself. The rocks felt cold and hard on my back. Looking up, the Afghanistan night unfolded before me, a brilliant sea of constellations and nebulae. The Milky Way, a gossamer blanket, stretched across the night as though God had tossed it softly into the blackness, its body frozen in time, but not really. To the east, I saw my friend. He had returned from his summer

* Yousuf Azimy, "Taliban Surrounded as Afghan Clashes Go On," Reuters, August 30, 2003.

hiatus. Orion—the Hunter. *Has it really been a year?* I whispered into the night.

I had come full circle watching the seasons change in Afghanistan. First fall, cool and crisp, which changed all too quickly to winter and its cold wet skies. Then finally, spring—thunderstorms and flowers—but that ended, too. Then summer. Its unrelenting heat and the shamals. Wind, more wind, and dust.

Orion was back. I smiled. I found a kinship with him that I did not find in others. Orion, the hunter who had challenged the gods, seemed akin to me. I loved looking at him. Transfixed by the tiny dots of life, I felt my body sucked upward into a labyrinth of time, spinning, twirling—I looked down and saw a young boy and an old man standing on the dry New Mexico plains. I watched the old man kneel down beside me and point up to the east, into the night, toward the hunter, introducing us. As I lay on the hard rocks, absorbing the universe—or it absorbing me—I forgot about Afghanistan, the war, and everything else. The heavens reminded me of my insignificance.

41

ONE MORE TIME

I lay motionless, trying not to make any sound that would alert the intruder. AJ was asleep. It was quiet. No explosions, no jets taking off, no helos landing. I listened patiently. I had heard the tiny feet, the scratching in the corner. I waited. *Crack!* I smiled, swung my feet out of bed, and turned on the light. But my sudden movement alarmed one that I had not marked. He came from beneath my rack and ran between my feet. I felt him brush my toe as he fled beneath the desk.

"Son of a bitch!" I swore, jumping out of bed. I was a nice guy. "Live and let live" was my motto. If I found a spider in my tent, I caught it and then freed it outside. But the mice had brought out the worst in me. It was a problem. First, there was one. We had seen the evidence on the bottom of AJ's Tootsie Roll bag. Then we heard them. They brought reinforcements. They lay quiet all day. But at night when the lights went out, their tiny feet scratched the floor as they looked for crumbs. When I heard the sounds on the bookshelf above my head, I drew the line. Besides, they might attract bigger critters, like "Jake." We hadn't seen Jake, but the fact they had found a six-foot cobra sleeping in the back of a helo was enough to convince me to take precautions.

I shuffled to the tent's corner and shined my light on the trap. It was empty—picked clean. I had eight traps carefully placed throughout the tent, but my kill rate had dropped in recent days. Now only the hard-core, street-savvy ones remained. I thought of them as al Qaeda. Looking at the empty trap, I realized I needed to raise my game. I would file the catches later.

I pulled on my flight suit and headed to breakfast. I briefed in an hour. The chow halls had improved remarkably over the previous year. For that matter, everything was better. But it wasn't enough to convince anyone to stay another three months. Yesterday we had finally received the official word we could go home. The Marines were happy but frustrated about the last-minute notice. Our departure date was three days away. My last combat mission was this morning.

We had packed 04 on pallets and shipped it to Cherry Point in a C-17. After shipping 04 home, the maintenance department struggled to keep the remaining five jets up. They broke frequently from the wear and tear. Several years of flights crammed into a year. It was akin to a runner completing the last miles of a marathon after pushing too hard. We could see the finish line, but we could only hobble toward it.

I met my wingman, Captain Chad "Eddie" Edwards, in Ops after breakfast. Eddie had joined our squadron the month before as a replacement for Stern, who was still going through a review process due to the mishap. I briefed the mission, covering all the details and potential "what-ifs" as I had done dozens of times before. I was hoping for an easy mission. No excitement, no gun runs, no firefights, no medevacs, and no body bags. I wouldn't hesitate to kill again if asked, but for my last mission I wanted simplicity. It was my last chance to capture the raw beauty of Afghanistan.

Our ships departed in the morning darkness on a typical XCAS mission. We toured Tora Bora and the Pakistani border, looking at the FOBs below. It was dark, quiet, and peaceful. I forgot there was a war. In the brief, I asked Eddie if he had seen the Buddhas near Bamiyan or what remained of them. He said, "No." I don't think many of the pilots had. After we topped off at the tanker and finished the last of our assigned ATO period, I pushed the flight west toward Bamiyan. The Hindu Kush, which stretched six hundred miles from the Helmand valley in southern Afghanistan to the Pamir Knot, where China, Tajikistan, Pakistan, and Afghanistan joined, had its center near Bamiyan. Here, in the heart of the Hindu Kush, the mountain had its own personality.

The sun's rays crested in the east and cast a warm

light in the valley below. The soft pastel colors reminded me of a Georgia O'Keeffe painting. The mountains bled a dark ruby red with segmented shades of purple, pink, and orange rock. The mineral-rich mountains below were a geologist's dream, except for thousands of discarded mines. Bamiyan had once served as a knot in the silk trade linking Rome with Guangzhou (Canton, China). Travelers on the Silk Road stopped at Bamiyan for a night's rest, and the commercial enterprises of the city grew over time. Bamiyan, once a vibrant community with an intricate irrigation system (Kareez, the Dari name), was perhaps where the name "Hindu Kush" or "Hindu killer" originated.

The bloodred cliffs appeared stained from the slaughter that occurred almost eight hundred years ago. The late Louis Dupree described Genghis Khan's army as "the atom bomb of its day." The historian Stephen Tanner added, "After a week's siege, Bamiyan was destroyed so completely that not only every person was killed but all the dogs and cats, and it was forbidden that anyone should ever live there again."* But Genghis Khan left the Buddhas intact. Perhaps he lacked the technology to destroy them, though that is doubtful, since he destroyed so much of Afghanistan, especially the complicated irrigation systems. Bamiyan never recovered from the Mongol destruction, though the Buddhas stood for another eight hundred

---

* Stephen Tanner, *Afghanistan: A Military History from Alexander the Great to the Fall of the Taliban* (Cambridge, Mass.: Da Capo, 2002), p. 95.

years. Then in 2001, under the guidance of Osama bin Laden, the Taliban destroyed them.

I looked down at the large empty sarcophagi. The crumbled sandstone bones lay piled in the feet of the upright caskets. Hundreds of tiny holes dotted the cliffs: dwellings, though I did not think anyone lived there now. Eddie and I remained silent, absorbing the beauty below. With thirty minutes of remaining fuel, I pushed the flight northeast to the Salang tunnel. Located at 11,100 feet, the 1.6-mile tunnel linked northern and southern Afghanistan, the only paved route across the Hindu Kush. It was a mess now. Built by the Soviets, the tunnel had served as a main artery for hundreds of T-62 tanks that poured south during the invasion of late 1979. Ten years later, the Salang tunnel witnessed their withdrawal, though fewer returned.

Snow now lined the pass and covered the surrounding mountains. I wanted to head east to Kuh-e Bandaka, to fly over the top of the world one more time, to look down into the Panjshir valley and view its inhabitants, who lived so deep and high in the mountains it made one question the limit of human endurance and suffering. I wanted to see where Alexander the Great had marched his army across Khawak Pass, but it was not to be. We didn't have the gas or the time. My last combat mission didn't involve any combat. Instead it was an aerial tour over historic battlefields that had witnessed the invasions of Alexander the Great, Genghis Kahn, Tamerlane,

Babur, the British, and the Soviets. Now we could add the Americans.

I looked to the northeast, to the endless line of snow-covered peaks that filled the northern horizon, and said good-bye. Then I turned toward Bagram and spiraled down. I recalled my first night landing, when the strong crosswinds served regularly by the Hindu Kush almost broke me. No more cockeyed landings in which the jet rocked up on its outrigger, threatening to flip over. No more approaches in blowing snow and freezing rain, wondering if I was going to break out. No more trying to stop on the wet runway, hoping I didn't run off into a minefield. The flight was as I had hoped—boring and uneventful. And for that I was glad.

42

TO WHOEVER INHERITS THIS LOT . . .

Kaboom! My chest and arms tightened; my legs kicked in an uncontrolled reflex. I dropped my pen and listened for the follow-up. Another Bagram mine. I had lived through a year of the unannounced explosions, adjusting my mind to their presence. But over the last month, my ears quit ignoring them. After each discharge, I waited for the next, cringing in anticipation. Sometimes they came. Sometimes they didn't.

The final weeks had been a whirlwind. After twelve months of a seemingly endless deployment, the end came quickly. There were good-byes and a sadness of leaving what had become comfortable. I found the sadness strange, since I hated Bagram. Then there were the tasks.

I had mailed the last of my letters and flags home. American flags that I had flown over Afghanistan. The last flag I mailed to an eleven-year-boy who did not know me. He was the son of Walid Majroh, the

Afghan interpreter I had met several months before who had been a mujahideen fighter in the 1980s and had met Osama bin Laden three times. Walid had known and worked for the Lion of Panjshir—Massoud. He had also shot down sixteen Russian jets. Abandoned by America after the Soviet withdrawal, he watched the Taliban rise. He then fled to America, where he raised his family. He gave all that away, returning to the battlefields once more, to help right a wrong. "Zak, my eleven-year-old son plays Little League baseball on a playground that is safe—that is without mines and unexploded rockets. We do not know how good we have it, Major Zak," Walid said to me before he departed. I could think of nothing better to give the man who had given so much.

Two days earlier, I said good-bye to U.S. Air Force tech sergeant Celio Castiblanco—Playboy 33. After his team emerged from the fight near Dai Chopan and back into the wire at Bagram, Cee-J stopped by to meet the Harrier pilots who had first supported him. Cee-J relayed the battle to us from his perspective and then introduced Yap and me to the rest of ODA 2056. They confirmed what I suspected. Being National Guard soldiers, headquarters had sent them to an obscure location in the Hindu Kush where fanciful reports of Taliban lacked substantiation. No one really believed there was much enemy there. But the mailman, EMT, air marshal, college student at OSU, small business owner, FBI agent, and others of ODA 2056 proved their worth, killing more enemy in one week than the combined ground forces of Afghanistan had accomplished in the prior year. There is an untold story there.

My tasks were now complete. I looked around my tent. Two cots, two empty desks, two chairs remained. My roommate, AJ, had left a few days earlier to prepare for the arrival of the Harriers in Al Udeid, Qatar. The day before, the remaining five jets flew out of Bagram to the cheers of the Marines. As we had done when we left Yuma, the CO led the jets out while I remained behind to close up.

The bookshelves inside my tent were bare. The pictures of my family were packed away. The B-hut, my home for the last year, was a hollow brown shell. Above my cot, the taped plastic garbage bag, my makeshift repair, remained. I felt sorry for the soul who would inherit my lot. I left him (or her) a note talking about the "goods" and the "bads" of my previous residence. And I left the mousetraps, which now had small ink marks on their sides, recording their scores. I also left a warning about "Jake" and relayed the story of the cobra they had found sleeping in the back of a helicopter not far from our tent. Finally I explained the plastic bag taped to the ceiling. Perhaps they would find a better way to keep the rains out. I signed the note and then finished the last of my e-mails to family and friends, ending with "Nightmares signing off from Afghanistan." I closed my computer, gathered the last of my belongings, and loaded them into my seabag.

The C-130 had arrived the previous night. After they shut down, I watched the aircrew drag large coolers into an abandoned tent. I looked the other way. It was our last night. I myself had a large bottle of Jim Beam I couldn't take home, so I did the next best thing. After eating dinner, I took the whiskey to the south side of Bagram and the barracks of my European friends. "Here you go," I said, holding out the bottle. "A gift from the Americans. I'm leaving tomorrow and can't take it with me."

"Well, do you wanna crack it, Zak?" asked Punk, in his heavy Dutch accent. Punk, an F-16 pilot, was serving as a liaison officer on the CJTF-180 staff and had become a recent friend. Lieutenant Colonel Pernille Hedin—the blonde—was there as well. Her soft Danish accent coaxed me. "Come on, Zak, it's your last night." Pernille and I had become good friends. We visited frequently, mostly at the pool. She was tall, beautiful, smart, and single—a perfect catch—but my heart resided elsewhere. Perhaps hers did, too. I didn't ask.

I thought about it. I hadn't broken the no-drinking rule once, based on Grouper's orders. I would have, had the CO given some sort of tacit approval, but he was a stickler for rules and I was there to enforce them. I had once caught the captains celebrating their success after a mission. I knew the CO would hammer them if he knew, so I told them to get rid of the booze. Then I left hoping they ignored me.

"What the hell. Yeah, uncork that fucker," I said.

Several hours later, I walked back to Camp Teufel-Hunden gazing at the stars, buzzed.

That was last night. Now it was time to leave. I picked up my bags and walked down to the flight line, where I joined the other Marines. We boarded the aircraft, squeezing sideways next to each other, shoulders pinched tight, lining the flimsy aluminum seats. The C-130 started and taxied out. The Marines turned and gazed out the windows looking at Bagram one more time. They smiled at each other but said nothing. The C-130 took the runway, ran up its engines, and began waddling down the rough tarmac with which I was so familiar. Bumpty, bump, bump we went. Finally, when enough air flowed across the fat wings, we lifted off. The Marines erupted in a spontaneous cheer. Yells and whistles reverberated through the aircraft as the Marines pumped their hands above their head and jumped in their seats. I was mad I did not have my camera at the ready.

After climbing above Bagram, the C-130 load-master gave the OK to unfasten our seat belts and to reposition if we desired. As I had done many times before, I picked my way to the back, to the hard steel cargo ramp that I knew well. I had jumped from it many times but it now served as a welcome bed. I rolled my helmet bag into a pillow and pulled my flight jacket over me as a blanket. I fell asleep quickly.

43

FAMILIAR AND UNFAMILIAR GROUND

The fat transport shook and made sounds that my senses found strange. They had sent warnings to my brain, alerting me that something was not right. I awoke and listened. Nothing. My nose, covered by my flight jacket, smelled the sweat within it. I had not wanted to wash out the luck, but Katie was right. I needed to clean it. The dream had been strange. But it didn't matter now. I was awake. I rose, stretched, and looked out the window. Tiny green islands dotted the blue waters below. I recognized the Maine coastline. America. Seeing it brought forth complex emotions that pulled me in different directions. I closed my eyes and thought of home. *That what lies ahead rests, waiting, while we approach slowly, one day at a time. Distant pieces we had once formed a whole with. A sunset and sunrise separate us though I do not think we are the same. How will the pieces fit now?* I opted for something less obtuse. My selfishness found it quickly.

I was happy not to be flying this leg. I had flown my Harrier across "the pond" enough times to know that all oceans look the same. Tomorrow the five Harriers would arrive in Maine. I reflected on our journey a year ago from North Carolina to Spain and wondered if AJ was wearing his diaper. The day before, I had flown the leg from Qatar to Spain. The headwinds had been light, lessening our flight time to nine hours. Our arrival in Spain was uneventful, which was a good thing as I recalled our landing there a year before. My stay in Spain was short, spending only one night before jumping on a C-130 to cross the Atlantic.

I looked down at Bar Harbor and thought of my time there with Katie a few years ago. Thirty minutes later, we touched down in Brunswick. The Marines grabbed their bags and stepped off the airplane onto American soil. There was no spontaneous eruption, though they smiled. They remained cautious, happy but unsure. Perhaps like me, they were thinking of home. I spun slowly in a circle, gazing at the towering firs and pines. I had forgotten the beauty of a green forest. We drove quickly to the hotel, where I put the Marines on liberty. I slipped off my flight suit and pulled on a set of Levis. They felt strange. I wanted to be alone. I walked down the street looking for a bar but found a bookstore. It seemed right.

I liked bookstores. Libraries were stuffy and cold. People whisper in the library. I liked bookstores more. I found myself in literature. I did not ask to go there. I just found myself there. I read the names. Faulkner, *too complicated*. Fitzgerald, *too verbose*. Hawthorne, *it might work. But you don't want a novel. Something short*. Hemingway. *Yes, Hemingway was always good*. I pulled the book and flipped through the pages of short stories I already owned. It had been a long time since I read them. "Big Two-Hearted River." *This is strange*. I smiled at the coincidence, tucked Nick Adams under my arm, and went to the cash register. I was thirsty.

I ran across the street, almost forgetting to look both ways. A tinted-windowed tavern stood between a flower shop and a gas station. The parking lot was full. I opened the door. Noise poured forth, but it pulled me in. Smoke filled the air. The bar and booths were filled. I saw an empty table. I moved forward awkwardly as people yelled around me. I looked at my watch—4 P.M. It was September and Sunday. TVs lining the room portrayed men in battle.

"What can I get you?"

I turned around. A short, skinny girl with hair pulled into a ponytail smiled. Her weathered face was pretty, but aging from cigarettes I knew she smoked. "I'll have a Sammy Adams and a menu, please."

"Regular or tallboy."

"Make it a tallboy."

She dashed off. The raucous crowd vaulted to their feet and screamed. I looked around at the people surrounding me. Most of them wore team colors and their hero's number. Large women slapped high fives with their male counterparts. A few babies sat in portable child seats, oblivious to the noise or at least accustomed to it. I was home. This was America. Barbecues, Barbie dolls, hot rods, and Harleys. Baseball, bikinis, rodeos, and racing. Rock, rap, country, and bluegrass. Fast food, fast cars, supersized meals, and supersized waistlines. And best of all—football.

It was not what I had dreamed about over the last year, but I found it comforting. Still, there was something amiss. I felt aloof. My mind fled to what it knew. Afghanistan—Bagram—dusty Disney Drive and explosions. *Those fucking explosions.* I thought of my friends. I stopped, caught myself, and breathed. It was OK.

Thousands of miles away, Americans were fighting for obscure reasons, though those who had just arrived there could easily explain them. I had been one of them, but I was different now. The hollering crowd seemed oblivious to this. Perhaps I was wrong. They were patriots, too, though I didn't think they understood the changes. I shrugged.

"Here ya ahr." The girl set the menu and beer down.

I waited until she left. Then I raised my glass. "Here's to you," I said. "I will not forget." I pressed my lips into the foam and realized I was a long way from Afghanistan, both physically and otherwise.

44

ROSES AND A CHANCE ENCOUNTER

We were over West Texas now, near Dalhart, cruising at 24,000 feet, the five of us in loose formation behind the single KC-10 tanker. Across the horizon stretched New Mexico. Arizona would follow soon. The Harriers had arrived in Maine following a short delay in Spain. After spending another night, we got up early, briefed the last sortie, and began our trip home. With the exception of dodging thunderstorms near Chicago, the trip to Yuma was going smoothly. I looked down to see how the roses were holding up. They were lying on top of my right console. I was afraid my cockpit's frigid air would turn them black and limp. My gift did not go over well with the other pilots. But I didn't care. I was going home.

The terrain below reminded me of eastern Afghanistan. I saw something familiar. *It can't be.* I pulled out my map. The coincidences were compiling at an alarming rate. I wondered if God was steering me. We were flying over Highway 39, a little east of

Mosquero, New Mexico. I recognized the land immediately though I had never seen it from above. I had spent my childhood summers below in and around the small town, population two hundred and decreasing. It was here that I had stalked imaginary Indians with my aunt's Red Ryder BB gun. It was here I swam naked in the cattle tank among the salamanders and water snakes, and ran across the pasture hoping to beat the bull. It was here I rode bareback, holding tight to my granddad's waist, moving through the herd, counting head. It was here that my granddad took me down into the canyons in the World War II–era Willys jeep. We stopped and he told me the stories. We were friends.

Forgotten memories surfaced from unknown depths, one after another, overpowering me in a collage of faces and seemingly irrelevant actions. I looked down on the canyon I knew well. Sparse vegetation dotted the hard-packed earth. I had hid in the cracks and crevices below, while hunting and while being hunted. I thought of Shkin. We flew on, over the town. I saw the tiny dwellings and quickly found my grandparents' home. I zoomed in using the targeting pod. The tool that had allowed me to deliver death with pinpoint accuracy now gave me a window into the past. The home looked the same as I had left it.

My grandfather was gone. I missed him. He had fought with the Marines on Iwo Jima as a navy Seabee. My mom recalled when he left for the war. She was a young girl, but she remembered it well—the train, the station, the tears, the stoicism of her mother when he left and the near fatalism of my grandfather's mother, who could not bear it. My grandfather in his mid-thirties had watched his father, my great-grandfather, struggle with his responsibility as a member of the Harding County draft board. As my great-grandfather sent the local boys to war, many who never returned, my grandfather's guilt grew. He knew his father would never send him because my grandfather's mother would never allow it. So my grandfather told his father, then mother, then wife, and his two daughters he was enlisting. Then he left.

They say there are no atheists in foxholes, but my grandfather returned from the Pacific a staunch atheist. He never went to church, and he begrudged God, arguing with his wife, saying that such a being didn't exist. My mom said the war changed him. "It didn't make him mean," Mom said, "just distant and somewhat hard to communicate with." I wondered about me. *Was I different now? Would Katie find me strange?* I didn't feel different. Clearly I hadn't seen things others had. I hadn't watched men die in front of me or held their hands as they bled out. I hadn't witnessed those things and was grateful for that. But I knew I had changed. I looked down at the tiny graveyard below. I needed him now.

"Nightmare flight, stand by for conditions at Yuma," called the copilot of the KC-10. After a short pause he continued. "Scattered at two thousand, overcast at four thousand, layered upwards to twenty thousand. Winds out of the north at five, light rain. Temperature sixty-five. Altimeter twenty-nine-point-seventy-five." The radio call broke my sadness. I nodded good-bye to my friend and then faced west.

As we approached the Arizona border the clouds became numerous and thick, forcing us to tighten our formation. We had taken the last of our gas from the KC-10, which departed and flew on to its base in California. Grouper began to descend slowly, staying smooth as he led the five aircraft into the goo. At 4,000 feet, twenty miles east of Yuma, we broke out. The flight of five Harriers moved into a small wedge on the CO's orders. We looped around to the south, flying over the airfield in a tight formation before coming back for the break.

We landed and taxied to the VMA-513 line. Our families and friends waited for us. Once the last Harrier taxied in, the CO gave the order to shut down. I completed my post-engine checks and climbed out of the cockpit. Then I saw a beautiful lady running toward me. In her arms was a tiny boy. I had forgotten how pretty she was. We embraced in a three-way hug. Tears rolled down two faces. I handed Katie the roses. She smiled and laughed, recalling my actions some eight years earlier when I returned from Japan. Caleb looked at me and hugged his mommy tighter.

Families cheered as the pilots shook hands with friends and fellow pilots from our sister squadrons. Soon the pilots and their families departed. I told

Katie I wanted to wait for the enlisted Marines in the C-130 to arrive before we went home. I spent the next hour walking around with Caleb, getting to know him or at least letting him get to know me. He wasn't as interested in me as he was in the jet. The C-130 arrived and disembarked the thirty Marines who served as the trail maintenance crew. Shouts of joy erupted on the flight line again as the families embraced. The Marines grabbed their bags and then did what anyone would have expected them to do. They disappeared. When there was no one else left, I turned to Katie and said, "Let's go."

45

LOOKING BACK

On September 30, 2005, I was awarded the Distinguished Flying Cross. I was surprised and confused. Two weeks earlier, a friend had sent a cryptic e-mail congratulating me for my actions and my award. I didn't know what he was talking about. He then sent me a link to an article stating that my wingman, Captain Mike Trapp, and I had been awarded the DFC. It didn't make sense. Grouper had placed me in charge of the squadron's awards after the deployment and we had been specific about what we submitted. Even more surprising, I learned the award was for my actions at Abdullah Kalay with Yap and not for my actions with Stroker near Shkin.

After returning from Afghanistan in October 2003, I worked with MAG-13 regarding our awards. Unlike the first set of air medals written under a headquarters' mandated deadline, I did my best to personalize each award. I included specific actions that each pilot had performed during his tour of duty in Afghanistan. The adjutant reviewed the awards and recommended that I submit some of them for a "Combat V" for valor. I told him, "No. Just take them as they are."

I consulted Grouper and he agreed, so we left it at that. Air medals without Combat V's. It was what the adjutant said that cemented my decision. The adjutant had used the word *some*—"some of these awards." Some of us dropped ordnance. Some of us did not. But we were all in it together. It didn't seem fair for some of the pilots to be recognized above and beyond their peers. I didn't want to be.

I wore the Distinguished Flying Cross twice though I remained on active duty for another two years. The medal was beautiful and alluring, but I cautioned myself. I knew there were others who had done and risked more, but they and their actions remained anonymous for various reasons. It wasn't fair, but as a friend said, "It is what it is." I returned the award to its blue plastic box and stored it inside a bigger box where I kept all my Afghanistan memorabilia. I stored the big box in my basement underneath a pile of other boxes. I moved on.

Over the years, other units, mostly infantry and ground units, made longer deployments. But the Nightmares of VMA-513 had spent a year in Afghanistan when most units did tours of six months or less. After we returned, we learned that no one back home was interested in Afghanistan. Everyone was focused on Iraq, where the United States experienced increasing casualties despite the fact that major combat actions were supposedly over. Perhaps the reporter who interviewed me back in Bagram was right. Maybe Afghanistan was a forgotten war.

While others thought of Iraq, I thought of Afghanistan, the Hindu Kush, and the friends I had left behind. I thought of the hospital and the children. Those who had lost limbs and whose families no longer wanted them. Those who couldn't digest their food and were dying of malnutrition. And I dwelled on the missions. The nerve-racking approaches in crappy weather and nasty crosswinds. In the end, I had flown 117 combat missions and had over 350 combat hours. But I do not recall the deployment fondly. As JC said, "I think Afghanistan brought out both the best and worst of us."

After I returned home, my friends and family asked me about Afghanistan, what it was like. They were careful and nonintrusive, not sure what I had seen. So I told them about this mission or that mission. The missions when I had killed, I buried. I did not reveal them but once. I told the story of Shkin and Abdullah Kalay but I got lost in the translation. It didn't feel right. After that, I never talked about them again.

When I thought of Afghanistan, I wondered about Playboy 33 and Lightning 21. Were they OK? Had they been in another ambush? What were they doing now? How were they getting along? Were they still alive? No matter how hard I tried, I couldn't get my mind off Afghanistan. So eventually I quit fighting it.

Several years passed and then Playboy 33 contacted me. We talked about old times. He told me the sad news. Mustang 56—Weapons Sergeant Michael Humphreys—had killed himself shortly after Christmas. The man Yap and I had helped in the rugged Hindu Kush was not able to make the adjustments back home. Somehow, I understood. A few years later I hung up my flight suit for the last time and retired from the Marine Corps.

While storing my uniforms in the basement, I saw the big box marked "Afghanistan." I pulled it out and opened it. Inside the big box was my DFC in its blue plastic box, next to my award citation in a bright red Marine Corps binder. There were other memoirs. There were maps. Survival and evasion maps, tactical pilot charts, maps of Shkin and Abdullah Kalay. There were newspaper articles and my pakol, the trusty Afghanistan wool cap made famous by Massoud. There was a coin that Playboy 33 had given me. There were letters from children in New Jersey and a stack of letters from the second-grade class of Prairie Trace Elementary School in Carmel, Indiana. Each letter was a drawing and I cherished them dearly. There was a leather wallet, with my name and a Harrier embossed in it. It was handmade and given to me by someone in ordnance. The artist was a former Marine who wanted to give something to those serving. I did not know him.

Then there was the shell, a gift from Jim Inglis. It was shined and engraved and I valued it more than anything except for the flag. The tiny flag. Grouper had given it to me. He said the Girl Scouts gave it to him. I took it and thanked him. It came with a small card. On it was printed the Pledge of Allegiance. An innocuous gift that took on greater proportions. I carried both with me whenever I flew. They became my reason.

At the very bottom of the box, there were three olive drab logbooks, each with an inscription: "Franzak, Vol. I, 7 Oct 2002–24 Dec 2002"; "Franzak Vol. II, 25 Dec 2002–17 May 2003"; "Franzak, Vol. III, 18 May 2003—." There was no final date on the last logbook. I had left it open, unsure how to end it. Maybe I needed the perspective of time. I opened the last volume and thumbed through it. I found my last entry:

> Best of all, I feel at home not like some stranger.
> It is natural and right. It's great to be home.

But as I soon discovered, that wasn't the truth. It wasn't "natural and right." But those entries never made it to the journal. Change had taken place: small, subtle changes, but they caused enough friction that I had a difficult time adjusting. I thought back to when I had stepped into the sports bar in Maine. A stranger, a transparent figure with dark secrets that I didn't want to share. I didn't understand why those around me weren't talking about the war. Then I came home. I had tried to find a normal routine but it didn't work. There was nothing normal about home. A week after returning, I fulfilled my promise. I told Katie I needed to go alone. I picked a Presbyterian church and tried to remain anonymous. But churchgoers are savvy. They recognize a new face. I was hounded with "Hi's" and "Hello's" and "Good morning, how are you?" and "Are you new in town?" and "Will you leave us your name?" and "Can you fill out this card?" and "Oh, you must bring your family" and "You are so nice. Thank you for visiting." I wanted only to thank God, alone.

I fulfilled my promise, but in doing so realized that my relationship with God was personal. I could neither explain it nor share it with others. Nor do I ever want to try again. Not long thereafter, the nightmares began. They were pretty much the same. I was alone in my Harrier over Shkin responding to a TIC, but the JTAC wouldn't answer my radio calls. His voice was there one minute, then gone the next. I just kept circling above, making unanswered radio calls, watching my gas burn down. Worse were the dreams about the hospital. Again I was alone, walking through the ICU looking at the bandaged children lying in the hospital beds, wrapped in gauze, missing arms, legs, eyes. I carried the lollipops in my hand. The wounded children just stared at me, expressionless faces. Their eyes followed me. Their empty, hollow faces revealed nothing. For some reason I kept repeating "It's going to be all right" when in fact I knew it wasn't. I looked around for a nurse, a doctor—someone—but there wasn't anyone.

But before going to bed, wondering if the nightmares would come, I took Caleb into our backyard to view the heavens. He no longer pointed up and said, "Moon, moon." Now he talked in sentences, paragraphs, questions. Questions I didn't understand. I wanted words, few and simple. I wanted everything to be as it had been, as it was before. It wasn't.

I hoisted Caleb in my arms and felt his weight. It pressed upon me. We stared up into the night. It was October and in the east stood the Hunter. Orion pulled me upward as I held Caleb tight. I was back in Afghanistan, Bagram, Camp Teufel-Hunden, near my tent, next to the blue outhouse, looking up. I didn't need to look down. I knew what was there, Hesco walls lined with concertina wire. But there was something different. It was quiet. No explosions, no gunfire, no medevacs dusting off, no Harriers blasting into the void. Only silence. Then a familiar smell returned, an unpleasant intrusion. It was unmistakable. Dust. That fine, talcum-brown soot of Afghanistan permeated everything—even one's soul.

CALL SIGNS

The following call signs were used in the Afghanistan AOR in 2002–2003. Because call signs changed during deployment, there may be more than one for a particular thing.

Blues	Dutch F-16.
Boar	USAF A-10 Thunderbolt.
Bone	USAF B-1 bomber.
Disney	Name of a coalition JTAC.
Elwood	Danish F-16.
Hardrock	JTAC assigned to the 82nd Airborne Division.
Irate	KC-10 refueling aircraft.
Joliet	USMC AV-8B from VMA-513.
K-mart	CAOC.
Malice	Navy SEAL team.
Misty	USAF A-10 Thunderbolt.
Nightmare	USMC AV-8B from VMA-513.
Nitro	U.S. Embassy in Pakistan.
Playboy	JTAC assigned to a Special Forces team.

Reaper	USAF AC-130 aircraft.
Rocky	Name of a coalition JTAC.
Saxon	British AWACS aircraft.
Scorcher	USAF J-STARS aircraft.
Shadow	CAOC.
Shell	KC-10 or KC-135 refueling aircraft.
Striker	JTAC assigned to Task Force Five, a subunit of Joint Special Operations Command.
Texaco	KC-10 or KC-135 refueling aircraft.
Tombstone	USAF ASOC.
Vicesquad	Marine Corps air control detachment located at Kandahar.
Warlord	USAF AWACS aircraft.

GLOSSARY

ACE. Air combat element. All Marine Air Ground Task
Force (MAGTF) comprise four elements. The ACE,
command element (CE), ground combat element
(GCE), and the combat service support element (CSSE).

AGL. Above ground level. Height above the ground, usually in feet. Differs from MSL (mean sea level), which
is an altitude referenced from sea level. Bagram's field
elevation is 4,895 feet. An aircraft that returns for
the break at 1,000 feet AGL would thus be flying at
5,895 feet MSL.

AMO. Aircraft maintenance officer. Senior officer in the
squadron responsible for the care and maintenance
of the squadron's aircraft and the Marines who work
in the maintenance department. The AMO in a Marine squadron is almost always a pilot, while the
assistant aircraft maintenance officer (AAMO) is almost always a warrant officer.

AO. Area of operations. An area of operations is an operational area defined by the force commander for
land, air, and naval forces to conduct combat and
noncombat activities. Used colloquially by military personnel in Afghanistan to refer to the area in
Afghanistan.

AOM. All-officer meeting.

AOR. **Area of responsibility.** The geographical area associated with a combatant command within which a combatant commander has authority to plan and conduct operations. Often mistakenly used to mean AO.

APU. **Auxiliary power unit.** In the AV-8B the APU provided an emergency backup to the main generator. The APU was required to be working on all night or instrument flights due to the importance of referencing and relying on a pilot's instruments during IMC or night conditions when there is no visible horizon.

ASOC. **Air Support Operations Center.** USAF organization responsible for planning and coordinating CAS missions in support of ground forces.

ATC. **Air traffic control** is a service provided by ground-based controllers who direct aircraft on the ground and in the air. The primary purpose of ATC systems worldwide is to separate aircraft to prevent collisions, to organize and expedite the flow of traffic, and to provide information and other support for pilots when able. Generally ATC has four separate divisions within it: Ground, Tower, Approach, and Center. "Ground" controls all movement on the airfield before or after a takeoff. "Tower" controls and coordinates the takeoffs and landings of aircraft. "Approach" controls the arrivals and departures of aircraft. Sometimes Approach is separated into "Approach" and "Departure." "Center" controls aircraft as they fly between one airport's departure corridor and another airport's arrival corridor. Due to the limited infrastructure (lack of radars, communication towers, and repeaters), ATC had a very limited role outside the area around Bagram and Kabul.

ATO. Air tasking order. Aviation order issued daily by the CAOC with the specific tasking for each squadron. ATOs provided details for each mission to include call signs, takeoff times, recovery times, unit supported, tanking times and locations, IFF codes, etc.

AWACS. Airborne Warning and Control System. The Boeing E-3 Sentry is an American military Airborne Warning and Control System (AWACS) aircraft based on the Boeing 707 that provides all-weather surveillance, command, control, and communications for U.S. forces and their allies. The normal crew requirement is four flight crew and thirteen specialists working the radar, radios, and other equipment.

BCP. Bagram Collection Point. Designated area where enemy personnel were kept.

B-hut. The living spaces for Marines in Afghanistan in 2002–2003. B-huts were simple plywood structures that housed eight Marines in an open squad bay. B-huts were covered with tarps for insulation, which often leaked. Due to their minimalist forms, B-huts were often called "hooches."

bingo. Fuel state in which aircraft are required to return to base.

Bitching Betty. Aural warning system in the AV-8B with a female voice.

blood chit. The common term for the written notice, in several languages, carried by aircrews in combat. If an aircraft is shot down, the notice identifies the aircrew as Americans and encourages the local population to assist them by promising them money in return. An identification number unique to each blood chit is printed in the four corners. The pilot can tear the corner off and leave the number with whoever assisted the aircrew. They can then turn that number over to a U.S. government representative for compensation.

bone. Slang term often used to describe the B-1 (originally from B-one) Lancer bomber.

break. An aircraft manuever in which the aircraft recovers at high speed over the airfield and lands flying an oval circuit. Used to minimize exposure to the enemy.

buster. Aviation slang term for going as fast as possible. For example, "Hang on, we're bustering."

CAOC. Combined Air Operations Center. In 2002–2003, the CAOC for Afghanistan was based first in Saudi Arabia and later in Qatar. A large staff working inside a large secure complex oversaw the air war over Afghanistan and Iraq. The CAOC is usually commanded by a USAF major general but it may be commanded by officers from another service.

CAP. Combat air patrol. Term used by pilots to describe a protective cover over friendly forces. Often stated as "capped" or "capping." For example, "We're capped above you now!"

CAS. Close air support. Missions flown in support of ground forces, who are usually in close proximity to the enemy. CAS missions require detailed coordination, to prevent fratricide.

CENTCOM. U.S. Central Command (in full, USCENTCOM). Located at MacDill Air Force Base, Tampa, Florida, CENTCOM is the unified command responsible for U.S. security interests in twenty-seven nations that stretch from the Horn of Africa through the Arabian Gulf region, into Central Asia. CENTCOM is one of nine unified commands in the Department of Defense. CENTCOM is responsible for operations in both Afghanistan and Iraq.

CG. Commanding general.

CJTF. Combined joint task force is a task force that includes elements of more than one service and elements of more than one nation. CJTF-180 was the specified task force for the Afghanistan AOR in 2002–2003.

CO. Commanding officer. Person charged with the responsibility and welfare of the unit as well as its operational success. During VMA-513's OEF deployment in 2002–2003, the CO was Lieutenant Colonel Jim "Grouper" Dixon.

DFC. Distinguished Flying Cross. Created by Congress eighty years ago, it is America's oldest military aviation award.

DSU. Data storage unit. Often called the "brick" due to its similarity in shape and size to a brick. Also known as the "black box" for the Harrier. Pilots plan missions on computers and then save the data to an electronic file. The electronic file can then be transferred to a DSU. The DSU is similar to a thumb drive but is more rugged and designed to withstand certain crashes. After the mission file is uploaded to the DSU, the DSU is loaded into the AV-8B in a receptacle next to the pilot's headrest. The data from the DSU can then be transferred to the jet's computers once the electrical system is turned on. This can save pilots lots of time. Instead of "finger-punching" data into a jet's computers after engine start, pilots simply transfer their mission from the brick to the jet with a push of a button. The DSU also records flight and engine parameters and is used by maintenance personnel to track the aircraft's systems after a flight. In the event of a crash, investigators will attempt to recover the DSU to determine what happened. Because of fire and other trauma, DSUs are sometimes not readable after a crash.

ECM. Electronic countermeasures. The AV-8B is cable of carrying the ALQ-164 jammer pod. Because the enemy in Afghanistan lacked a sufficient radar capability, VMA-513 elected not to fly with a jamming pod in 2003–2004. ECM gear on the AV-8B also includes the radar warning receiver (RWR).

EEO. Equal employment opportunity. "It is the policy of the Commandant of the Marine Corps to provide equal opportunity in employment for all persons; to prohibit discrimination in employment because of race, color, religion, sex, age, national origin, or physical or mental disability; and to promote the full realization of equal employment opportunity through continuing affirmative efforts." Marine Corps Order 12713.6A, December 5, 1997.

ELINT. Electronic intelligence.

EOD. Explosive ordnance disposal. Specific military members trained and designated to remove UXOs and IEDs.

FENCE checks. Combat checks done by a pilot before crossing into enemy territory. *FENCE* refers to Fuel, Engine, Navaids, Communication, and Equipment. The typical FENCE checks done by Harrier pilots used the acronym *CWAIVER*. C—combat thrust engaged, communications (radios checked), clock set; W—weapons checked (mode, quantity, fuse set); A—ARBS (Angle Rate Bombing System) camera checked, bore-sighted, and set; IFF (identification of friend or foe) modes 1, 2, 3, and 4 set and checked with positive "reply" light; V—VRS (video recording system) tape inserted and set to record; E—expendables: flare, chaff, jammer, and "all" (emergency defense) programs checked and set, positive dispense of switch actuation, ECM (electronic countermeasures) set, jamming pod in repeat; R—RWR (radar warning receiver) set, RADALT (radar altimeter) altitude set.

firebase. See FOB.

fitrep. Fitness reports are part of the Marine Corps performance evaluation system. All Marines in the grade of sergeant through major general have a fitrep written on them by their reporting senior (the Marine's immediate boss) on at least an annual basis. A Marine's career and promotion are based largely on that Marine's fitness reports.

FLIR. Forward-looking infrared is a technology that senses infrared radiation. Instead of using light magnification to view objects in the dark as NVGs do, FLIRs sense the IR radiation (thermal heat) of an object and are thus able to portray it in an electrical image. FLIRs do not need any ambient light to function but like NVGs they cannot see through clouds.

FOB. Forward operating base. Outposts from which ground forces operate. Also referred to as a safe house or firebase.

FOD. Foreign object damage. Any object can be sucked
up by a jet engine, thus damaging the motor. Due to
the high tolerances of jet motors, a small rock, rivet,
or paper clip ingested by the motor can seriously
damage the motor. Large objects can be sucked up as
well. When the author was a young sailor serving in
VF-1 (U.S. Navy F-14 squadron based at Naval Air
Station Miramar in the 1980s), a sailor in the neighboring unit, VF-2, was sucked up into the intake of
an F-14. Amazingly, he survived since the pilot was
able to shut the motor down as the sailor was lifted
from his feet and began the horrible journey down
the long intake toward the motor's sharp blades. The
sailor's jacket was shredded and the motor was a
complete loss but the young man lived. He also never
worked on the flight line again.

Four. Short for S-4 or the logistics section. Might also
imply the logistics officer of the unit. For example,
"Have you seen the Four?"

fpm. Feet per minute. Descent rate used by aircraft.

fragged. Being tasked by higher headquarters; for example, "The CAOC fragged us for the 0200 launch."

fratricide. Unintended attack on friendly troops in which
injury or death ensues. It is literally the killing of
one's brother or sister.

Gatling. In 2002–2003, Afghanistan's geography was divided into specific areas for aviation reference. The
areas were labeled Gatling Alpha, Gatling Bravo/
Charlie (previously two separate areas), Gatling
Delta, and Gatling Echo. When pilots were tasked
with XCAS missions, they were usually designated to
a specific Gatling area.

GAU-12. The "Equalizer." Manufactured by General Dynamics, the 25 mm, six-barrel gun pod can be mounted on the centerline of the Marine Corps' AV-8B Harrier. It has a 300-round capacity with a Lead Computing Optical Sight System (LCOSS) gunsight. The Equalizer normally uses PGU-20/U armor-piercing incendiary (API) or PGU-22 or PGU-25 high-explosive incendiary (HEI) ammunition and fires at a rate of 3,600 rounds per minute or sixty rounds a second. Due to the gun's strength and "kick" when firing, Harrier pilots are taught to fire one- or two-second bursts. Due to the high rate of fire and limited ammunition, the gun's rounds can be emptied quickly.

GCA. Ground-controlled approach, a type of service provided by air traffic controllers whereby they guide aircraft to a safe landing in adverse weather conditions based on radar images. Most commonly a GCA uses information from either a Precision Approach Radar (PAR, for precision approaches with vertical, glide path guidance) or an Airport Surveillance Radar (ASR, providing a nonprecision Surveillance Radar Approach with no glide path guidance). Technically, the term GCA applies to the precision radar approach with glide path guidance. The AV-8B, like most navy and Marine Corps tactical aircraft, did not have an ILS (instrument landing system) that was compatible with civilian or air force systems. Thus when the weather was below nonprecision minimums, we were reliant on air force controllers who provided us GCAs (PARs). The PARs provided by air force personnel in 2002–

2003 were excellent, providing their equipment was operating.

GCAS. **Ground close air support.** Designated missions where pilots stand ready to launch if they are needed. The CAOC scheduled GCAS missions when the weather deteriorated.

GPS. **Global Positioning System.** A device that interprets signals for satellites and provides an exact georeference.

g-suit. **Part of a fighter pilot's ensemble.** Normally a set of trousers fitted with pneumatic or hydrostatic bladders that can zip up over a pilot's flight suit and cover the abdomen and legs. The g-suit inflates during increased g maneuvers and squeezes the pilot's legs and lower abdomen. The higher the g-force the more the suit inflates and squeezes the pilot, forcing blood in the lower extremities up toward the head. During high-g maneuvers, blood pools in the body's lower extremities. When blood drains from the head, a pilot is susceptible to g-loc (g-induced loss of consciousness). Acceleration (g) is one of the major physical stresses associated with combat flying. If a pilot sustains too many g's for too long a period, then the pilot will g-loc. A pilot may not recover from a g-loc for thirty seconds and will take another thirty seconds to acquire his or her bearings. Pilots who fly into the ground at high speed with no attempt to maneuver their aircraft are assumed to have g-loc'd. A g-suit does not increase a pilot's g threshold but makes it possible to sustain high g longer. A g-suit will typically add one to two g's of tolerance. Pilots still need to practice the g-straining maneuver that consists of tensing the abdominal muscles in order to tighten blood vessels so as to reduce blood pooling in the lower body. High g is not comfortable, even with a g-suit.

gunner. A nickname for a warrant officer in a Marine aviation squadron. The nickname is frequently used in reference to the ordnance officer in the squadron but is often used as a generic term for all warrant officers.

H-E. High explosive. Often used to denote a type of artillery round.

HEI. High-explosive incendiary. A type of ammunition designed to penetrate armor. Common round carried in the AV-8B's Gatling gun.

Hesco. The Hesco barrier or bastion is a modern gabion used for flood control and military fortification. It is made of a collapsible wire mesh container and heavy-duty fabric liner, and used as a temporary to semipermanent dike or barrier against blast or small arms. It is named after the British company that developed it, HESCO.

HOG. Short for Warthog, often used to describe the A-10 Thunderbolt.

HUD. Head-up display. An electronically generated display of flight, navigational, attack, or other data superimposed on a piece of glass in the military pilot's forward field of view.

HVT. High-value target. Enemy personnel whose capture or death would greatly affect enemy operations.

ICU. Intensive care unit. A specific section of the military hospital on Bagram where patients in need of critical care were kept.

IED. Improvised explosive device. A homemade bomb usually cunningly crafted by the enemy and detonated remotely.

IFF. Identification of friend or foe. A cryptographic identification system designed for command and control. It is a system that enables military and national (civilian-located ATC) interrogation systems to distinguish friendly aircraft, vehicles, or forces, and to determine their bearing and range from the interrogator. IFF is used by both military and civilian aircraft and normally employs four modes referred to as modes 1, 2, 3, 4. Modes 1, 2, and 4 are for military use only. Mode 3 is used by both civilian and military aircraft for separation and avoidance. Mode 3 is often used in conjunction with mode "C," which is a barometric altitude-reporting function in addition to the geographical location so as to provide a three-dimensional location. Pilots refer to their IFF code as their "squawk." For example, "Approach, Joliet 12 is squawking five-two-one-four."

IFR. Instrument flight rules are regulations and procedures for flying aircraft by referring only to the aircraft instrument panel for navigation. Even if nothing can be seen outside the cockpit windows, an IFR-rated pilot can fly by referencing a pilot's instruments. An IFR-rated pilot is authorized to fly through clouds using air traffic control procedures designed to maintain separation from other aircraft.

IMC. Instrument meteorological conditions, sometimes referred to as blind flying, are weather conditions that normally require pilots to fly primarily by reference to instruments, and therefore under instrument flight rules (IFR), rather than by outside visual references under visual flight rules (VFR). Typically this means flying in clouds, bad weather, or at night.

initial. A designated point, usually six miles from extended runway centerline, in which returning aircraft pass before entering the break and landing.

INS. Internal navigation system.

IR. Infrared (IR) radiation is electromagnetic radiation whose wavelength is longer than that of visible light (400–700 nm), but shorter than that of terahertz radiation (300 gigahertz) and microwaves. Infrared radiation spans more than three orders of magnitude (roughly 700 nm to 300 μm). NVGs operate in the near infrared spectrum, 0.7–1.5 μm. FLIRs operate in the far infrared spectrum, 8–15 μm. IR missiles (handhelds or MANPADS) operate in different portions of the IR spectrum depending on their technology.

ISAF. International Security Assistance Force.

JDAM. Joint Direct Attack Munition. The Joint Direct Attack Munition is a guidance kit that converts existing unguided gravity bombs, or "dumb bombs," into all-weather "smart" munitions. JDAM-equipped bombs are guided to their target by an integrated inertial guidance system coupled with a GPS receiver for enhanced accuracy, giving them a published range of up to fifteen nautical miles (twenty-eight km) from the release point. Because JDAMs rely on GPS signals for guidance and not the reflected energy from a laser, they can be released through the weather with devastating accuracy. In 2002 and 2003, the AV-8B did not have a JDAM capability. Currently it does.

JOG. Joint Operations Graphic. A chart with a 1:250,000 scale. Provides more detail than a TPC (tactical pilot chart) but covers less area.

J-STARS. Joint Surveillance Target Attack Radar System is a U.S. Air Force airborne command and control platform that conducts ground surveillance to develop an understanding of the enemy situation. It is designed to support attack operations and targeting that contributes to the delay, disruption, and destruction of enemy forces. The E-8C is a modified Boeing 707-300 series commercial airframe remanufactured and modified with the radar, communications, operations, and control subsystems.

JTAC. Joint terminal area controller. A qualified military service member who, from a forward position, directs the action of combat aircraft engaged in close air support and other offensive air operations. The term used historically and in other countries and the relevant NATO standard is *forward air controller* (FAC).

kts. Abbreviation for knots, a reference to nautical miles per hour. A jet traveling at 500 kts equates to 575 mph.

lase. To designate a target with laser energy. Pilots might also say "sparkle" or "sparkle on" to signify they are designating a target. Others who are able to ensure the laser energy is good, that their weapon systems see the laser energy, are apt to respond "Good sparkle."

LGB. Laser-guided bomb. The Harrier can carry the GBU-12 (500-lb LGB) and GBU-16 (1,000-lb LGB). Although they are precision weapons with devastating accuracy, LGBs have limitations. LGBs can miss the target if the laser is turned on too early or if the weapon is released too early. During certain delivery profiles when the LGB sees laser energy as soon as it is released, it can turn from its delivery profile too soon and miss by falling short of the target. To prevent this, the laser designator must be turned on at the time that will preclude the bomb from turning down toward the target prematurely. Normally the pilot knows the proper moment for laser on. The specific LGB and the delivery tactics of the fighter/attack aircraft dictate the minimum designation time required to guide the weapon to the intended target. The effects of smoke, dust, and debris can impair the use of laser-guided munitions. The reflective scattering of laser light by smoke particles may present false targets. Rain, snow, fog, and low clouds can prevent effective use of laser-guided munitions. Heavy precipitation can limit the use of laser designators by affecting line of sight. Snow on the ground can produce a negative effect on laser-guided munition accuracy. Fog and low clouds will block the laser-guided munition seeker's field of view, which reduces the guidance time. This reduction may affect the probability of a hit. LGBs are excellent precision weapons and have greatly aided pilots who fly CAS missions, but they have their limitations and need to be understood so as to prevent unintended consequences.

lima charlie. Phonetic slang for loud and clear. For example, "I hear you lima charlie."

litening pod. Proprietary targeting pod developed by Northrop Grumman. The AN/AAQ-28(V) Litening system is a self-contained, multisensor weapon-aiming system that enables fighter pilots to detect, acquire, auto-track, and identify targets for highly accurate delivery of both conventional and precision-guided weapons. The Litening targeting pod features advanced image processing for target identification; coordinate generation for GPS weapons; a 640 x 512 pixel forward-looking infrared sensor for effective day and night operations; a new 1,024 x 1,024 pixel charge-coupled device (1k CCD) television sensor; a new dual-waveband infrared laser designator and range finder; a laser spot tracker; an infrared laser marker; and an optional air-to-ground data link and digital video recorder.

LSO. Landing signal officer. LSOs are designated pilots who trained to facilitate the safe and expeditious recovery of navy and Marine Corps aircraft aboard ships. They are often referred to as "Paddles," due to their lineage in World War II, when they held colored paddles or flags in the air in different positions to guide and direct aircraft to safe landings.

LSS. Landing sight supervisor. Similar to an LSO but trained to perform the same functions in regard to recovering Harriers into confined spots such as roads or landing pads. Under the CO's direction, VMA-513 always had one pilot in a vehicle that monitored the takeoffs and landings of the Harriers. The CO referred to this person as the "missile watch" officer but in reality he performed many other functions and greatly aided the operations and safety of the AV-8Bs during the deployment.

LZ. Landing zone. Location where helicopters can land.

MAG. Marine Air Group. A MAG normally comprises four to five squadrons but may have more. MAGs are usually commanded by a colonel, often called a "bird" colonel in reference to the eagle that designates such rank or a "full" colonel to separate from the rank one below it, lieutenant colonel, which is often called a "light" colonel.

MALS. Marine aviation logistics squadrons are squadrons designated by the Marine Corps to provide a central point of advanced maintenance activities to support flying squadrons. During VMA-513's 2002 OEF deployment, representatives from MALS-13 were attached to VMA-513 and deployed with us for the duration. They were also indispensable.

MANPAD. Man-portable air defense system is a generic term used to reference a small handheld IR SAM.

MARCENT. Marine Central Command. Commanded by a Marine lieutenant general (three stars), MARCENT worked directly for the CENTCOM commander (four stars). MARCENT was VMA-513's direct superior during the 2002–2003 deployment.

MAW. Marine Aircraft Wing. Currently there are four MAWs in the Marine Corps, three active MAWs (1st, 2nd, and 3rd) and one reserve MAW (4th). MAWs are normally commanded by a major general (two stars).

MAWTS-1. Marine Aviation Weapons and Tactics Squadron One. It is the premier aviation school in the Marine Corps and similar in pedigree to the U.S. Navy's Top Gun and U.S. Air Force's Fighter Weps schools. Each spring and fall, the school provides six weeks of instruction for selected pilots, weapons systems operators, and ground combat officers and support service officers from the Marine Corps and other U.S. and foreign services. Students receive classroom instruction combined with a rigorous flight curriculum. The course hones their knowledge about weapons and their delivery, platform tactics, and integration among Marine aviation and other Marine, joint, and foreign aviation platforms and command and control systems. After successfully completing the Weapons and Tactics course, pilots are designated WTIs (weapons and tactics instructors) and return to their commands to serve as warfare instructors and planners. MAWTS-1 instructors are also responsible for designating ACTIs, NSIs, and, with the aid of the squadron WTI, LATIs. See also WTI.

mike-mike. Millimeter.

Milk run. Easy mission. Sometimes used to refer to a logistics resupply mission.

mishap. An aviation accident, classified into four categories: class A, B, C, and D. A class A mishap is the most serious and denotes either a death or the loss of an aircraft or both.

MP. Military Police. VMA-513 deployed with augments from other units. Some of these augments were MPs and were charged with establishing and maintaining the security of the Marine camp in Afghanistan.

MSL. Mean sea level. The average (mean) height of the ocean's surface (especially that halfway between mean high and low tide); used as a standard in reckoning land elevation. Pilots fly altitudes based on MSL to maintain separation from each other.

MWR. Morale, welfare, and recreation. VMA-513 built

a specific building to house all the MWR gear we brought with us or acquired later. The MWR gear was stored in the MWR tent (B-hut) before the building was erected.

MWSS. Marine wing support squadron. Like the MALS, Marines from the MWSS were absolutely essential to the operation and success of VMA-513 during its 2002–2003 OEF deployment. Additionally, the author was extremely fond of the Marines of MWSS-373 who attached to our unit. They were some of the sharpest, most motivated Marines the author ever served with.

nav bag. Navigational bag. See PILOT BAG.

NCO. Noncommissioned officer. An enlisted Marine or soldier.

nine-line. Formal brief given by the JTAC, FAC, or FAC(A) to aircraft that allows them to conduct a CAS attack. The nine-line consists of nine lines, each line containing specific information on how to attack the enemy without accidentally engaging any friendly forces. The nine-line is standardized and designed to rely on brevity so that targets may be engaged quickly and effectively.

NOD. Night optical device. A ground term for NVGs. During our deployment we used PVS-7 NODs for driving at night and standing duty as the LSS (landing sight supervisor) when aircraft launched and recovered.

NSI. Night systems instructor. A senior aviator in the squadron with extensive experience in night systems missions that include but are not limited to operations regarding NVGs and FLIRs. NSIs are responsible for training and qualifying squadron pilots in night systems.

NSQ. Night systems qualified. A squadron pilot who has completed the requisite sorties and training and is thus designated to fly combat missions involving night systems.

NVG. Night vision goggles. Harrier pilots use the AN/ AVS-9 NVGs. NVGs allow pilots to see in the dark using light amplification. In this method, small amounts of light (usually moonlight and starlight) in the surrounding area are converted into electrical energy. Electrons pass through a thin disk and are multiplied; these electrons bounce off a phosphor screen, which converts them back to light. This light is what the viewer sees and enables him to see in the dark. NVGs must have some light in which to work. If there is no light, then the NVGs have nothing to magnify and convert to electrical energy. The darker the night, the less capable the NVGs. NVGs work well on half-moon nights or brighter, but on moonless nights or when the clouds block starlight, the NVGs' performance is seriously degraded. NVGs also have limiting features such as a narrow field of view (FOV), 40 degrees with AN/AVS-9s, and no depth perception. Lights are also magnified greatly, which produces the dangerous illusion that a near aircraft is far away and that a faraway aircraft is near. Lights of an aircraft at one mile distant and lights of another aircraft at twenty miles distant appear to the viewer wearing NVGs to be the same distance away. Many pilots have crashed into each other due to these dangerous phenomena.

ODA. Operational Detachment Alpha. The Special Forces Operational Detachment-A, or A-Team, is the fundamental building block for all Special Forces groups. There are six "A" detachments in each Special Forces company. A captain leads the twelve-man team. Second in command is a warrant officer. Two noncommissioned officers, or NCOs, are trained in each of the five SF functional areas—weapons, engineering and demolitions, medicine, communications, and operations and intelligence—and make up the remainder of the team. All team members are SF-qualified and cross-trained in different skills as well as being multilingual.

ODO. Operations duty officer. Direct representative of the CO who monitors and tracks the squadron's daily flight schedule. The ODO keeps abreast of aircraft as they leave and return from missions. The ODO is also responsible for tracking the status of all squadron aircraft, whether they are "up" or "down," and briefs pilots on current weather and airfield conditions.

OEF. Operation Enduring Freedom. The war in Afghanistan.

OIF. Operation Iraqi Freedom. The war in Iraq.

ONC. Operational navigational chart. It has a scale of 1:1,000,000. Often used by pilots to provide a big picture of their operating area with markings of divert fields, unit locations, and boundary lines. Pilots might refer to an ONC as a "divert chart."

1:50. A 1:50,000 map commonly called a "one to fifty." Provides more detail than TPC or JOG and is useful to attack pilots for detailed coordination required in CAS missions. Unfortunately, because of its scale it does not cover much ground. Thus pilots may have to carry a number of these maps if they do not know the specific area in which they are going to support ground troops. That is often the case in Afghanistan.

OPREP. Operational Report. An "OPREP-3 SIR (Serious Incident Report) provides the commandant of the Marine Corps, through the Marine Corps Operations Center, 'information on any significant event or incident that is not of national-level interest or otherwise reported under another flagword.' An OPREP-3 Navy Blue report provides the chief of naval operations, through the Navy Operations Center, 'information on any significant event or incident that is not of national-level interest. When operating under the command of a senior U.S. Navy Headquarters, refer to reference.' " Marine Corps Order 3504.2, June 8, 2007.

OPSO. Operations officer. Senior officer in the squadron responsible to the CO for coordinating flight schedules and pilot training. The OSPO for VMA-513 during its OEF deployment in 2002–2003 was Major Andrew (AJ) Heino.

optempo. A slang term for operational tempo, though it has gained in acceptability. Optempo usually defines how hard or fast one or a unit is working.

PAX. Short for personnel or passengers. For example, "I'm carrying six pax."

PFT. Physical fitness test. Mandatory test for all Marines required twice a year. In 2002–2003 the USMC PFT consisted of as many dead hang pulls as one could accomplish in one attempt, the maximum number of sit-ups (crunches) in two minutes, and a three-mile run. Twenty pull-ups, one hundred sit-ups in two minutes, and a three-mile run in less than eighteen minutes equated to a perfect score of 300.

pilot bag. A small bag in which pilots carry the essential charts, maps, approach plates, and documents necessary for a mission. Pilots often call these bags "nav bags."

popeye. Naval aviation brevity word for IMC; when a pilot is in the clouds and thus requires vectors.

powerline. Denotes a specific maintenance shop that combines mechanics from power plants (engines) and line personnel commonly referred to as plane captains. Plane captains are qualified and designated personnel who prepare a pilot's aircraft before launch.

PT. Physical training.

PUC. Person under control; people under custody. Enemy combatants held in detention facilities.

push. Aviation jargon for changing radio frequencies or identifying a specific frequency. For example, "Nightmare flight, push magenta on the left." Flight lead is directing all members of the flight to change their left or primary radio to the frequency assigned to the magenta color. A pilot might also say, "I'll monitor this push," thus letting others know he'll monitor that frequency while he talks to someone else on another frequency, using another radio. Most tactical aircraft are equipped with two radios that can be used simultaneously.

QRF. Quick reaction force. Designated ground force, usually on standby, that can respond immediately to a TIC. Normally carried in a Black Hawk helicopter although sometimes they respond in vehicles.

RADALT. Radar altimeter. Provides a pilot with height

above ground in feet. Altitude readout from RAD-ALT is commonly referred to as AGL (above ground level) and differs from MSL (mean sea level) altitude, which is provided by the barometric altimeter, commonly called the "baro." Most civilian aircraft, both commercial and private, use baro altimeter readings in MSL as their reference. Military pilots, who often fly low to the ground, require a more accurate and immediate reference. Thus the use of RADALTs.

ready room. Designated area where pilots receive briefings and training. Also a place where pilots tend to lounge and relax when briefings or training is not taking place.

ROE. Rules of engagement. These determine when, where, and how force shall be used. Although commanders desire to keep the ROE simple so that they can be understood by all military personnel, this is not always the case.

RTB. Return to base.

RWR. Radar warning receiver. The AV-8B uses the ALR-67, which provides pilots indications when target-tracking radars are locking on to a pilot's aircraft.

S-1. Administration section. Marine Corps tactical units are broken down into different sections. S-1 refers to the admin section, S-2 the intelligence section, S-3 the operations section, and S-4 the logistics section. Military personnel often use slang terms such as "the Two," "the Three," or "the Four" to reference a specific section. For example, "I'm going to the Two for a debrief." Or "Has anyone seen the Four? We're out of toilet paper again."

safe house. See FOB.

SAM. **Surface-to-air missile.** Can refer to a radar-guided SAM or an IR SAM. IR SAMs (heat seekers) are commonly referred to as handhelds or MANPADS because they are man-portable. The IR SAM was considered the most dangerous threat in Afghanistan in 2002–2003.

sanitize. Stripping one's body and flight suit of all information other than a military ID card and dog tags. The thought is that if one ejects and is taken prisoner, the standard answer is to provide only "name, rank, and serial number." The dynamic has changed. One is just as likely to get his head cut off if taken prisoner no matter what he is carrying.

SIPRNET. Secret Internet Protocol Router Network.

sitrep. Situational report.

six. The six-o'clock position behind a pilot, the unseen area where bullets and missiles come from.

SNCO. Senior noncommissioned officer.

SOF. Special operational forces.

SOP. Standard operating procedure.

STO. **Short takeoff.** Due to the AV-8B's unique ability to use vectored thrust, the most common and preferred takeoff is a STO. STOs combine the elements of a conventional takeoff with those of a vertical takeoff into a hybrid takeoff. The pilot normally adds full power and waits until the Harrier reaches a designated speed (dependent on gross weight and field elevation). He then rotates the nozzles down to 50 degrees. The jet jumps off the deck and the pilot raises the gear and flaps and begins to "nozzle out." Harrier pilots nozzle out by rotating the nozzles back to aft slowly as the jet's speed increases and the jet thus becomes airborne solely on "wing lift."

STOL. Short takeoff or land. Also, a specific position for the flaps in the AV-8B.

TACAN. TACtical air navigation. A navigation system used by military aircraft that provides the user with bearing and distance (slant-range) to a ground or shipborne station. In the AV-8B, pilots used the TACAN in the air-to-air mode and thus received ranging from their wingman. This was especially useful at night, when distances between aircraft were hard to determine while wearing NVGs.

TAC lead. Tactical lead, a flight designation that assigns responsibility for the flight (two or more aircraft) to one individual. The TAC lead is usually the most experienced leader in the flight but may not be the most senior member.

TAD. Tactical air direction (net). Radio frequencies designated for JTAC use.

TIC. Troops in contact. Used by military personnel to describe when friendly forces become engaged with enemy forces. Also known as a "firefight."

torso harness. Part of a fighter pilot's ensemble. Fits over the g-suit and covers the lower legs, chest, and shoulders. A pilot attaches the torso harness to the ejection seat before flying. The torso harness is very uncomfortable to wear or walk in. It is designed to protect the body during an ejection when instantaneous g-forces of twelve to fourteen g's are experienced. If a torso harness is not properly fitted, a pilot may break his neck during an ejection. Even if the torso harness is properly fitted, a pilot may still break his neck during an ejection. During my military career, two Harrier pilots died due to the forces on their bodies during the ejection. One was a friend, mentor, and former boss. The author also ejected from a TA-4 and recognizes the importance of a properly fitting torso harness, despite the discomfort.

TPC. **Tactical pilot chart.** Supports high-speed, low-altitude, radar, and visual navigation of high-performance tactical and reconnaissance aircraft at very low through medium altitudes. Scale: 1:500,000. Commonly used by attack pilots.

TST. **Time-sensitive target.**

UAV. **Unmanned aerial vehicle.** Pilotless aircraft such as the Predator.

up-front-control (UFC). A box located below the HUD with a numbered keypad, digital display readout, and function select keys. In the AV-8B, pilots input most of the tactical information (navigation waypoints, radio frequencies, weapon selections, RAD-ALT warning altitudes, etc.) via the UFC. When VMA-513 deployed to Afghanistan in 2002, the squadron's aircraft had the newest radios, but due to budget shortfalls, the software was incomplete. Thus all radio frequency changes had to be completed "heads down" using the radio in the right console.

USAF. **United States Air Force.**

USMC. **United States Marine Corps.** Finest and most feared fighting organization that has ever existed.

UXO. **Unexploded ordnance.** In Afghanistan, and especially Bagram, the ground was littered with unexploded Soviet mines, mortar rounds, rockets, etc.

Any unexploded ordnance strewn about was referred to as a UXO.

VFR. Visual flight rules are a set of regulations that allow a pilot to operate an aircraft in weather conditions generally clear enough to allow the pilot to see where the aircraft is going. To avoid collisions, the VFR pilot is expected to "see and avoid" obstacles and other aircraft. Pilots flying under VFR assume responsibility for their separation from all other aircraft and are generally not assigned routes or altitudes by air traffic control (ATC).

VL. Vertical landing. Due to the AV-8B's unique ability to rotate its nozzles 90 degrees, the jet can hover, providing it has enough thrust to equal its weight. An empty AV-8B weighs approximately 17,000 lbs. The Pegasus motor provides approximately 23,000 lbs of thrust at sea level. Thus an AV-8B is generally capable of hovering at sea level carrying an additional 6,000 lbs of fuel or ordnance. Due to the decrease in oxygen as elevation is increased, the amount of thrust produced by the motor is decreased. At 5,000 feet of elevation, the AV-8B no longer has the ability to hover. Thus at that elevation it must rely on a conventional landing or hybrid landing, often called a rolling vertical landing (RVL).

VMA-513. Attack squadron 513 of the U.S. Marine Corps. All Harrier squadrons in the USMC have a VMA designation. V—an antiquated reference to a "fixed-wing" platform; a reference system developed by the navy and Marine Corps before World War II. M—Marine. A—attack. Thus *VMA* means "Marine fixed-wing (not helicopter) attack" squadron. The numbers 513 also have a lineage. The number 5 represents the fifth air wing. The number 1 represents the first group. The number 3 represents the third squadron. Thus when the unit was activated it was the third squadron in the first group of the Marine Corps' fifth fighter wing. As units (wings and groups) are disbanded due to the needs of the nation, the squadron keeps its nomenclature and is reassigned accordingly. Marine Attack Squadron 513 was first commissioned as VMF-513 on February 15, 1944, at Marine Corps Auxiliary in Field Oak Grove, North Carolina, flying the Grumman F6F Hellcat. Sixty years later it had long been redesignated VMA-513 and was assigned to MAG-13 (Marine Air Group 13) under the 3rd MAW (Marine Aircraft Wing). Marine Corps squadrons are normally commanded by lieutenant colonels.

VMC. Visual meteorological conditions. Clear of the clouds. In aviation, visual meteorological conditions are those in which visual flight rules (VFR) flight is permitted—that is, conditions in which pilots have sufficient visibility to fly the aircraft maintaining visual separation from terrain and other aircraft. They are the opposite of instrument meteorological conditions (IMC).

VRS. Video recording system. The AV-8B used an 8 mm tape normally of sixty to ninety minutes in length. The VRS is bore-sighted to the HUD (head-up display) and is used to record important aspects of the flight: takeoffs, landings, and gun, missile, or rocket firings.

Winchester. Out of ordnance.

WTI. Weapons and tactics instructor. A graduate of the MAWTS-1 WTI curriculum who is responsible for teaching aviation warfare and advanced aviation tactics in his or her squadron. WTIs are often the most capable and best pilots in the squadron. To become a WTI, Harrier pilots must have the following qualifications: division leader (capable and designated to lead a flight of four aircraft), air combat tactics instructor (ACTI), low-altitude tactics instructor (LATI), and night systems instructor (NSI). WTIs are colloquially referred to as Jedis due to their advanced tactical knowledge, onerous training, and the selectivity of their position. Because the cost of training a WTI is extensive and sometimes prohibitive, squadrons usually have only one or two of them. Any pilot who has completed the WTI course maintains that qualification throughout his or her career.

XCAS. Airborne "on-call" CAS. Missions in which aircraft are designated to fly and be airborne but not in support of any specific unit.

XO. Executive officer. The direct representative of the CO (commanding officer) and second in command in the squadron. The author served as XO during VMA-513's OEF deployment in 2002–2003.

AUTHOR'S NOTE & ACKNOWLEDGMENTS

For every loss, there are people and pieces of a life left behind—people who must pick themselves up and move on though the desire to do so remains questionable and the path uncertain. The families of our fallen servicemen and servicewomen know all too well the grief and pain associated with the loss of a loved one. They are the ones that need help both in the days and weeks following the tragedy, and in the years to come.

The Tragedy Assistance Program for Survivors (TAPS) is a nonprofit organization that provides both immediate and long-term support for anyone suffering from the loss of a military loved one, regardless of the relationship to the deceased, the geography, or circumstance of death, be it combat, mishap, accident, suicide, or other. TAPS reaches across barriers and stigmas because the loss of an American serviceman or servicewoman is always the same—tragic.

TAPS is the first place anyone suffering from the loss of a loved one can turn to. They are partnered with hundreds of organizations that provide niche support, and they know how to navigate turbulent waters, because they've been there. They know the pain and cost of losing a loved one. TAPS is there when tragedy strikes, and they are there years later. TAPS doesn't forget. TAPS can be reached at 1-800-959-TAPS (8277). More information is available via their website, http://www.taps.org.

A portion of the proceeds of this book will go to the Tragedy Assistance Program for Survivors (TAPS).

This is a story about war. It is a story told from one perspective—mine. I have done my best to tell the story truthfully. I relied heavily on my journals, photographs, and research. I take all responsibility for any errors or inaccuracies. As with most books, its journey was long and lonely, plagued by doubt. But in the end my gratitude extends beyond my pen to those who aided me. Please forgive me if I forgot to mention you personally.

I want to thank my mom and dad for raising me, instilling values of right and wrong, and above all, providing unconquerable love and a sterling example of what a mother and father should be. I want to thank my brother, Mark, for sharing the sacred country with me, where the crimson and golden slashed cutthroats swim fast and free. May it always be so. I want to thank my sister, Judi, and her husband, Herb, for help in the editing process and perhaps most important—telling me what didn't work.

I am extremely grateful to Bing West, Steven Pressfield, and my former mentor, Jay Stout. They provided advice, guidance, and assistance throughout. I thank those who offered to read the manuscript before it was released. Thank you, Nate Fick, Quang Pham, Thomas X. Hammes, Craig Mullaney, Donovan Campbell, General Richard Myers, and General Anthony Zinni. I owe special thanks to my good friend Brad Graft, who provided continual support and outstanding advice, especially when doubt consumed me. *Wolverines!*

I thank every Marine, soldier, sailor, and airman I served with as well as every pilot with whom I flew. I learned something from each of you. For the lonely grunt who asks little, takes less, but gives so much, I personally thank you. For those on the home front, thank you for not forgetting.

I am especially indebted to my publisher, Anthony Ziccardi, who took a chance on an unknown entity, and my agent, EJ McCarthy, who made it possible. I owe many thanks to Kathy Sagan and Tom Pitoniak. Their editing greatly aided the manuscript. Thank you, Jessica Webb, for all of your unseen work. To my publicist, Sarah Reidy, who was instrumental in countless ways, thank you. To all at Simon & Schuster and Threshold Books who assisted me, thanks.

Finally, I must thank those most important to me. Caleb and Zoë, thank you for your laughs, hugs, and kisses and letting me do what I need to do. To my eldest son, Ryan, thank you for your technical support with the web design but more important, for your love and friendship. I am very proud of you. And to the most beautiful woman in the world, Katie, thank you for everything. Words will never convey what you mean to me. *Te amo.*